European Media in Crisis

**THE
EURO**MEDIA
**RESEARCH
GROUP**

When the financial markets collapsed in 2008, the media industry was affected by a major slump in advertising revenues and a formerly highly successful business model fell into a state of decay. This economic crisis has threatened core social values of contemporary democracies, such as freedom, diversity and equality. Taking a normative and policy perspective, this book discusses threats and opportunities for the media industry in Europe. What are the implications of the crisis for professional journalism, the media industry and the process of political communication? Can non-state and non-market actors profit from the crisis? And what are media policy answers at the national and European level?

Josef Trappel is Professor of Media Policy and Media Economics in the Department of Communication Studies at the University of Salzburg, Austria.

Jeanette Steemers is Professor of Media and Communications in the Faculty of Media Arts and Design at the University of Westminster, UK.

Barbara Thomass is Professor for International Comparison of Media Systems at the Institute for Media Studies at the Ruhr University Bochum, Germany.

Routledge Studies in European Communication Research and Education

Edited by Claudia Alvares, Lusofona University, Portugal; Ilija Tomanić Trivundža, University of Ljubljana, Slovenia and Fausto Colombo, Università Cattolica del Sacro Cuore, Milan, Italy.

Series Advisory Board: Nico Carpentier, François Heinderyckx, Denis McQuail, Robert Picard and Jan Servaes.

ECREA

http://www.ecrea.eu

Published in association with the European Communication Research and Education Association (ECREA), books in the series make a major contribution to the theory, research, practice and/or policy literature. They are European in scope and represent a diversity of perspectives. Book proposals are refereed.

European Media in Crisis
Values, Risks and Policies

Edited by Josef Trappel,
Jeanette Steemers and Barbara Thomass

Routledge
Taylor & Francis Group

NEW YORK AND LONDON

First published 2015
by Routledge
711 Third Avenue, New York, NY 10017

and by Routledge
2 Park Square, Milton Park, Abingdon, Oxon OX14 4RN

Routledge is an imprint of the Taylor & Francis Group, an informa business

Library of Congress Cataloging in Publication Data

European media in crisis : values, risks and policies / edited by Josef Trappel, Jeanette Steemers and Barbara Thomass.
    pages cm. — (Routledge studies in European communication research and education)
Includes bibliographical references and index.
    1. Mass media—Europe. I. Trappel, Josef, 1963– editor.
    II. Steemers, Jeanette, editor. III. Thomass, Barbara, editor.
P92.E9E96 2015
302.23'094—dc23   2015005215

ISBN: 978-1-138-89891-2 (hbk)
ISBN: 978-1-315-70824-9 (ebk)

Typeset in Sabon
by codeMantra

Printed and bound in Great Britain by
TJ International Ltd, Padstow, Cornwall

Contents

PART III
Crisis in Journalism Values, Public Communication and Representation

PART IV
Looking to the Future: Policy Perspectives

Conclusions

Preface

Josef Trappel, Jeanette Steemers
and Barbara Thomass

In 1986, the Euromedia Research Group published its first two books, *New Media Politics* (Sage) and the *Handbook* on European media systems (Campus). They were the first tangible products of a group of scholars who met for the first time in 1982. In November 2014, the Euromedia Research Group gathered for its 56th meeting, finalizing its 13th book in a series of books reflecting upon the transformations of mass media and public communication. What unites these scholars is their consistent interest in how media and communication policy acts and should re-act in response to these transformations.

The latest book is on *Media in Crisis*, and its various implications on values and risks for society. This issue fits well into the long term perspective of the Group which observed and experienced an exciting array of what has been called innovations during these more than 30 years. Cable and satellite television, digitalization of all formats of communication, personal computers and, finally, the internet, the world wide web and social media have demanded and provoked critical appraisal and reflections.

It has proved a suitable cycle to meet twice a year. In these meetings, group members inform one another on recent developments in the countries they know best, followed by reports on their individual or collective research efforts. Most interesting and stimulating, however, are the subsequent debates on research papers, often preliminary versions of book chapters. Contrary to blind peer-reviews by mostly anonymous scholars, the Euromedia Research Group developed a culture of open and constructive criticism. Such critique is by no means less direct than in any blind peer-review process. But it has the advantage of offering the option of starting a debate or conversation. Often, this process uncovers unknown knowledge – if not wisdom – by Group members and frequently teams of book chapter authors changed subsequent to the exchange of opinions, with critics joining as authors.

Thereby, writing a book becomes a true Group exercise. No chapter finds its way into our books without being discussed time and again. All meeting participants contribute their fair share to each chapter, in accordance with their specific field of competence. As a result, most chapters have more than one author, and some authors contribute to more than one chapter. This line-up of authorship reflects the interactive way of working within the Euromedia Research Group.

To us, the members of the Euromedia Research Group, the book is the manifestation of our debates over several years. And to our readers, we hope, the book is inspiration for further reflection.

For more information about the Euromedia Research Group and its publications, please visit our website: www.euromediagroup.org

Foreword

Denis McQuail

THE EARLY ORIGINS OF A CRISIS OF OUR TIMES

'Crisis' is a hyperbolic term and too easily applied to developments and events that simply alter or upset the on-going course of arrangements. Here we are concerned with various branches of the media industry, especially for those that are closest in their functioning or effects to the political and social centre of the society. The more that developments seem to threaten what are presumed to be essential interests of a society, the more justified the term seems to be. Historically, in most current nation states, the 'media' (initially little more than the newspaper press) were largely marginal to significant political, economic and cultural affairs. A long and uneven progress of political change gradually brought a much enlarged range of media into active engagement in public life. This process accelerated during the twentieth century and a number of essential features of society came to depend on the viability, cooperation and wider influence of print and broadcast media. The contribution of media to democratic politics and to a 'good society' depended on their voluntary adoption of appropriate goals and values and their effectiveness in the sphere of public communication. In practice, this would mean a flow of information, ideas and opinions universally distributed.

The scope for perceiving some element of genuine crisis grew along with this increasing dependence and influence. Fundamental matters of freedom, justice and democracy had become entwined with the fate of the once peripheral business of publication. In countries claiming to operate on principles of freedom, different perceptions of emerging threats were to be found. One concerned the low or varied quality of information provided to (or demanded by) the mass of the public by a press medium primarily devoted to profiting from mass advertising and mass sales. This seemed to require an excess of sensationalist and trivial content. Another threat derived from the observation that the mass or popular newspapers of the early twentieth century were falling largely into the hands of a few monopoly owners who used their undue power of influence on behalf of their own class in an unresolved class struggle. In autocratic states, there was little room for different interpretations. There was simply and open and fundamental subversion of the principles of freedom of expression and enlightenment espoused in ideal terms by many early editors and journalists.

Leaving aside these circumstances of plain abuse of public communication, there was much vocal criticism of the media of press and film, but little in the way of organised public policy or action until the second half of the twentieth century, apart from monitoring or limited censorship on grounds of morals and public mores, plus exhortation to greater responsibility. The main exception to this remark can be found in the various, mainly European, moves to develop radio within a setting of public ownership and close supervision. However, the reasons had little to do with any earlier critical responses to the failings of the press. They were on cultural and moral grounds plus a wish of governments to manage the infrastructure centrally and efficiently as well as to control access to channels of public communication. This usually entailed a neutralisation of political conflicts, as well as the promotion of various cultural and educational purposes. In this story up to the mid-twentieth century we see no clear perception of crisis and much optimism about the potential of media to contribute to social and economic progress.

AN EMERGING 'MEDIA SOCIETY' AND ITS DISCONTENTS

In the aftermath of World War II, the idea of crisis began to take on some of its contemporary character. The rise of television post-1950 had a number of wider repercussions for media systems, gradually undercutting the financial basis of the worldwide film business and, more slowly still, providing strong competition for the advertising income on which most newspapers depended. However, while television continued its rise and rise in respect of extent, influence and financial significance, the press was perceived as threatened from other sources. One was a gradual process of social and cultural change to a more secular, privatised, mobile and consumerist society, less politicised and ideologically driven. It was also a society in which literacy, even when near universal, ceased to provide the only key to social and cultural participation for the public.

Another source of challenge was a growing awareness of the dependence of democratic political process on the chances of media access and influence (especially by way of television) that were not evenly distributed. From the 1970's onwards the mass media of both broadcasting and press were widely seen as being at the heart of democratic governance and as such should not be left to the arbitrary forces of commerce and ownership concentration. However, this was not a universal perception and vulnerable to the charge that any attempt to prevent abuse or support the goal of public service to the political process would itself introduce new distortions and limitations, offending against the fundamental principle of freedom of publication.

The challenges indicated were not essentially new and were dealt with in partial and often ineffective ways. In general, there was no sustained sense of crisis, except on the part of critical theorists and radical reformers, for whom crisis was the way forward. Broadcasting, in Europe at least, was largely protected on consensual grounds from the ills referred to, while the troubles of the press seemed to be containable by professional adaptation, greater efficiency and continuing loyalty of readerships, with stable media habits and political allegiances. In retrospect, it appears that the successive impacts of changed circumstances and the growth of the new media of the time were normal events, even if problematic for one media sector or another. Declining media were not actually disappearing and the fears expressed by various cultural and political elites were both predictable and never realised as predicted. If there were new dangers to be seen, there are also new hopes and possibilities for the benefits of society.

The current situation, sketched below, on the other hand, is being experienced as a true crisis, since it has fundamental roots affecting all branches of media and is experienced across all media, and more widely, with quite uncertain outcomes. It was preceded by a phase during the 1980s and 1990's of shocks largely delivered to the cocooned world of broadcasting. The reasons for an acceleration of concern are still mixed, but most powerful was the rise (partly an American import) of a new ideology of economic freedom and competition that favoured releasing all or most media, new or old, from existing limitations. This phase was characterised at the time as the Age of Media Moguls – Big Beasts that were establishing new transnational media empires. The names of Berlusconi, Bertelsmann, Murdoch and others come to mind. This coincided (by chance) with the discovery and trial of new means forms of communication that could transform existing structures and the means of operation, control, finance and functions of major institutions of public communication. The key innovations were the expanding capacity of computers, associated digitisation of all communications and availability of new means of transmission, including satellites, wireless, cable systems and portable content. The greatest new challenge for media industry was to find business models by which to exploit new opportunities.

Governments initially hoped to encourage and manage innovation and expansion in the hope of securing national economic advantage. Sooner or later these aims proved impossible to fulfil within a public framework and the case for deregulation became a matter of pragmatics as well as ideology.

The sudden transformation of national media systems in East and Central Europe after 1990, that coincided and fitted well with big changes in the West, gave an extra impulse to change. A large slice of media industries were de facto released from state control and obliged to make their own way in a highly contested market place. There were potentially rich pickings for western entrepreneurs.

DIMENSIONS OF THE CURRENT CRISIS

The crisis for media that is developing, nearly everywhere, according to this account has several dimensions. The most self-evident and inescapable signs of crisis are found in the profound economic shock to established media industries, with steadily declining audiences for certain 'old media', redistribution of audience interests and, above all a decline and great uncertainty in once reliable sources of advertising income. One cause may be found in a general economic crisis of a conventional kind, but a more fundamental and more permanent cause lies in the rapid innovation of new media devices and applications, often using mobile technology, displacing existing forms and market arrangements.

While it is quite possible to see the impact of 'new media' as essentially positive in the longer perspective, opening up many new opportunities for growth, certain key features of emerging 'new media', especially digitisation and convergence, seem to make established forms of public communication, especially broadcasting and the mass press, obsolete or simply ineffective. The future will be threatening for some key existing interests of society and change will be accompanied by many strains and uncertainties.

Inter media- competition and pressures towards concentration are accentuated, accompanied by very strong pressure to speedy monetization of the various applications of new media systems, in which large sums and hopes have been invested.

The rise of what seems like an entirely new media sector, under the heading of 'social media', brings with it unknown consequences for clients and producers of media services. Growing globalization of media ownership, production and audience formation, threatening local and domestic media functions and even their survival.

Most relevant in the context of this book are the challenges to current regimes and frameworks of media policy, often assembled on a piecemeal and provisional basis and with considerable difficulty over time. The arrangements and principles in place are threatened with varying degrees of increasing irrelevance. A weakening of currently agreed normative frameworks for the operation of media in their (still presumed) public functions would be a serious loss. Standards that were once formulated with confidence for the essential work of journalists are already no longer agreed and are less commonly enforced or enforceable. On many issues of media accountability public opinion is still divided and uncertain.

Under emerging conditions of rapid media development and steadily increasing globalization, the practicality of any public control or guidance by way of public policy is called into doubt. Where public control still exists, as for instance in the case of the surviving public broadcasting institutions, systematic pressure is now being widely brought to bear, for reasons mentioned, in the direction of privatization and more commercial behaviour.

Although technological innovation seems to be at the root of the seismic shifts described, there is no intrinsic reason why the innovations in question have to lead to crisis, rather than to varied solutions to changing problems of public communication. There are many voices and much experience and evidence to support the alternative development of the same technologies for other purposes. The notion of crisis can indeed be reformulated as one of struggle between competing versions of the place of communication in a 'good society' (itself a contested concept. Perhaps increasingly so). What this actually means depends on the particular issues that are identified as problematic in the time and place. This is the crux of the matter at the moment.

There are some relatively new and uncontrollable underlying forces at work as well as changed priorities and perceptions on the part of society. These arguably involve a reduction in control of national media systems in a more global and multichannel media environment. It does not seem an exaggeration speak of a 'crisis of public media policy' as a distinct dimension of the general crisis. In which case, it looks s if we have a range of new issues, new problems to solve from the perspective of the 'public good' and a loss of the means for dealing with the situation.

THE TRADITIONAL INSTRUMENTS OF
PUBLIC POLICY FOR MEDIA

The main traditions of media policy in Europe have involved a series of measures designed to cope with particular problems associated with mass media. These have related, first of all, to expectations that the that they will, in various important ways, support a number of vital social processes, or at least not cause harm in these matters. Support is generally perceived as necessary for the democratic political system and justice system, and for maintaining social order. A variety of cultural goals and values are also at stake. Freedom of publication and expression sets limits to what policy can achieve, but much is still possible by way of structural intervention (to limit monopoly especially, but also to encourage fair access and wide distribution of diverse information and ideas). In cultural matters subsidy and protectionism have been employed and some direct legal restraints applied, where charges of individual or public harm can be upheld. As noted, the public control of broadcasting has, since the beginnings, given exceptional effectiveness and legitimacy to many public policy initiatives. Exhortation by governments has had some influence on established self-regulatory media institutions.

Most, if not all, of the familiar means of implementing policy (already enfeebled) have been challenged under current circumstances on grounds of ineffectiveness, if not of illegitimacy. Subsidies have become largely irrelevant, as the media sphere is expanded and globalised. Control of monopoly is limited at best to certain limited spheres of media activity within national control. Protectionism, except in very disguised forms, is either ruled out of court by free trade agreements or seen as marginal to any good outcome, given the open and fluid nature of tastes and audience choices. Restrictive laws or forms of censorship are unable to cope with the multiplicity of new media outlets, especially with open media frontiers. The areas of media operation that have been generally subject to some degree of self-regulation and voluntary public accountability (mainly the mainstream and more 'respectable' newspaper press) have already shrunk, leaving much outside of the scope of any actual or potential jurisdiction.

The possibility of new instruments of public policy being developed cannot be excluded, once new structures and systems are more stable and better understood (if that ever happens), but it is hard to escape the conclusion that a serious challenge to media policy – in the name of either commercial freedom or even true freedom – has acquired a powerful new momentum and is difficult to challenge.

Even more problematic than the diminishing means of implementation may be the increasing lack of fit between traditional normative standards for media conduct and the changed circumstances of media performance. The former were developed in an age of active policy making to suit national societies, with somewhat different priorities than today. On the other hand, while reigning social mores are generally thought of as more permissive, there has been increased alarm and more pressure for action in those areas where Internet use has become a source of perceived harm, especially to young people and other vulnerable sectors of society. This is in some respects a reversion, although with much better reason, to early restrictive attitudes to the film, pornographic publication and, later, to some popular music. The key factor here is not so much intrinsic revulsion, denial of freedom, but the question of unregulated use and exposure.

MEDIA POLICY IN CRISIS

The policy instruments referred to were developed to deal with the main perceived problems of twentieth century (mass) media. Many of these stemmed from tendencies towards monopoly and concentration, especially where these impinged upon the conduct of democratic politics. In particular, freedom of publication and diversity were highly prized and held to be in danger. Another set of concerns related essentially to issues of quality of the output of the media, either in informational or cultural terms (as variously defined). A third category covered questions of actual or suspected harm. More peripherally, policy dealt sporadically with questions of access and distribution, from an audience or 'consumer' perspective. The terrain of public media policy had little or no bearing on private communications, whether personal or business.

In the later period of the 'old order' of media, much close attention was paid to specifying and defining the relevant norms and qualities, mainly for the purpose of monitoring and evaluative or critical research. The earliest focus was on overt 'bias' (usually political or ideological) of attention in news reporting and publication resulting more from routine selection patterns by editors than from propagandist intent. This developed into more sophisticated concepts and methods for discerning systematic covert bias stemming from conscious ideology or simply unintended preconceptions or misconceptions. The possibilities ranged from clever propaganda to unwitting prejudice or blindness in news information that purported to be 'objective' (a blanket word for various informational qualities).

A principle of equal potency that soon gained wide currency was that of diversity, with its multiple potential applications. It could refer not only to the range of content available, but also to the differences of sources and channels and to the composition of audiences reached. Although higher diversity was generally more valued, its various different kinds were also to be distinguished. Diversity could be applauded where all citizens were equally open to the whole spectrum of ideas and information and culture of their own society. Or a version of it could relate to a condition of accurate reflection of the actual spectrum of tastes and interests. A narrower meaning of diversity set a value on there being provision in a pluralistic society for different 'communities of interest' to co-exist, on the basis of ethnicity, politics, religion or social demographics, with a self-sufficiency to communication possibilities of their own. In general, the diversity value was a response to a basic expectation attributed to mass media: that their intrinsic logic would drive them inevitably towards greater (and undesirable) homogenization of society and cultural and informational 'levelling' (downwards).

The third main principle in the pantheon of normative principles was that of 'freedom', which did not seem to need defining and has always been difficult to measure and monitor, except in terms of the degree of limitations and obstacles imposed.

The sources of such potential threats varied. The most obvious enemy was the oldest one – government or the state in its many manifestations. For some, the only definition of freedom needed was 'freedom from government'. In this view, media policy itself could also be included as a threat. However, an alternative perspective led to the questions: "Freedom for what?" Freedom for Whom? Where are the limits to freedom, if any, to be set?"

These three principles, objectivity, diversity and freedom, each owed its significance in policy debate to assumptions about mass media and its typical structures: large public or commercial organisations that tended towards an extension of power and control. They do not exhaust the range of relevant normative ideas but between them they provide a path towards analysis of the main issues relating to media. Certainly they once did so, but the question has to be faced whether they are adequate or as relevant in their most widely current formulations and applications to the new world of media that is now gradually taking a new shape.

NORMATIVE CRITERIA OF PERFORMANCE IN QUESTION

Of the three principles discussed above, that of freedom still takes priority, even if it remains in theoretical dispute. At first sight, the emerging new media conditions do not require any adaptation of standards or of ways of estimating their observance. It seems, however, much less problematic to achieve, as long as the potential of the Internet can be realised. This in turn is basically to be settled by the nature of the society, not its media system. An unfree society will not have media freedom and a poor society may lack the infrastructure, consumer technology and skills. Otherwise there is no high barrier to access as an Internet publisher (of any kind of content), whether economic or legal. Problems of monopoly control or licensing should not arise. The capacity to receive freely may be limited by costs of some content or lack of facilities, but the principle of freedom was rarely judged by its practical chances of realisation.

In the days of early unfolding of the possibilities for the Internet as a medium of public communication, no longer a matter of speculation, it was widely credited as being a liberating force in almost every respect. This was without plan or policy, although it did result from a conscious decision to create an open communication network and it was consistent with the then deregulatory climate of its homeland, the USA. At the current stage of development, this is still largely the guiding assumption. Some shadows are, however, being cast on the assumption by two contemporary tendencies.

One is the enormous valorization of the whole Internet media world, with resulting pressures to produce more revenues from users, by one means or another and also new forms of monopoly control by major media owners and service providers. Forces of concentration are at work, even if the consequences are not so evident in the vast detail of what is on offer. The drive for income from on-line traffic has generated a large industry devoted to monitoring use and converting the results into valuable data for advertisers.

Another, still somewhat murky, trend is towards surveillance of uses and users by public agencies of various kinds for various kinds of socially approved objectives ranging from safeguarding national security to protection of Children. This can lead to direct and arbitrary intervention in particular instances, without much appeal, often by service providers who answer only to their commercial interests. It can also lead to covert 'chilling' of some sources. The threats to freedom to publish or receive that now arise are likely to be either hidden or arbitrary or both. In general, there are no laws or conventions designed to safeguard the presumed new freedoms. In a sense, these limitations are quite consistent with a conditions of freedom that are not guaranteed or based on principle, but just circumstantial.

The once obsessive attention to the value of 'objectivity' begins to seem either mistaken or simply out of date, for somewhat similar reasons. In general, the vast supply of information, often mixed with ideas and opinions that circulates via the Internet carries no general claim to being 'true' and any judgment about reliability depends on the user's assessment. Amongst the whole supply there will be many sources that are still produced within the old rules of 'objective journalism', but they may be less easy to identify. It is not that accuracy, balance and other informational qualities are any less valuable than they were, but detailed evaluation and monitoring are no longer possible if only because of the scale of the task.

The third widely applied principle of media performance, that of 'diversity', seems similarly at risk of obsolescence. The Internet is by definition extraordinarily diverse. The number of sources and 'channels' cannot be counted, never minded assessed for the quality of this diversity. This does not rule out selective enquiries, for instance into the news offered by major providers or consumed by large 'audiences', or into the range of content types and/ or sources that is actually attended to by large numbers. Concentration of attention still occurs, based on a combination of decisions by suppliers and audiences/users. The Internet behaviour patterns of particular groups can be analysed and compared according to the diversity criterion. Moreover, there is an increasing tendency for Internet as a communication network to take on much the same functions as traditional broadcasting, albeit on the basis of much more user selection. Perhaps rather than obsolete, the diversity criterion needs to be re-imagined and re-engineered for the new circumstances, when it becomes clearer what these are.

TOWARDS A NEW PARADIGM FOR MEDIA POLICY?

The view advanced in this Foreword has largely centred on a deconstruction of an 'old' and tried paradigm, in the face of new realities. Too much media activity and experience has irretrievably escaped the scope of media policy, without even trying to account for new 'social media', also a growing component in the spectrum of public communication. Despite this inescapable conclusion, there are still some persistent survivals of older impulses. These include: a recognition that media can cause harm (personal and public) and can achieve positive collective benefits, when directed to the task. They can also be legitimately called to account by 'society', of which they are still a part. The values of freedom and confidentiality still need to be upheld. The protection of culture, language and identity still matters to many and requires collective effort. What is now increasingly missing or weakened is the institutional means for advancing and protecting values of public communication that have not been diminished. But if media can change and adapt, so can the institutions within which they operate. The search for a 'new paradigm' in these terms is the central thematic of this book.

Part I

European Media in Crisis

Problems, Perspectives
and Definitions

1 What Media Crisis? Normative Starting Points

Josef Trappel, Hannu Nieminen, Werner A. Meier and Barbara Thomass

DEBATING THE "C" OF MEDIA DEVELOPMENT

When the Euromedia Research Group, which is the collective author of this book, started its internal debate on the current state of the media, the letter "C" swiftly became of significance. For some – and those are in the good company of academic scholars – the "C" is best interpreted as crisis, if not collapse. Referring, for example, to the results of the interview-based description of the British news media by Andrew Currah (2009), news brands are being "hollowed out" (2009, p. 130) and journalism in digital newsrooms is experiencing "collateral damage." (ibid., p. 123) Núria Almiron (2010) found a permanent crisis of journalism that has been deepened by the financialisation of corporate media.

For others, however, the "C" stands for change, challenge or even chance. The media – their argument goes – have always been characterised by constant change, probably on a faster and more permanent track than other industries. Exposed to rapid technological innovations in production and susceptible to cutting-edge distribution technologies, the media industry has managed to turn critical developments into chances for future developments. When radio, and later television, was successfully introduced into media markets formerly controlled by the printed press, the latter reinvented itself, adapting to the changing environment by catering for the changing needs and wants of their readers. Seemingly, the media industry lives up to the saying "Never let a good crisis go to waste," credited to Winston Churchill.

On what both schools of thought – the "C" for crisis and the "C" for chance – might agree upon is another understanding of the "C," introduced by Robert McChesney (2013). In his analysis of the implications of capitalism on the Internet, he argues media history can be understood as being driven by critical junctures. These are "rare, brief periods in which dramatic changes are debated and enacted. (…) Most of our major institutions in media are the result of such critical junctures." (ibid., p. 66f) Critical junctures, he continues, occur when revolutionary new communication technologies undermine the existing system, journalistic content is increasingly discredited or seen as illegitimate and when there is a major political crisis in which the dominant institutions are increasingly challenged (ibid., p. 67). All three conditions hold, so the time of another critical juncture has come. Being a media activist as much as an academic scholar, McChesney's analysis might contain elements of wishful thinking. Nevertheless, through the meaning of critical juncture the "C" is even more tightly knit into the fabric of contemporary media development.

In this chapter – and actually in the entire book – we intend to contribute to the better understanding of the ongoing media developments that apparently shake up and potentially destroy the existing order. Regardless of whether we call this process change, crisis or critical juncture, some agents and stakeholders profit to the detriment of others, and public communication irrevocably transforms. We are interested in the various forms and the implications of this process. Our joint research question therefore is:

> In what way and to what extent are the current processes of media change critical to the pursuit of democratic norms and values in contemporary societies?

This is a highly relevant question as it concerns simultaneously the conditions of access to public communication, the conditions of media fulfilling their part of the social contract within democratic societies, and the conditions of journalistic production and content dissemination. There is a price to be paid when these conditions deteriorate: "Vast areas of public life and government activity will take place in the dark (…)." (Nichols and McChesney, 2010) And this would definitely not be desirable.

In this first chapter of the book we take a closer look at the development of the media from various angles. First, we pay tribute to the notion of crisis in the context of social sciences. Second, we argue that any debate on critical developments is associated with underlying values and norms, as a crisis for one might at the same time be a chance for others. Based on these values, we then observe and discuss drivers of change. We then reflect on the history of crises and their implications on public communication and the media. Finally, we conclude by returning to our research question.

INSTITUTIONAL MEDIA CRISIS

Crises appear to be long-sellers in social sciences. It is indeed a suitable starting point for reflecting social changes – and social life changes all the time. The term crisis holds an explicit dramatic undertone and it is more persevering than the tedious terms change or transformation.

Austrian economist Joseph Schumpeter might be credited for pioneering and introducing crisis (and innovation) into mainstream social science research. He criticized the oversimplified understanding that crises happen whenever something of sufficient importance goes wrong. Rather, he argues, crises are incidents of cyclical processes and cannot be regarded as "isolated misfortunes that will happen in consequence of errors, excesses, miscon-duct" or any other failure (Schumpeter, 1942, p. 41). And he states these cyclical processes "by nature [are] a form or method of economic change and not only never is but never can be stationary." (ibid., p. 82) Apparently, Schumpeter had economic developments in mind, but his notion of cyclical occurrence of crises became prominent for the analysis of other fields as well.

Scholars interested in public communication have used the term fre-quently but somewhat inconsistently. During the relatively prosperous 1990s, Jay Blumler and Michael Gurevitch published their book *The Crisis of Public Communication* (1995). They bemoaned the decay of institutions and traditions of public communication. "Institutions that previously organized meaning, identity and authoritative information for many people structured their political preferences and simplified the process of democratic power-seeking – notably political parties, the nuclear family, mainstream religion, neighbourhood and social-class groupings – all have waned in salience and influence." (Blumler and Gurevitch, 1995, p. 2) Furthermore, journalism, in particular its watch-dog role, "is often shunted into channels of per-sonalization, dramatizations, witch-huntery, soap-operatics and sundry trivialities." (ibid., p. 1) In short, Blumler and Gurevitch stipulate: "It would be no exaggeration to describe this state of affairs as a *crisis of civic communication*." (ibid., p. 1) emphasis in the original

In the context of the 2009 ECREA summer school, Hannu Nieminen put a question mark on the title of this contribution, *Media in Crisis?* (Nieminen, 2009) He contextualizes the media crisis within a much wider "epistemic turn" (ibid., p. 36) that rearranges the place of the media in society at large. "It seems plausible that the more complex society and people's everyday life become, and the faster the everyday life choices and decisions have to be made, the less the traditional universal newspaper seen as a department store of information can offer solutions to people's epistemic needs." (ibid., p. 39) In this sense, media need to adapt to the changing social life and if they do, they can avoid the crisis.

More recently, Núria Almiron (2010) identified a severe crisis of journalism, following from the financial market crises that started in 2007. In her reading, the culprits are to be found among financial capitalists. "In the media sector, the 2007–2009 crisis had a strong impact. (...) Nevertheless, the financial and economic turbulence that began in 2007 was by no means what made corporate journalism enter a crisis. Nor was it the Internet or ICTs and digital convergence and their new business models waiting to burst. Nor was it the advertising slump or changing consumer patterns. Rather, financialized corpo-rate logics have been demolishing the democratic foundations of journalism throughout the last decade." (Almiron, 2010, p. 176)

Equally in 2010, a special issue of *Journalism Studies* (Vol. 11, issue 4) was published. In his foreword, Jay Blumler suggests to think of a crisis "with two legs": "One is a crisis of viability, principally though not exclusively financial, threatening the existence and resources of mainstream journalistic organizations. The other is a crisis of civic adequacy, impoverishing the contributions of journalism to citizenship and democracy." (Blumler, 2010, p. 439) In the same issue, James Curran puts a critical question mark behind the claim of British publishers that there is no crisis and "the future of journalism is safe in their hands." (2010, p. 465)

In 2012, a group of scholars around Manuel Castells and Gustavo Cardoso published an edited volume, *Aftermath: The Cultures of the Economic Crisis* (Castells et al., 2012). There, John B. Thompson further elaborates on one of Jürgen Habermas' early works (*Legitimation Crisis*, 1988). Crises occur when systems of some sort break down. Habermas differentiates system crises from identity crises. The former occurs when the self-regulation mechanisms of a system break down, the latter when social integration breaks down: " (…) it arises when members of a society become aware of the major disruption and feel that their own lives or 'collective identity' is in some way threatened." (Thompson, 2012, p. 62) Thompson argues there are overlaps and the distinction is somewhat artificial as system crises may become identity crises and vice versa. Instead, he suggests making a distinction between political crisis, which involves a breakdown of the political system or some serious challenge of the government, and social crisis, "which is a broader social malaise in which people feel that their world is being disrupted in some fundamental way." (ibid., p. 64)

This comprehensive and by no means exhaustive literature review demonstrates the diversity of scholarly understandings of (media) crisis. Blumler and Gurevitch use the term crisis to describe the malaise of public communication they observe. Nieminen refrains from calling a mid- to long-term transformation process a crisis, while Almiron argues journalism is in a permanent state of crisis. Thompson, again, limits crisis to the possible or expected breakdown of systems, which in its social variation also includes the disruption of people's lives.

By way of applying Habermas' and Thompson's line of thinking to the media field, system or political crises translate into institutional media crises. Such crises consequently occur when media (self-) regulation mechanisms collapse and media institutions are critically challenged. Institutional media crises are likely to carry the characteristics of system or political crises, but they do not – at least not until now – qualify as social crises. Various institutional stakeholders are affected in their core business by the critical changes, thus qualifying as a Habermasian system crisis. Journalists, newspaper publishers, advertising retailers, online media providers are among them. Contrary to these centrally affected stakeholders, people (audiences) are much less concerned about the media crises, as there is a plethora of new ways and means to be entertained and informed through Internet-based channels, far beyond incumbent media organizations. The media crisis is much more the crisis of media institutions than a social crisis of the people. People's attitudes might be ignorant and inadequate but this understanding as institutional crisis has important repercussions on the range of possible remedies to cure the media crisis. Such institutional media crises are likely to occur in (Schumpeterian) cycles when McChesney's conditions apply: revolutionary technologies, discredited journalism and challenged institutions.

To conclude, media crises are understood as cycles of institutional crises, which occur when media order and regulation in significant segments of the media field break down, forcing actors and stakeholders to take disruptive decisions. Institutional media crises may transform into social media crises if the conduct of people's lives is upset by these crises. Media change, in contrast, refers to the constant process of transformation over time.

VALUES AND NORMS

Institutions, order and regulation are essential subjects for the understanding of media change and media crisis. All three subjects are closely related to the set of norms and values that are socially agreed upon and enacted in any form of democratic society. Processes of change (and crises), therefore, will impact on this set of norms and values – change and crises are never neutral when it comes to implications and their assessment.

Therefore our analysis of media changes affecting the pursuit of civic virtues needs to make explicit those norms and values that constitute contemporary democracies. Christians et al. (2009, p. 37ff) identify several concepts of values for public communication that are bound to concepts of the order of society. In a corporatist order, which builds strong links inside social groups, truthfulness of public discourse is the prominent value that allows for a peaceful exchange of ideas and decision making. Freedom for those participating in the public sphere is the distinguished normative requirement in a liberal order as no other regulating force than the notorious invisible hand of the market and consequently the marketplace of ideas ensures unrestricted deliberation and decision-making. Deficits in this market-oriented understanding of communication led to the idea of social responsibility in public communication, which is the leading understanding of communication values in pluralist democracy. And civic participation became an important orientation in the postmodern period where individualism and fragmentation of members of society require new forms of exchange and decision-making. A normative perspective of communication thus tries to answer the question: How should public discourse be organized to find solutions (and take decisions) in cases of conflicting interests in society?

Modern pluralist democracies share fundamental values for public communication. Freedom of opinion, of speech and of information, democratic deliberation, protection and promotion of culture, promotion of diversity, universal access and privacy rights are among these values, which are present in all pluralist democratic societies (Babe, 1990; Napoli, 2001). Furthermore, the values of empowerment and participation are highlighted in particular in relation to news. "News (...) can empower citizens by informing them about the social, political and economic events and issues that shape their lives. News (...) is the informational fuel considered vital for a democracy to remain healthy." (Cushion, 2012, p. 43f) Similarly, Blumler and Gurevitch stress the role of the media in activating citizens by providing incentives "to learn, choose and become involved, rather than merely to follow and kibitz over the political process." (1995, p. 97)

These values are firmly rooted in the era of enlightenment, which established the normative fundamentals for the modern political order with civil and human rights and fundamental principles for public communication. Free citizens should have the right to free speech, which should be performed in a public sphere, where public issues are debated and decided following the better arguments. Civil and human rights, the freedom of assembly, of opinion and of the press and the right to elect the government brought a new balance to power.

Today, the public sphere can be understood as a forum where conflicting interests are mediated and debated, where legitimacy and performance of economic and political actors and their agencies are controlled. Public sphere takes the idea of citizens for granted who are connected by common ground. Thus the functions of public sphere are the answer to the requirements of contemporary pluralist democracies (Calhoun, 2003).

Requirements for a well-functioning public sphere can be transferred onto the media. The principle (and value) of universality stipulates no one and no opinion shall be excluded from the public sphere. In the media field, universality means everyone should have access and should be able to make himself or herself heard. All ideas and expressions of culture should be present. Universality as the inclusion of all individuals, groups, opinions and issues is translated in the media into diversity of opinions, issues and actors. Michael Schudson (2010, p. 104) considers advocacy for various viewpoints as one of the essential functions of the media in democracies.

Objectivity is the principle (and value) that describes the effort to be accurate in facts, sound in argumentation and free of personal or vested interests. This principle applies to the journalistic part of the media. Objectivity can also be read as truthfulness and professionalism.

Balance is reflected in the journalistic norms of fairness and accuracy. Arguments, not emotions, should dominate the discourse and any undue bias should be avoided. Linked to the value of balance is the notion of relevance, referring to efforts to concentrate on issues of common interest and not on partial or marginal topics. These principles, from the perspective of the journalistic professional discourse, usually are summarized under the notion of quality – which, as a catch-all word, is then again spelled out by scholars to different criteria as mentioned above.

Without respect for these principles of forming opinion and control of government and power-holders in society, the understanding of a citizenry is impossible. Respect for these principles is essential for a vital democracy.

In an attempt to summarize requirements for the public sphere in contemporary pluralist democracies, Karmasin, Rath and Thomass established the following list of norms and values:

- freedom
- diversity
- the enlightened citizen
- participation, integration, reflection, deliberation
- self-determination of individual
- society as a democratic commons
- orientation towards a welfare and participatory idea of society
- integration of individual and social concerns
- sovereign conduct of life with self-determination, participation and responsibility
- peaceful comity of nations

(Karmasin et al., 2013, p. 475)

Given this extensive – but not exhaustive – list of norms and values for a well-functioning public sphere, our research interest asks how processes of change (and crises) might affect their performance. Most of these norms are well established in national constitutions and broadcasting and press legislation. However, legal or even constitutional certificates do not necessarily guarantee delivery by media institutions and organizations. Processes of critical change might disrupt good intentions laid down, for instance, in internal mission statements of broadcasters or newspapers. Internet-based forms of public communication might be even less inclined to adhere to these values from the outset, perhaps beyond Google's indefinite claim "not to be evil."

Scholars have observed flaws in fulfilling some (or all) of these values. In their study *Media for Democracy Monitor*, Trappel, Nieminen and Lund (2011) compared the performance of the leading news media in ten countries in fulfilling democratic requirements. Their findings unveil considerable differences, some of them linked to national culture and respect for media freedom, others obviously linked to the financial resources at the disposal of the scrutinized news media. Crises following from disruptive economic downturns are likely to impact negatively on the adherence to democratic norms and values. For Britain, Currah reports the observation that the value of enlightened, well-informed citizenry might suffer from the retreat of hard news: "(…) the underlying civic function of news publishers – to gather information and inform society – is steadily being replaced by a softer, more lightweight model that is dependent on the personal views of a relatively small coterie of heavy-weight commentators and celebrity journalists." (Currah, 2009, p. 130) This shift is at least partially caused by cost-benefit considerations, as commentators generally cost less than investigative reporting. Again, the economic downturn might have triggered this trend.

To conclude, research on media change and media crisis is necessarily normative. Contemporary pluralist democracies adhere to a common set of norms and values that has developed over the centuries but needs to be constantly defended. Media change and media crises must therefore be carefully observed with regard to the potential erosion – or indeed re-enforcement – of these norms and values.

DRIVERS OF CHANGE: THE USUAL SUSPECTS

As change is ubiquitous, drivers of change are abundant. Social settings are forceful drivers of change, such as the increase of relative wealth, of mobility, of the amount of free (leisure) time, the availability of social security and the loosening ties to institutions that organize meanings (schools, parties, churches, labour unions etc.) in (post)modern societies. Another set of usual suspects to drive change is the complex of technology and innovation. Perez provides an extensive overview of technological revolutions that changed society. She distinguishes five periods: first, the Industrial Revolution in the late eighteenth century; second, the Age of Steam and Railways, starting in 1829; third, the Age of Steel, Electricity and Heavy Engineering from 1875 onwards; fourth, the Age of Oil, the Automobile and Mass Production from 1908 onwards; and finally, fifth, the Age of Information and Telecommunication beginning in 1971. (Perez, 2009, p. 9) Another driver of change are the lifestyles and habits of people who modify their preferences of consumption and of past-time, certainly in response to changes in the supply of available goods and services.

Joseph Schumpeter acknowledges the complexity of change and suggests capitalism as such as the main driver of change. What counts, according to Schumpeter, is not competition as such but competition for new commodities and new technologies: "(…) competition which commands a decisive cost or quality advantage and which strikes not at the margins of the profits and the outputs of the existing forms but at their foundations and their very lives." (ibid., p. 84)

So there are good reasons to look more closely at features of capitalism to better understand media change. We concentrate on three such drivers of change, which are related to the capitalist order and which have been discussed extensively by communication scholars in the past. These are (a) technology; (b) the Internet; and (c) commercialization and advertising. These driving forces are obviously interrelated.

Technology

Raymond Williams called technological determinism "an immensely powerful and now largely orthodox view of the nature of social change" (1974, p. 13). According to this somewhat ideological position, new technologies and the process of research and development are considered to set the conditions for social change and progress. Williams, a great opponent to this view, suggests analysing and understanding the role of technology in the process of change as symptomatic, rather than deterministic. Technology, in his view, becomes an element in the process of change, which is occurring in any case. This view "considers particular technologies, or a complex of technologies, as *symptoms* of change of some other kind. Any particular technology is then as it were a by-product of a social process." (ibid.) Williams then uses the rise of the press to illustrate this process. The press in Britain was not driven by print technology but by the need of two powerful agents, the political elites and trade representatives. Both had a need to address large audiences with their messages. "Early newspapers were a combination of that kind of messages – political and social information – and the specific messages – classified advertising and general commercial news – of an expanding system of trade." (ibid., p. 21)

Contemporary scholarly writings elaborate this perspective further. Graham Meikle and Sherman Young conclude their analysis of the rise of the Internet by stating: "But our point is that *the development of media technologies is an ongoing process, not an event.*" (2012, p. 33) In their view, technology needs to be understood as "produced and developed within complex relationships between people, institutions and technical possibilities." (ibid., p. 21) It is therefore not the technology itself that changes society but specific members of the changing societies, who provide the means and resources to develop technologies. Williams reminds us that technologies that promise to cater for the needs of those who are in power are more likely to succeed: "A need which corresponds with the priorities of the real decision-making groups will, obviously, more quickly attract the investment of resources and the official permission, approval or encouragement (…). We can see this clearly in the major developments of industrial production and, significantly, in military technology." (Williams, 1974, p. 19)

Lister et al. (2003, p. 81) condensed Williams' view into a non-deterministic research agenda for technology and change: "Williams' emphasis called for an examination of (1) the reasons for which technologies are developed, (2) the complex of social, cultural, and economic factors which shape them, and (3) the ways that technologies are mobilised for certain ends (…)."

For these reasons, technology is not an appropriate starting point to study and explain social change. Media and communication technologies are no exception. The technologies that enabled the rise of the press, radio, television and lately the Internet responded to changes in society and the desire of the political and economic elites to keep the Schumpeterian cycle of capitalism in motion.

Internet

Ideas of technological determinism returned in a surprising move when the Internet (or the World Wide Web) was introduced in the early 1990s.

According to some enthusiastic scholars, the Internet holds the promise not only for social change but for improving democratic agency, participation, empowerment and many more desirable values in contemporary democracies. Almost twenty-five years after the launch of the World Wide Web, some more realistic perceptions of the emancipatory potential of the Internet have prevail. In his bleak analysis of the Internet as being turned against democracy by capitalism, Robert McChesney contends "[t]he Internet and the broader digital revolution are not inexorably determined by technology; they are shaped by how society elects to develop them." (2013, p. 216) And this society, it seems, elects to use the Internet primarily for commercial reasons.

Media and public communication are affected by the Internet in their core business and in fulfilling their role in society. Colin Sparks (2004) assessed the consequences of the first severe crisis of the then still early Internet on incumbent media. After a pronounced overheating of expectations and a considerable flow of investment money (venture capital) in the late 1990s, the so-called dot.com bubble burst in 2000/2001. While online media had to reduce staff, cut costs and reduce investments, the implications of the Internet on incumbent media easily survived the dot.com crisis. The first in Sparks' list of impacts of the Internet on media business models is the erosion of previous distinctions of content and delivery technology, "replaced by a single kind of content – digitized information – transmitted along common channels and available through common reception technologies." (Sparks, 2004, p. 311) Indeed, as a consequence, competition between formerly separated media increases as digital content is available (for the time being) on a non-discriminatory and network-neutral basis. Incumbent media are forced to compete with start-ups and global giants like Google, Facebook and Twitter in addition to their earlier competitors.

Küng et al. (2008) further elaborated the impacts of the Internet on the mass-media industry from an economic perspective. Network effects, price discrimination, customization and personalisation, bundling and unbundling, convergence are just a few of these impacts. Together with uncertainties concerning regulation in this contested field (in particular copyright legislation and network neutrality requirements), the authors draw the conclusion that – in their terminology – an "isoquantic shift" is to be expected, which refers "to a significant technological advancement that dramatically changes the way people do things and completely reorientates people's concepts of how things are done." (ibid., p. 36) Such an isoquantic shift, following from the various implications the Internet has on incumbent media, is most likely to result in what we defined as institutional crisis of the media.

Commercialization and Advertising

As discussed above, media organizations are centrally affected by the commercialization of the Internet. Incumbent media organizations are confronted with the decay of the link between journalistic content and advertising. Sparks explains that the Internet "allows for the disaggregating of editorial and advertising material. (...) It is no longer necessary for the reader to be exposed to the advertising messages in order to gain access to editorial material, nor is it necessary to be exposed to editorial material in order to gain access to advertising." (Sparks, 2004, p. 314f) Ten years later, this process of disaggregation is far advanced and one of the main concerns of incumbent media organizations and the institution of journalism. "Indeed, what is especially ominous for the future of journalism is that some advertising has shifted not from traditional news media to their satellite news web-sites, but has leapfrogged instead to other parts of the Web, which have nothing to do with journalism." (Curran, 2010, p. 468) With regard to news production, Currah reports from his interview-based research in Britain that the Internet erodes the economic viability of news production: "The principal conclusion is that increasing commercial pressure, mainly driven by the inherent characteristics of the digital revolution, is undermining the business models that pay for the news (...)." (Currah, 2009, p. 5) Denis McQuail agrees with this conclusion and states: "The steady commodification (monetarisation) of the internet displaces early ties of obligation to the public and society (...)" (2013, p. 175), resulting in increasing commercialization and superficiality of content.

To conclude, while neither (digital) technology nor the Internet (World Wide Web) as such can be considered to be drivers of change, their implications for public communication and, in particular, incumbent media organizations are severe. The Internet by and large reflects larger shifts in society and enables new economic actors to introduce new rules to public communication. As the media order, as well as regulation in journalism and news provision, is eroding, if not breaking down, it is well justified to talk about an institutional media crisis. Actors and stakeholders are required to take disruptive decisions.

LEARNING FROM FORMER CRISES

How does the current institutional media crisis correspond with earlier times of crisis and change in the media field? Given the commercial character of most media organizations, economic prosperity or deficiency might also serve as apparent predictors for the (economic) success or failure of the media. But this analysis would fail to encompass the complexity of the matter if media were merely counted as economic subjects. Instead, we argue that prosperity and crisis of the media are closely linked to the social role media played – or were expected to play – in different stages of contemporary history. Our argument rests on the assumption that media have been pivotal in the social and cultural construction of modern nation states. Thus media can be compared to other major nation-building institutions, such as education, church, army and civil service. All these institutions can be characterized as being epistemic, creating and reproducing a form of knowledge that is centrally constructed around national concepts and symbols. Furthermore, contrary to the above sketched, oversimplified argument, we hold that economic crises are not necessarily bad times for the media.

We start this retrospection with the Second World War. Since then, four distinct socio-political and socio-cultural periods can be distinguished:

Post-War Until Late 1960, Early 1970:
Media Constructing the Nation

This period was characterised by the deployment of an extensive mode of reproduction (in contrast to the intensive mode adopted later). The central metaphor was large-scale industrial production: factories, Taylorism, division of labour, etc. For the effective organization of industrial production, a policy of social and political pacification and softening down the class differences was adopted. A large number of social reforms were carried out by the early 1970s. In a number of countries, the left-wing parties, previously excluded from political life, were now invited into national negotiations and consensus building efforts and new ways of workers' participation were experimented in industrial relations, etc. Ralf Dahrendorf's concept of the peaceful settlement of societal conflicts was influential in these processes. (cf. Dahrendorf, 1959) The first oil crisis of 1973 ended the period of continuous economic growth, also called the "long boom."

In order to enhance the values and ethos of national reconstruction, the main epistemic institutions were engaged in this work. This concerned equally education, church, cultural institutions (arts, museums and libraries), universities and sciences, as well as the media. In broadcasting, new innovations took place, both in the form of television and in the improved transmission technology in radio (FM), promoting also new institutional models such as the co-habitation between BBC and ITV in the UK. The newspaper press, experiencing a rapid period of reconstruction and renewal, organized competing interests between different classes and other social forces but situated this competition sternly within national frames – which required a recognition of differing interests sharing, however, a common framework or symbolic reservoir.

Late 1960s Until Late 1980s: Media Serving
Social Welfare

By the early 1970s, the Western economy started to suffer from structural problems. Starting from the US, economic growth stagnated, joined with rapidly rising inflation. Social and political stability, long reigned by the fruits of growth, faltered and resulted in increasing signs of mass discontent (France, 1968) and terrorist activities (Germany, Italy, US).

The basic mode of capital accumulation changed from the extensive to the intensive mode, which did not require any more of the same kind of integrative social and cultural policies. Instead of the policy that aimed at equalising societal differences, policies promoting social disintegration and segregation were adopted as they promised better economic benefits – at least in the short term. This was the promise of the neoliberal turn, which started to gain a foothold, first in the US and the UK in the late 1970s and later in most European countries.

At the same time, the traditional global system based on a negotiated balance between nation states (of which the UN was an emblematic example) appeared to have run its course. The political and economic sovereignty of nation states now created an obstacle for global capital accumulation. If European countries and companies were willing to compete with the US and Japan in the global market, it required the establishment of a single European market, supported and enhanced by respective social and political structures.

In this period, television (and previously radio) represented a different form of interest organization. Instead of particular interests as presented by newspapers – and the form of external pluralism they represented – radio broadcasting epitomised public interest, in the sense that particular interests were negotiated and organized within one medium. Against the class-based citizenship, this form of internal pluralism promoted the idea of universalist citizenship. The commercialized newspapers, which gradually took over from the party press, offered still another way of organizing national interests based on universalized internal pluralism: a market-based organization (consumer identity).

Late 1980s Until 2000: Media Marketized

During this period, economic and political relations consolidated. The European Union accepted new members and the internal market grew accordingly. However, the conditions for the traditional relations of social production, which used to be based on the principles of full employment and national social and cultural integration, no longer existed. Societies segregated according to economic wealth. Impulses for economic growth were sought from several directions: lowering the costs of industrial production; transferring production to low-wage countries; flexibilizing labour contracts (crushing the union power); substituting computerized work processes for human labour (post-Fordism); removing global and regional trade barriers; reconstructing the financial mechanisms to promote growth: expanding the non-productive sector of economy (banking, insurance, taxation); creating global financial markets; inventing new instruments to intensify the circuit of capital (options and other incentives, hedge funds); exposing previously non-market functions of society and culture to market logics; privatisation of public utilities and services; adopting New Public Management principles to public administration; commodification of culture and symbolic production (education, universities, arts and other cultural institutions, the media); re-redistribution of wealth: promoting private monopolies through privatising public utilities (windfall profits); rewarding the capital owners and other high-income groups by tax redemptions paid for by cuts in public services.

In order to manage and co-ordinate all these different elements of the transformation of capitalism, two basic conditions were needed. Politically, a new elite consensus was required to replace the old one, based on a modelled Keynesian economic ideal. Technologically, the new global economic and financial formation required a constant monitoring and controlling of both the processes of production and trade and the flow of financial transactions. A new global information network (the Internet) with very high capacity was necessary.

The media were supposed to support the new (global and European) order and were expected to contribute as mediators between national and European interests and as economic actors themselves. In particular, the entertainment and cultural industries were becoming increasingly important economic areas. Furthermore, the new political consensus needed popular legitimacy. The media had a major role in constructing public consent to support the new policies – which, in many respects, were undermining the previous achievements on social policy and labour relations. Most importantly, however, the new global economic and financial order required the rapid expansion of the Internet as a computerized information network. In the name of efficiency, all societal institutions and organizations needed to be linked to the network: industry, administration, households. The Internet (or new ICT more generally) promised to fulfill several mutually beneficial economic functions. It provided a necessary conduit for economic and financial information (business-to-business); it created a new business area in itself (Google, Microsoft, Apple, Facebook, mobile connectivity); it opened up new global business opportunities and models for business; and it offered new ways for interaction between public administration and citizens.

2000 Until Today (2014): Co-Ordination Challenges

The period is characterized by an increasing imbalance between the three levels of global media and communication policy: national, regional and global. Because of the decentred nature of the Internet, national governments lack the means for its regulation. As long as the service-providers are located outside the national jurisdiction, there is no legal means to regulate them on a national level. To a different degree, the same problem concerns the EU. Its competence is restricted to the media activities that take place in the territory of its member states. And again, on the global level, there are no such political organs or international organizations that have full competence over the functions of the Internet, although the ITU has certain authority over some of its technical aspects.

As the economic balance in the realm of the media is increasingly tipping from the other industrial branches (print media, television, recorded media) to the Internet, this is met with a simultaneous development in the area of global political system from a multi-centred order to a US-led mono-centred regime. One concrete result of this development is the global intelligence operation by the NSA, capable of spying on all Internet and telecommunication traffic. In the sphere of media-content services, the US-run companies Microsoft, Facebook, Google, Netflix and others dominate the Internet-based communication. In the case of conflicts between the jurisdictions, the companies prefer to negotiate directly between the European governments and to strike bilateral compromises, instead of negotiating with the EU about all-European solutions.

Instead of what was wished for in the early 2000s, the developments in Europe are characterized by increasing tendencies of disintegration. The anticipation of a European public sphere, uniting European people and establishing a space for open dialogue and democratic will, has changed to the fragmentation of Europe. The European media, instead of promoting a collective European identity and solidarity, reflects the increasing social and political polarization of European societies.

To conclude this retrospect, we argue that media crises correspond with the role played in different periods of contemporary history and the evidence supports this argument. The media played pivotal roles in accompanying the epistemic turn from the post-War reconstruction period to the current global, neoliberal economic order. Lately, the media are losing relevance as major nation-building institutions, causing a crisis that clearly goes deeper than short-term economic problems.

CONCLUSIONS

By returning to our research question, "In what way and to what extent current processes of change might be critical to the pursuit of democratic norms and values?" we conclude the current media change qualifies as an institutional media crisis. Over the last six decades, the media followed the political and economic orders, playing a pivotal role as major nation-building institutions themselves. Lately, however, this institutional role has eroded in parallel to the rise of new channels and distribution technologies that network political elites with citizens and business with consumers. The institutional crisis is therefore deeper rooted than in the more obvious economic turmoil caused by new competitors on the Internet and shifts in advertising budgets from incumbent media organizations to Internet-based businesses. This process of erosion has repercussions on the pursuit of democratic norms and values. In times of crisis – i.e. when significant segments of the media field break down and disruptive decisions need to be taken – media organizations might no longer be in a position (and willing) to adhere to their underlying and inherited norms and values. Media policy, therefore, needs to reflect upon and enact measures to establish framework conditions that ensure the pursuit of democratic norms and values.

REFERENCES

Almiron, N. (2010) *Journalism in Crisis. Corporate Media and Financialization.* Cresskill, NJ: Hampton Press.

Babe, R. E. (1990) *Telecommunications in Canada: Technology, Industry and Government.* Toronto: University of Toronto Press.

Blumler, J. G. (2010) Foreword. The two-legged crisis of journalism. *Journalism Studies,* 11(4). pp. 439–41.

Blumler, J. G. and Gurevitch, M. (1995) *The Crisis of Public Communication.* London: Routledge.

Castells, M., Craca, J. and Cardoso, G. (eds) (2012) *Aftermath. The Cultures of the Economic Crisis.* Oxford: Oxford University Press.

Calhoun, C. (2003) The Democratic Integration of Europe: Interests, Identity, and the Public Sphere. In: Berezin, M. and Schain, M. (eds.), *Europe Without Borders: Remapping Territory, Citizenship, and Identity on a Transnational Age* (pp. 243–74). Baltimore: Johns Hopkins University.

Christians, C. G., Glasser, T. L., McQuail, D., Nordenstreng, K. and White, R. A. (2009) *Normative Theories of the Media: Journalism in Democratic Societies.* Urbana, IL: University of Illinois Press.

Currah, A. (2009) *What's happening to our News: An investigation into the likely impact of the digital revolution on the economics of news publishing in the UK.* Oxford: Reuters Institute of the Study of Journalism.

Curran, J. (2010) The Future of Journalism. *Journalism Studies,* 11(4). 464–76.

Cushion, S. (2012) *The Democratic Value of News: Why Public Service Media Matter.* Hampshire, NY: Palgrave Macmillan.

Dahrendorf, R. (1959) *Class and Class Conflict.* Stanford: Stanford University Press.

Karmasin, M., Rath, M. and Thomass, B. (eds) (2013) *Normativität in der Kommunikationswissenschaft.* Wiesbaden: Springer VS.

Küng, L., Picard, R. and Towse, R. (2008) Theoretical perspectives on the impact of the Internet on the mass media industries. In: Küng, L., Picard, R. and Towse, R. (eds) *The Internet and the Mass Media* (pp. 17–44). Los Angeles, London, New Delhi, Singapore: Sage.

Lister, M., Dovey, J., Giddings, S., Grant, I. and Kelly, K. (2003) *New media: a critical introduction.* London: Routledge.

McChesney, R. (2013) *Digital Disconnect: How Capitalism is Turning the Internet Against Democracy.* New York: New Press.

McQuail, D. (2013) *Journalism and Society.* London, Thousand Oaks, New Delhi, Singapore: Sage.

Meikle, G. and Young, S. (2012) *Media Convergence: Networked Digital Media in Everyday Life.* Hampshire, NY: Palgrave Macmillan.

Napoli, P. M. (2001) *Foundations of Communications Policy: Principles and Process in the Regulation of Electronic Media.* Cresskill, NJ: Hampton Press.

Nichols, J. and McChesney, R. (2010) How to Save Journalism. *The Nation.* 25 January 2010. Retrieved from: http://www.thenation.com/article/how-save-journalism-0#.

Nieminen, H. (2009) Media in crisis? Social, economic and epistemic dimensions. In: Carpentier, N., Pruulmann-Vengerfeldt, P., Kilborn, R., Olsson, T., Nieminen, H., Sundin, E. and Nordenstreng, K. (eds) *Communicative Approaches to Politics and Ethics in Europe: The intellectual work of the 2009 ECREA European media and communication Doctoral summer school* (pp. 31–43). Tartu, Estonia: Tartu University Press.

Perez, C. (2009) Technological revolutions and techno-economic paradigms. *Working Papers in Technology Governance and Economic Dynamics*, 20. Retrieved from: http://hum.ttu.ee/wp/paper20.pdf.

Schudson, M. (2010) News in Crisis in the United States: Panic – and Beyond. In: Nielsen, R. K. and Levy, D. A. L. (eds) *The Changing Business of Journalism and Its Implications for Democracy* (pp. 95–106). Oxford: Reuters Institute for the Study of Journalism.

Schumpeter, J. (1942) *Capitalism, Socialism and Democracy*. 3rd edition. New York, London: Harper & Brothers.

Sparks, C. (2004) The Impact of the Internet on the Existing Media. In: Calabrese, A. and Sparks, C. (eds) *Towards a Political Economy of Culture: Capitalism and Communication in the Twenty-First Century* (pp. 307–26). Lanham, MD: Rowman & Littlefield Publishers.

Thompson, J. B. (2012) The Metamorphosis of a Crisis. In: Castells, M., Craca, J. and Cardoso, G. (eds) *Aftermath: The Cultures of the Economic Crisis* (pp. 59–81). Oxford: Oxford University Press.

Trappel, J., Nieminen, H. and Nord, L. W. (eds) (2011) *The Media for Democracy Monitor: A Cross National Study of Leading News Media*. Gothenburg: Nordicom.

Williams, R. (1974) *Television: Technology and Cultural Form*. New York: Schocken.

2 Systemic Media Changes and Social and Political Polarization in Europe

Auksė Balčytienė and Kristina Juraitė

INTRODUCTION

This paper contributes to the debate on evolving uncertainty and crisis in the European mediascape. While in many countries economic factors are often blamed for dramatic modifications of media operations, this chapter follows a different approach. It suggests the adjustment of European media to shifting contextual (economic, technological) conditions is also affected by mounting societal changes and transformations, amongst which the individualization of consumption is the dominating one. The paper argues that audience interests and growing personalized access opportunities to information reinforce media fragmentation, which, furthermore, leads to audience segmentation and increasing political and social polarization within and across various nations in Europe. Individualized information consumption appears to be critical for European democracy since it affects the cohesion of society. By diverting public attention away from shared and communal dialogues to private interests and soft issues in the media it challenges the notion of good community. By reducing civic involvements it intensifies public anxieties and increases uncertainty, skepticism and distrust. As argued, younger Central and Eastern European democracies appear to be more seriously affected by these societal changes, as well as by their outcomes and effects, than Western European societies where long-lasting democratic practices and traditions have secured certain conditions and mechanisms for healthier performance of their media and public engagement in communal matters. The chapter makes the suggestion that contemporary societal developments call for the reinvention of the normative vision and recognized ideals of professional journalism.

SYSTEMIC TRANSFORMATIONS AND THE ATMOSPHERE OF CHANGE

Changing European societies and their media landscapes have recently been undergoing multifold challenges of an economic, technological and institutional nature, including declining revenues, shrinking audiences and emerging new technologies that create an unstable, volatile and stressful environment. As widely discussed in the literature on institutional development analysis, change is always accompanied by instabilities and concerns including uncertainties and feelings of loss (Giddens, 2013; Bauman, 2000). To us, this observation is important and it forms the theoretical basis of our chapter. More specifically, we view the process of institutional change as being primarily a social phenomenon, and thus a historical and cultural (and not just an economic or technological) progression. Applied specifically to the analysis of media transformations in today's Europe, such a perspective calls for a closer look at historical and cultural legacies as manifested in people's mentalities and traditions, their values and behaviours as well as a sense of the right timing for pursuing and managing societal change (Hoyer, 2001). Such an approach rests on the idea that all decisions are made by people or groups of people and organizations. Hence enduring traditions, norms, values, fashions and ways of life, and also the feelings, emotions, perceptions and impressions associated with required adjustments, should not be neglected, misjudged or underestimated.

This chapter looks at the evolving trends in the European mediascape and discusses changes in media performance occurring simultaneously with societal change. In both established democracies in the West as well as in transitional democracies in Central and Eastern Europe, a growing proportion of the public is less inclined to consume political news (Aalberg et al., 2013). At the same time the rise of political disengagement and a decline in support for conventional party ideologies and party membership (and politics in general) are echoed in various European States (as seen in the data presented in Tables 2.1 and 2.2).

Our analysis is based on the cross-national data from the European Social Survey (ESS), which has been conducted every two years across Europe since 2001.[1] In this chapter, the Round 6 data collected from twenty-nine European countries in 2012 is analyzed. For the analysis, selected CEE and Western European countries have been compared in terms of public consumption of politics, legitimacy of institutions, public and political participation, social well-being and democratic values.

Table 2.1 Public perceptions of media, democracy and social well-being in CEE, % (ESS, 2012)

	Bulgaria	Czech Republic	Estonia	Lithuania	Poland	Slovenia	Slovakia
Media are free to criticize the government (6–10)	59.2	**74.4**	62.5	59.9	**70.9**	**76.9**	**70.6**
Watching news/ politics/current affairs (more than 1 hour daily)	**38.6**	**24.6**	25.9	24.1	18.5	15.4	25

(Continued)

	Bulgaria	Czech Republic	Estonia	Lithuania	Poland	Slovenia	Slovakia
Heavy TV watching (more than 3 hours daily)	43.4	31.7	21.6	25	15.4	11	30.5
Interested in politics	51.1	22.1	39.6	21.1	39.7	41.3	31.4
Trust in national parliament (6–10 points)	7.2	16.7	25.4	15.8	12.9	14.9	15.6
Trust in political parties (6–10 points)	4.1	14.1	13.8	11.5	5.6	6.8	9.6
Trust in legal system (6–10 points on 10 point scale)	9.7	29.1	41.7	27.9	19.5	18.2	15.2
Voted in last national election	72.5	59.7	59.3	53.9	65	69.7	75.1
Being active in political party	2.8	1.9	2.3	3.8	2.5	2.6	1.8
Being active in other organizations	1.2	6.3	4.8	2.8	7.3	1.9	4.8
Current member of the trade union	4.7	5.6	5.2	3.3	5.5	13.4	6.7
Assessing one's **country as democratic** (6–10 points)	26.9	61.6	54.6	51.4	55.1	36.8	52.3
Satisfied with the way **democracy** works in country (6–10)	10.8	42	40.1	29.6	39.7	20.4	40.1
Satisfied with country's **economy** (6–10 points)	3.7	27.1	26.9	22.9	29.4	8.7	18.4
Most people can be trusted (6–10 points)	17.7	31.4	48.4	46.2	26.1	34.6	26.2
Feeling **happy** (6–10 points on 10 point scale)	56.3	70.7	73.6	66.3	79.6	77.2	71.9
Feeling **optimistic** about one's future (6–10 points)	55.3	58.1	68.6	58.2	68.4	73.2	56.6
Felt **anxious** last week	83.4	42.2	59.1	69.7	39.6	28	56.1

Table 2.2 Public perceptions of media, democracy and social well-being in Western Europe, % (ESS, 2012)

	Belgium	Denmark	Finland	Germany	Ireland	Netherlands	Norway	Portugal	Spain	Sweden	Switzerland	UK
Media are free to criticize the government (6–10)	84.4	95.5	90.9	89.9	85	91.1	93.7	62.2	73.7	93.1	85.3	82.4
Watching news/politics/current affairs (more than 1 hour daily)	18.9	16.7	12.9	14	30.3	23.7	12.1	31.7	18.1	9.8	5.8	34
Heavy TV watching (more than 3 hours daily)	18.2	34.6	26.5	18.8	26.8	30.4	30.1	37.2	27.4	19.4	10	24.4
Interested in politics	45.1	69.9	54.6	64.3	43.4	64.7	50.7	29.6	34.8	58	62	49.6
Trust in national parliament (6–10 points)	34.2	62.6	61.4	37	24.5	51.8	66.3	9.3	21	60.4	62.8	29.5
Trust in political parties (6–10 points)	29.7	48	41	17.1	12.3	47	42.6	3.1	7.1	38.2	41.4	18.1
Trust in legal system (6–10 points on 10 point scale)	43.8	85.6	81.5	57.9	46.2	66.2	82.1	18.9	24.9	65.4	70.5	51.7
Voted in last national election	78.5	85.3	79	73.1	69.6	80.9	75.3	64.5	72	82.1	55.5	68.6
Being active in political party	4.4	3.9	3.1	4.6	3.5	3.5	7.9	1.4	7.7	4.4	6.4	2
Being active in other organizations	18.4	25	37.2	31.6	11.4	25.2	32.1	4	22	34.3	17.4	7.9

(Continued)

	Belgium	Denmark	Finland	Germany	Ireland	Netherlands	Norway	Portugal	Spain	Sweden	Switzerland	UK
Current member of the trade union	31	58	51	11.5	13.2	17.1	48.7	4.3	–	45.6	9.5	13.1
Assessing one's country as democratic (6–10 points)	73.7	93.4	88.8	76.2	70.3	82.3	89.8	57.3	51.7	89.5	92.1	71.6
Satisfied with the way democracy works in country (6–10)	62.2	83.3	81.2	51.7	50.2	73.3	85.2	24.6	32.8	80.2	86.3	52.2
Satisfied with country's economy (6–10 points)	43.2	53.3	68	59.1	11.9	48.6	91.3	5.3	6.1	66.2	82.3	20.1
Most people can be trusted (6–10 points)	45.8	78.4	74.4	38.9	45.7	64.3	75	20.1	44.3	62.5	53.5	47.8
Feeling happy (6–10 points on 10 point scale)	91.9	95.5	95.2	87.3	78	93.5	94.3	69.2	86.9	91.2	93.5	84.4
Feeling optimistic about one's future (6–10 points)	64.6	81	75.6	81	75.1	66.9	76.9	53	62.3	76.3	83.8	71.6
Felt anxious last week	69.8	21.3	33.9	19.2	43.8	69	18.2	60.4	34.6	38.9	63.7	46

The cross-national data of the European Social Survey (2012) show great variations are found across different European countries on how people assess their country's democratic features, as well as their own emotional and economic well-being characteristics (see Table 2.1 and Table 2.2). Simultaneously, public participation in political parties, trade unions and NGOs, as well as people's trust in political institutions (parliament, government, political parties, legal system), is particularly low in the CEE countries (see Table 2.1). Furthermore, current democratic processes and economic developments have been more critically judged in CEE and certain countries of Southern Europe than in the rest of the European continent (see Table 2.1 and Table 2.2). For instance, Bulgaria (and also Russia, which we included into our analysis for comparative reasons) differs from other countries in the ways in which people express their unhappiness, frustration and disappointment with their country's democracy, economy and politics (see Table 2.1 and Figure 2.1).

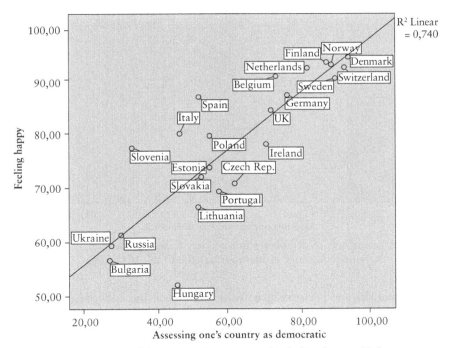

Figure 2.1 Assessment of democracy in a country by feeling happy, % Source: Authors' estimations based on ESS (2012) data.

On the other hand, the biggest optimists in terms of how democracies are performing and a general climate of social trust, satisfaction and happiness can be found in the Nordic nations, as well as in Switzerland, the Netherlands, Belgium and Germany (see Figure 2.1), i.e. those countries that not only have stable economies but also stronger democratic traditions, civic skills and experience. People in these countries are engaged and participate in public matters; they also show their strong commitment to democratic ideals (they participate in elections, they are active in professional and communal organizations) (see Table 2.2). They also express stronger trust in other people (see Figure 2.2), which creates a healthier and more favourable climate for social cohesion and solidarity.

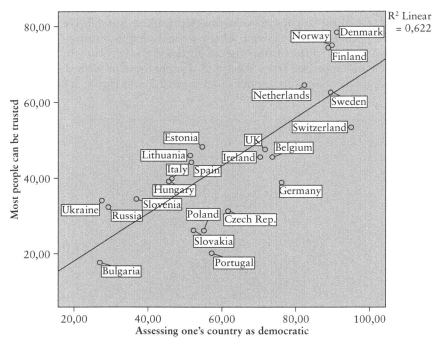

Figure 2.2 Assessment of democracy in a country by trust in people,
          % Source: Authors' estimations based on ESS (2012) data.

Media qualities and performance (its independence and adherence to watchdog recommendations) in Northern and Western Europe are also measured as following strong professionalism ideals, which, once again, show stronger satisfaction among people with how democracies work in their respective countries (see Figure 2.3). In contrast, transitional societies and countries with former authoritarian or totalitarian experiences (predominantly those from Southern Europe and the CEE) do not show similar results of strong optimism and satisfaction. Nor do they assess their media operations as highly professional (see Figure 2.3). All in all, these illustrations visibly follow the vision of Daniel Hallin and Paolo Mancini: three models of media and politics and their corresponding country clusters of Northern and Western Europe, as well as CEE and Southern Europe (Hallin and Mancini, 2004).

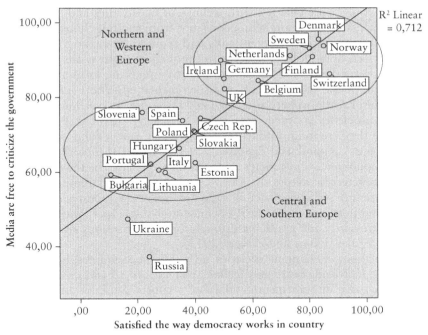

Figure 2.3 Assessment of democracy and media freedom in a country,
% Source: Authors' estimations based on ESS (2012) data.

Our main assumption in this paper is that these differences and dissimi-
larities in public perceptions could also be observed as variations found
across European media – for example, in democratic performance quality
characteristics as well as other features, predominantly in such functions
as public-service orientation, accountability, professional solidarity and the
like. But before we look specifically at media operations, we would like to
address here another matter, namely making a minor but essentially significant distinction between transitional CEE countries, which in the past two
decades experienced an inflow of very intense and varied transformations
(Sparks, 2012; Jakubowicz and Sükösd, 2008), and the rest of European
countries, predominantly from the Western part of the same continent.
Western societies and their media indeed display transformative characteristics as well. As extensively discussed, many of those are related to economic
fluctuations and technological innovations, but as we argue here, changes
that Western nations and their media are going through are less dramatic
and complex when compared to transformations in the CEE because these
are occurring within well-established and functioning mechanisms and societal structures and within the frameworks of agreed-upon policies, customs
and traditions. With this line of thinking, it may seem as if Central and
Eastern Europe live in an endless cycle of intense fluctuations and instability,

in a social atmosphere charged with feelings of uncertainty and flux. As a matter of fact, such an impression comes not from societal change as such but from the abundance of urgent calls and requests emanating from and inspired by not only global pressures (technological innovations or financial crises or geopolitical changes) but also by mounting local ambitions, demands and public hopes. Hence, an issue touched upon here is related to the socio-cultural atmosphere as created and fashioned by systemic changes. Transitional societies are predetermined to be in a certain 'flux' (Balčytienė, 2013) since they are in an 'enduring change.' They lack a solid 'social and ideological base' (Rupnik and Zielonka, 2013; Sparks, 2012; Norkus, 2011) and thus impulsiveness, instability and volatility appear to be the dominant cultural characteristic across the CEE. Conversely, such extreme volatility is not apparent in societies of the West, where societal structures and institutional conditions are more clearly defined and stable and where change occurs progressively and gradually through formal institutions and through agreed-upon rules (Ekiert and Ziblatt, 2013).

As we suggest, in changing societies, all public uncertainties, hesitations and doubts, increasing fears and feelings of loss lead to and culminate in various concerns, disagreements and value conflicts. Such an atmosphere negatively affects both people and institutions, and thus calls to be described as uncertainty, discontent or, even more, as crisis. Its reflections are also recognized in all social fields, politics and media.

FROM NORMATIVE VISIONS TO ACTUAL CHALLENGES

According to the normative point of view, the ideal for media performance in healthy democracies should be as a source of objective information that is widely available to citizens and interest groups (Trappel et al., 2011; Christians et al., 2009). Democratic media have a number of functions. They should support free speech and act as a check (watchdog) on the activities of powerful institutions. This ideal vision also foresees that democratic media should promote a discursive space for the emergence of rational debate. The media should act as mediators and social mobilizers. In a modern society, the media should be a pillar together with other societal institutions such as education, healthcare, or cultural structures and systems, consolidating societies and keeping nations together (Deuze, 2008).

However in the twenty-first century, serious pressures, challenges, drawbacks and the media's failure to adhere to ideals of professional journalism are reported throughout Europe. To secure journalistic independence and autonomy, various models have been developed to counter both internal and external pressures (see, for example, the discussion in Chapter 4). However some recent failures of journalistic professionalism happened because of the stresses of market competition, which can place high standards and ethical principles under pressure in the battle for market share. Market pressures reveal the vulnerability of journalism's democratic function of public service, both in older and young European democracies (Schudson, 2010; Štetka, 2013).

Economic change is often pinpointed as creating shifts in journalistic production and a dramatic modification of media operations in various countries (Wiik and Andersson, 2013; Štetka, 2013). The financial fluctuations and global economic crises of recent years have affected media business operations and financial models in weak and strong economies, in small and large markets, in European countries with long-standing traditions of professional journalism and in those nations where professional journalism is under greater political pressure, such as Central and Eastern Europe or Southern European states. Alongside the financial crisis and uncertain media business models, newspaper circulations, advertising shares and media incomes have fallen, undermining the economic structures of print media even in countries with strong newspaper circulations such as the Nordic countries or Germany. In spite of the fact that newspaper operations were challenged in all European markets, responses to the challenges were not identical. Although certain countries have escaped the dramatic shifts in the newspaper business, very serious outcomes could be seen in a number of states with specific market conditions and public policies. In some Western countries (Germany, the Nordic countries), professional journalism and newspapers are still geared towards the classical mission of journalism (Esser and Bruggemann, 2010). Likewise, the media of those nations enjoy higher trust and popularity (see, for example, Table 2). But in many CEE markets, journalism follows and subscribes to less formalized, less institutionally and professionally committed purposes that rightly are described as a clientelist role (Rupnik and Zielonka, 2013; Örnebring, 2012). The professional status of CEE journalists is also weaker (Lauk, 2008; Dobek-Ostrowska et al., 2013). Solidarity among journalists is poor, competition and rivalry are increasing. Also the public trust in the media in CEE is generally lower than in other European States (see Table 2.1).

Furthermore, as observed in media monitoring efforts such as the Freedom House reports, the global economic crisis has affected media independence and journalistic professionalism in all European countries. Variations between different countries and professional cultures can be observed here as well, but especially critical was the effect of the global economic crisis on media operations in Europe's younger democracies. State interventions, increasing media instrumentalization, compromises and neglect of professional ideals are just few trends identified as outcomes related to economic pressures and market share uncertainties in CEE (Štetka, 2013).

In addition to the global economic crisis, technological factors also challenge traditional media operations. Conventional media have moved online and many younger users have changed their media consumption habits in favour of online media. This shift in consumer lifestyles and consumption habits has seriously undermined the press. For many young Europeans the Internet has become the main information and news source (Vihalemm et al., 2012; Balčytienė et al., 2012a). Changing media access routines also challenged media's conventional business models. New technologies have already transformed journalism by changing news production cycles, which in turn affected media agendas and choices made by journalists. New technologies have indeed pluralized public communication – they have diversified news sources and offered new access opportunities for various readers (Lunt et al., 2014). Specifically, this feature has been stressed as a core factor contributing to the diversification of opinions and democratization in the CEE (Jakubowicz, 2012). But by doing so, the impact of technologies and journalistic shifts has also intensified opposite trends such as news competition and, thus, tabloidization and sensationalism.

Hence an increasing economic pressure on media and a decline in the quality of public debates also affects public engagement and political participation. In the turbulent times of crises, changes and uncertainties, the idea of citizenship and how it is embodied and fulfilled is changing towards more networked and individualized experiences, based on personal likes, wants and needs, rather than long-term commitments, duties and loyalties (Deuze, 2008). Rather than voting, joining a political party or trade union or demonstrating, citizens look for other meaningful, self-expressive, less hierarchical but more creative and engaging experiences that are offered by the new information and communication tools. In comparison to the broadcast era (Prior, 2013), people have more opportunities to choose between different types of content on different platforms, which leads to greater polarization and fragmentation in the public. Individual preferences for content indeed affect political behaviour, and selective exposure to certain information might increase interest and participation in politics. As a result, partisan media are thriving on the Internet, as they are on cable television (ibid.). In contrast, people without strong political interests are less likely to encounter the news at all (Iyengar et al., 2010). As shown, media content changes also depend on issues that attract consumer attention. As Vihalemm et al. (2012), mainly in reference to CEE changes in media access, point out:

> When news, public affairs, culture, the environment and history have traditionally been regarded as topical areas of universal interest, having a strong integrating potential for the national mass media, it is more difficult to discover such integrating topics for the different media usage types of today. Interest in gossip and scandals seem to be the most widespread common element for different media usage clusters. But these are themes that are not integrating but, rather, alienating and fragmenting media audiences.
>
> (Vihalemm et al., 2012, p. 49)

Similarly, another tendency is related to the role of intellectuals, leaders and authorities as echoed in the media. As Bennet (2012) argues:

> Modern era dutiful citizens were urged by educators, politicians, civic leaders, and other authorities to follow the news, join community organizations, and, above all, vote. By contrast, the younger generations breaking away from these norms in the current era of personalized politics have few clear guidelines to follow in fashioning a public life.
> (Bennet, 2012, p. 30)

Therefore, it appears the media are affected by altering existing media business models, by technological pressures but also by changing public expectations and habits that both disrupt existing and create emerging roles and functions for professional journalism. 'Individualization of consumption' (Bauman, 2002; Beck and Beck-Gernsheim, 2002) appears to be one of the most significant developments triggered by commercialization and technological diffusion as well as other cultural-societal factors. As envisioned by Hallin and Mancini (2004) and others (Bennet, 2012; Deuze, 2008), with secularization on the rise, and when ideologies and other formal group identifications (e.g. party, union, church or class) decline as mechanisms for organizing civic life, individuals start to define their social and political attachments through the values of personal lifestyle. In Western Europe, as a result of increasing liberalization, many of the ideals of the previously dominant logic of the social contract were marginalized or dropped (Nieminen, 2010). As a result of liberalization and shifts in public policies towards deregulation and marketization, many of the European nation-states were gradually transformed into market states, backgrounding many of the ideals of the social contract. It is not difficult to observe that such developments not only 'institutionalize' individualization (Beck and Beck-Gernsheim, 2002) but they also maintain and support individualism and, subsequently, contribute to the rise of a notion of living in an 'epoch of singularity' (ibid.). Such developments also noticeably change the field of media and professional journalism. As Starr (2012) succinctly shows, the primary mistake in such thinking in the media field was ignorance of the fact that journalistic product such as news is a public good, and that public goods tend to be systematically under-produced in market-driven circumstances.

But in addition to economic fluctuations or technological progressions, what are the social and individual responses to global and national turbulences? To what extent is evolving individualized consumption and political alienation affecting democratic regimes in Europe?

The perspective we are suggesting here for understanding crises in the media is the approach that views societal changes and also reviews long-term institutional transformations and social effects. A number of questions seem to be of particular importance: What is the critical determinant of variations in European media transformation and performance qualities? How could European media reactions to changing conditions be classified? What similarities and differences could be observed between older and younger European democracies? How do arising social trends of increasing individualized consumption and political alienation affect the functioning of democracy in Europe, and what is the role of journalism in this respect?

INDIVIDUALIZED ENCOUNTERS AND CULTURAL RESPONSES TO CHANGE

In the CEE, the trend of social and political polarization appears to be especially critical and requires a deeper analysis. After the collapse of communism in Central and Eastern Europe, Ralph Dahrendorf (2004) raised the alert that new political, institutional and economic formations in the region might outrun social and cultural developments, which means it could take much longer until proper social foundations are laid to consolidate and sustain democracy and civil society in the region. Indeed, despite more than two decades of liberal democracy, rule of law, market economy and free media, public engagement and political participation in the region have been lagging behind most of the established democracies. Passive political culture, clientelist practices and imitative behaviours with deep roots and long-lasting antidemocratic traditions put in question the sustainability and resistance of democratic reforms against global and regional challenges (Balčytienė, 2013; Örnebring, 2012).

Despite the fact that many of the mentioned drawbacks could be witnessed to various degrees across European media (professionalism compromises among journalists, tabloidisation, the rise of sensationalism, commodification of politics), these qualities have predominantly contributed to the assignment of CEE countries and their political and media arrangements as mirroring journalism and political cultures of highly polarized Southern European societies (Hallin and Mancini, 2004). Although there is no direct connection between polarized political culture and public engagement and participation, in the longer run all this might be negatively influenced by the actions of both actors: politicians and the media. Generally, in the CEE, politics is strongly shaped by its connections with and its presence in the media (Rupnik and Zielonka, 2013; Bajomi-Lazar, 2014). Having relatively fresh histories of democratic development, low membership of political parties and fragile organizational structures, the political parties in CEE are particularly dependent on and determined by the media. The media is the only channel through which public consent and attention can be mobilized on political matters. Even more, politicians are genuinely convinced the media have a major influence on voting habits and behaviours. Hence they employ enormous efforts to systematically control and manage public opinion (Mungiu-Pipidi, 2008). The CEE media, on the other hand, are not without sin either. They are prone to heavy manipulation, populism and sensationalism (Gross, 2013). Indeed, very clear differences are found across the CEE countries. Certain CEE countries (Estonia) democratically perform better than others, but still there is a general impression that politics and the media in most of CEE countries uphold their actions through reciprocal cohabitation and functioning symbiosis shaped through joint, clientelist interests.

As seen today across most of CEE, conflict, disagreement, volatility and flux (and, therefore, the lack and absence of long-term political thinking and public-policy visions) appear to be amongst the most illustrative features of today's political and social life in this part of Europe (Rupnik and Zielonka, 2013; Balčytienė, 2013). As argued elsewhere, such a climate of high polarization in CEE may be seen as encouraged by the atmosphere of political, economic and social transformations and of extreme instabilities and intense changes. Thus it may be treated as a natural outcome of changing and shifting preferences of their elites (Sparks, 2012; Norkus, 2011).

Combined with rising political communication professionalisation, such a trend of the existence of polarized interests of elites might lead to a critical condition where public communications space is saturated with controversial issues and citizens are unable to find out about core matters. Such a critical condition might lead to citizens' passivity, disappointment and gradual withdrawal from public life. Some symptoms might be already seen in public assessments of their well-being and feelings about the state of democracy in selected CEE countries (see Table 1). As data of the European Social Survey 2012 indicate, the population in the CEE countries is more pessimistic about the performance of public institutions and less engaged with public and political organizations. It is also more skeptical about the way democracy and its main instruments, including political parties, the legal system and the media, work in their countries (see Figure 2.3). Clear differences in comparison with individual feelings of happiness, optimism and frustration can be seen as well. Apparently, people in CEE (and also in Southern European countries) are faced with more challenges and difficulties in their personal lives than their counterparts in Western Europe. There is more disappointment, anxiety and suspicion about the future of the country, the world and the self.

Still, variations are found across the CEE. Despite common denominators that could be found in explaining the links between media and politics in CEE, extreme variations are found across countries in the same region. In certain CEE countries, political interventions in the media take the leading role, resulting in varying types of media capture and colonization (Hungary, Bulgaria, Romania) (Bajomi-Lazar, 2014). Also, people's perceptions, attitudes and behavioural patterns are diversified across the region. For instance, Bulgaria stands out with the highest skepticism with regard to the democratic and economic situation, as well as high personal frustration and low democratic values. On the other hand, Bulgarians are among the most interested in politics in the CEE region, are heavier consumers of TV and heavier consumers of political news on television, even though they are more skeptical and critical about media freedom in their country (see Table 2.1).

Another evident inconsistency and paradox of social life in today's CEE is that supplementary political and societal components and structures that should activate public control, awareness and participation, such as trade unions, civil society, public-service channels, professional independent media and others, are unusually weak or marginal (see Table 2.1). However, with certain exceptions, sustainable democratic instruments and political culture traditions in Western European countries do contribute to positive perceptions of politics, the economic situation and society. On the other hand, political, economic and social insecurity is more threatening in CEE countries because of transformations and democratic instability (higher internal political polarization and unresolved value conflicts among elites), enduring corruption in certain countries, power manipulations among elites and public disengagement from civic life.

In the longer run, such an existing dichotomy between the highly polarized and active (political, business, media) elites and the passivity of the public ultimately may lead to a critical condition about the state of democracy in several CEE countries. As a result of rising sensationalism and commodification of politics, increasing political news management that parallels dominating group interests and media instrumentalization, the public sphere in most of the CEE countries appears to be saturated with controversial, polarized, conflictual, divergent issues. Citizens, correspondingly, may find themselves as permanently, deliberately uninformed, manipulated and misrepresented voters. Naturally, their disappointment and gradual withdrawal from public life may also be shaped by political and media performances (see Table 2.1 and its data specifying degrees of public engagement and satisfaction with how democracy works in their country). Thus it is no surprise that conflict, disagreement, volatility and flux (and, therefore, the lack and absence of long-term political thinking and public-policy visions) appear to be amongst the most illustrative features of today's political and social life in most of CEE.

Amongst those dominating features (and also paradoxes) of CEE media is that, although contributing to the function of pluralization, of information provision, even of interests-mediation, which are amongst the core functions of a democratically performing media, in fact such dominant particularistic political interests and clientelist cultural practices (Rupnik and Zielonka, 2013; Örnebring, 2012) prepare a ground that turns out to be risky for democracy. In such a context, the media – which are principal players in the webs of networks of politicians, lobbyists, celebrities and business owners – are predetermined to neglect potential ethical issues and missions of professional journalism, and therefore are mainly concerned with maintaining their ideologically-charged mission, thus providing only partial stories of events described (Gross, 2009; Balčytienė, 2013). Likewise, such media conduct greatly contributes to social and political polarization in CEE.

Indeed, varying accounts are given to explain those developments towards individualized access and selective exposure that are witnessed not only across the CEE countries. As seen from Western experiences, economic pressures and financial cuts in media are blamed for intensifying news competitions and even sensationalism and tabloidization (Starr, 2012). Other studies refer to public policy shifts towards increasing liberalization (Nieminen, 2010), followed by audience lifestyle changes and arising new consumption fashions of politics (Mancini, 2013). The strongest rhetorical point in the latter case is the argument that consumers themselves appear to be more interested in sports, entertaining content, crime news and local issues than hard news (Bennet, 2012). On the other hand, as also proved in various studies in Europe, engagement with politics and hard news issues takes place through alternative means and is manifested in political activism and public engagement with political issues in social media and blogs (Lunt et al., 2014; Balčytienė et al., 2012b). Truly, the new mediated, networked and interactive environment provides a different context and modes for social and political development, interaction, participation and identity formation. However, not only the media but also consumer culture, which is always of individual character, transform citizenship into more individualized, anti-hierarchical and creative patterns of public engagement (Poster, 2006). Indeed, in recent years the use of the Internet and interactive communications has increased dramatically in all EU countries and among all age groups, which generated suggestions that Internet-based media should be 'intellectualized' to adhere to democratic needs and requests (Vihalemm et al., 2012; Lunt et al., 2014).

All in all, no matter which cultural traditions and prescribed missions the media of the European countries follow, their operations are equally challenged by developments towards individualized consumption, audience interests shaped by information access, selectivity and engagement, which gradually may also have serious effects and consequences on the quality of critical and rational debate and political participation. Still, as we argue here, changes are not neutral; they need to be contextualized. As explained, a number of European countries – predominantly those younger democracies of Central and Eastern Europe (Bulgaria, Romania) but also economically weaker Southern European countries (Spain, Portugal) – appear to be more seriously affected by such inclinations than countries in the West. We suggest that specific social and cultural attributes – weaker associational and civic cultures and a weaker notion of the idea of common good, higher reliance on the medium of television, weaker media democratic performance and weaker professional solidarity among journalists – may create hypothetically favourable conditions for the emergence of definite destructive trends, such as the dominance of particularistic interests, leading to high political and social polarization that may be further enhanced by media performance and audience selections.

Although recent political, economic and social developments in CEE may appear relatively homogeneous and uniform, especially in a broader comparative research, there are significant cross-national differences inside the CEE region, as also seen from our analysis (Balčytienė, 2013). As seen in Table 2.3, at least three groups can be identified on the basis of public perception and social-formations data.

Table 2.3 Clusterization of CEE countries by public perceptions of media and democracy

	Bulgaria	Czech Republic, Slovakia, Lithuania, Hungary	Poland, Slovenia, Estonia
Consumption of politics on TV (interest in politics, exposure to TV news)	High	Medium	Low
Legitimacy of institutions (trust in political institutions)	Low	Medium	Medium
Participation in national elections	High	Medium/High	Medium
Participation in associations (NGOs, trade unions)	Low	Low	Low
Democratic values (satisfaction with democracy)	Low	Medium	Medium
Public anxieties	High	Medium	Low

* Based on ESS Round 6 (2012) data.

Apparently, Bulgaria can be distinguished for its rather extreme public frustration, pessimism and disappointment with democratic processes in the country. A more moderate cluster includes Czech Republic, Slovakia, Lithuania and Hungary, while the third grouping represented by Poland, Slovenia and Estonia can be characterized by a rather smooth and more stable democratization. Existing political, economic and social divides are reflected in public perceptions and assessments of the ongoing processes in their countries, including the role of media in supporting democracies (see Figure 2.4 and Figure 2.5).

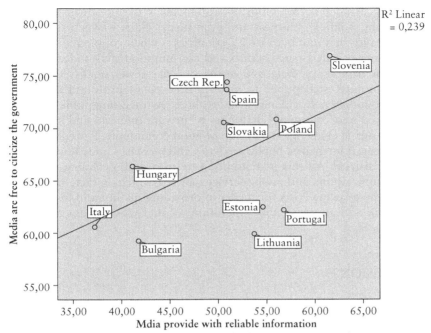

Figure 2.4 Assessment of media freedom and reliability in CEE and SE countries, % Source: Authors' estimations based on ESS (2012) data.

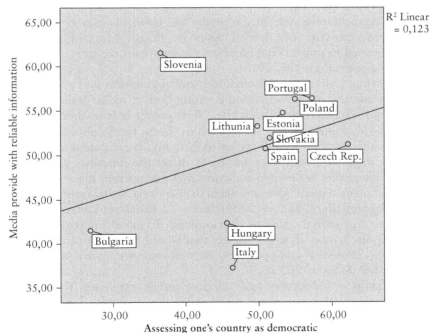

Figure 2.5 Assessment of democracy and media reliability in CEE and SE countries, % Source: Authors' estimations based on ESS (2012) data.

All things considered, the competitive atmosphere of unresolved value conflicts among political, business and even media elites – which still appear to be a reality in a number of CEE countries – when coupled with the rise of consumer-oriented news access and consumption may indeed become critical for democracy. Polarized media produce fewer quality opportunities for the interested public to give an account of profound changes in their surrounding political and social realities. By diverting public attention from shared and communal dialogues to private interests and soft issues, polarized media challenge the notion of good community. By reducing civic involvement, it intensifies public anxieties and increases uncertainty, skepticism and distrust. All this is in addition to an overall declining interest in general public affairs and public service matters, which, in fact, may be also triggered by growing costs for media in providing quality and investigative journalism, and also by public migration to alternative interactive online media spaces.

CONCLUSIONS

Indeed, the idea that contemporary societies may polarize over time appears to be justified. As explained, in the 'epoch of information abundance' individual preferences of the public for content may affect their media exposure as well as political behaviours, which might lead to increasing partisan assemblages and public groupings contributing to media fragmentation and audience segmentation and, thus, to social and political polarization. There are obvious signs that such developments are already happening, the most commonly used example being Fox News and its selective aims in targeting certain audiences (Mancini, 2013).

The starting point in our discussion is the assumption that all identified trends, specifically of individualized consumption, of media fragmentation, of group polarization and others, affect how people reason about, react to and act in the political world (Poster, 2006). These trends also have effects on the quality of the rational critical debate and its maintenance characteristics – in other words, they indirectly affect the functions and performance of the media. Segmented audiences make democracy more vulnerable since a fragmented media does not seem to encourage social integration and community-building (Bauman, 2000). It doesn't foster the kind of common knowledge and shared-opinions development that could make possible a more integrated, more dynamic society that would be more open to change by seeking necessary compromises, negotiations and consensus-finding (Gross, 2009; Mancini 2013).

Individualized encounters and selective public exposures indeed may affect what citizens know about politics, but they may also lead to exclusion and group polarization. Particularly, this trend has raised concerns about the quality of democracy. Individualized encounters with information certainly may increase interest in certain issues. Nonetheless, it may limit the diversity of arguments that viewers possess. Hence the most uncertain issue is the question of what the democratic consequences of such individualized and selective political exposure could be.

All these developments and trends of individualized access and consumption appear to be more critical in the young democracies of Central and Eastern Europe. Such an account is based on specific contextual conditions and socio-cultural particularities of those countries, predominantly on economically weaker market structures (which directly affect economic conditions of media), on specific features of their political cultures defined as having stronger notion of particularism and weaker appreciation of the idea of public good, and also on various types of instabilities and public anxieties driven by changing conditions requiring quick reactions and people's adjustments.

In contrast, in most countries from the West, where economic changes are less dramatic and traditions of media financial support from various resources are stronger (for example, through state support and financial subsidies, or public donations and local community initiatives), effects of changes on the general media economic climate may not be as harsh as in younger markets of CEE, where such public-support models are not that well developed – although in many countries they exist but their effect is marginal. For example, in Germany, quite similarly to the Nordic countries, both media industry and policies have provided adequate responses to the changing economic situation, and thus journalism in those countries is still well prepared to fulfill its functions of producing accountable and professional quality and investigative journalism.

Indeed, building a democracy and civil society is a process, which requires autonomous and professional journalism to provide 'social cement of democracies' (Deuze, 2008). Apart from monitoring public life and informing citizens on major public issues, the role and power of journalism are to amplify social tensions, connect people and engage them in a dialogue for social cohesion and democratic consolidation. Taking into account different social textures of the CEE countries, as well as the scope of multifold changes in the region, including relatively new political and institutional formations, economic crises, social tensions and other difficulties, media and journalism should be considered as a critical social foundation of democracies and civil societies.

To conclude, a number of conditions must be met to ensure media democratic operations and, hence, public political engagement in Europe. Among the most significant appear to be adequate policy provisions, as well as a media culture influenced by the idea of the public sphere. Additionally, a no less important requirement appears to be a general feeling of stability, both of political and economic, in a particular society. Another observation arising from this discussion is the finding that universalistic trends (such as the rise of individualized consumption leading to media fragmentation and, hence, to political and social polarization) are differentiated across various European countries. In a number of these, although for different reasons (for example, in Hungary), effects of obvious transformations are registered and are heatedly debated, since their effects are accelerating hazardous developments that are critical and threatening for democracy (Bajomi-Lazar, 2014). But discussions and effects of various developments in the European mediascape – such as declining revenues from traditional advertising, shifting audience preferences for interactive media encounters, decreasing political engagement – should not be overlooked in those states, mostly traditional Western democracies, where instabilities, fluctuations and uncertainties caused by economic or other societal transformations have not been that dramatic. All in all, the tendencies of group polarization, of rising discontent as well as many other uncertainties should be assessed as matters of rising significance and universal concern. A shorter-term perspective allows us to get hold of political, economic and legal changes and media adjustments, whereas a more thorough analysis is required to get hold of effects of socio-cultural factors on observed trends.

NOTE

1. ESS Round 6: European Social Survey Round 6 Data (2012). Data file edition 2.0. Norwegian Social Science Data Services, Norway – Data Archive and distributor of ESS data. Retrieved from: http://www.europeansocialsurvey.org/.

REFERENCES

Aalberg, T. et al. (2013) Media choice and informed democracy: Toward increasing news consumption gaps in Europe? *The International Journal of Press/Politics,* 18(3). pp. 281–303.

Balčytienė, A. (2013) A conceptual guide to the analysis of Central and East European transformations. In: Trivundža, I. T., Carpentier, N., Nieminen, H.,. Venerfeldt, P. P, Kilborn, R., Sundin, E. and Olsson, T. (eds.) *Past, future and change: Contemporary analysis of evolving media scapes* (pp. 29–39). Ljubljana: Slovene Communication Association & European Communication Research and Education Association.

Balčytienė, A., Vinciūnienė, A. and Auškalnienė, L. (2012a) Access, loyalty and trust: Changing audiences and media life in contemporary Lithuania. *Media Transformations,* 6. pp. 64–91.

Balčytienė, A., Vinciūnienė, A. and Auškalnienė, L. (2012b) Mediatized participation and forms of media use and multiple meaning making: The Baltic perspective. *Media Transformations,* 7. pp. 4–34.

Bajomi-Lazar, P. (2014) *Party colonization of the media in Central and Eastern Europe.* Budapest: CEU Press.

Bauman, Z. (2000) *Liquid Modernity.* Cambridge: Polity Press.

Beck, U. and Beck-Gernsheim, E. (2002) *Individualization: Institutionalized individualism and its social and political consequences.* London: Sage.

Bennet, L. W. (2012) The personalization of politics: Political identity, social media, and changing patterns of participation. *The ANNALS of the American Academy of Political and Social Science*, 644. pp. 20–39.

Christians, C., Glasser, T., McQuail, D., Nordenstreng, K. and White, R. (2009) *Normative theories of the media: Journalism in democratic societies*. Urbana, IL: University of Illinois Press.

Dahrendorf, R. (2004) *Reflections on the Revolution in Europe*. New Brunswick, NJ: Transaction Publishers.

Deuze, M. (2008) The changing context of news work: Liquid journalism and monitorial citizenship. *International Journal of Communication*, 2. pp. 848–65.

de Vreese, C. and Boomgaarden, H. (2006) News, Political Knowledge and Participation: The Differential Effects of News Media Exposure on Political Knowledge and Participation. *Acta Politica*, 41. pp. 317–41.

Dobek-Ostrowska, B., Barczyszyn, P., Michel, A. and Baranowski, P. (2013) Polish journalists: from politics to market. In: Anikina, M., Dobek-Ostrowska, B. and Nygren, G. (eds.) *Journalists in three media systems. Polish, Russian and Swedish journalists about values and ideals, daily practice and the future*. Moscow: Faculty of Journalism, Lomonosov Moscow State University.

Ekiert, G. and Ziblatt, D. (2013) Democracy in Central and Eastern Europe one hundred years on. *East European Politics and Societies*, 27(1). pp. 90–17.

ESS Round 6: European Social Survey Round 6 Data (2012) Data file edition 2.0. Norwegian Social Science Data Services, Norway – Data Archive and distributor of ESS data.

Esser, F. and Bruggemann, M. (2010) The strategic crisis of German newspapers. In: Levy, D. and Nielsen, R. (eds.) *The changing business of journalism and its implications for democracy* (pp. 39–55). Oxford: RISJ.

Giddens, A. (2013) *The consequences of modernity*. Cambridge: Polity Press.

Gross, P. (2009) The menace of post-objective journalism in the U.S.A. In: Bohrmann, H., Klaus, E. and Machill, M. (eds.) *Media industry, journalism culture and communication policies in Europe* (pp. 41–64). Köln: Herbert von Halem Verlag.

Hallin, D. C. and Mancini, P. (2004) Comparing Media Systems. Three Models of Media and Politics. Cambridge: Cambridge University Press.

Hoyer, S. (2001) Diffusion of journalistic innovations: A cross national survey, paper presented at the 15th *Nordic Conference on Media and Communication Research Conference*, Reykjavik, Iceland, August 11–13, 2001.

Iyengar, S., Curran, J., Lund, A., Salovaara-Moring, I., Hahn, K. amd Coen, S. (2010) Cross-National versus Individual-Level Differences in Political Information: A Media Systems Perspective. *Journal of Elections, Public Opinion and Parties*, 20(3). pp. 291–309.

Jakubowicz, K. (2012) Democracy and New Media in Central and Eastern Europe. *Central European Journal of Communication*, 1. pp. 139–45.

Jakubowicz, K. and Sükösd M. (2008) Twelve Concepts Regarding Media System Evolution and Democratization in Post-Communist Societies. In: Jakubowicz, K. and Sükösd, M. (eds.) *Finding the right place on the map: Central and Eastern European media change in global perspective* (pp. 9–40). Bristol: Intellect.

Lauk, E. (2008) How will it all unfold? Media systems and journalism cultures in post-communist countries. In: Jakubowicz, K. and Sükösd, M. (eds.) *Finding the right place on the map: Central and Eastern European media change in global perspective* (pp. 193–213). Bristol: Intellect.

Lunt, P., Kaun, A., Pruulmann-Vengerfelgt, P., Stark, B. and Van Zoonen, L. (2014) The mediation of civic participation: Diverse forms of political agency in a multimedia age. In: Carpentier, N., Schroder, K. C. and Hallett, L. (eds.) *Audience transformations: Shifting audience positions in late modernity* (pp. 142–57). London: Routledge.

Mancini, P. (2013) Media fragmentation, party system, and democracy. *The International Journal of Press/Politics*, 18(1). pp. 43–60.

Mungiu-Pipidi, A. (2008) How media and politics shape each other in the New Europe. In: Jakubowicz, K. and Sükösd, M. (eds.) *Finding the right place on the map: Central and Eastern European media change in global perspective* (pp. 87–101). Bristol: Intellect.

Nieminen, H. (2010) The unravelling Finnish media policy consensus? In: Levy, D. and Nielsen, R. (eds.) *The changing business of journalism and its implications for democracy* (pp. 55–67). Oxford: RISJ.

Norkus, Z. (2011) Estonian, Latvian, and Lithuanian post-communist development in the comparative perspective. In: *EHDR: Estonian Human Development Report: Baltic way(s) of human development – twenty years on* (pp. 22–31). Tallinn: Eesti Koostoo Kogu.

Örnebring, H. (2012) Clientelism, elites, and the media in Central and Eastern Europe. *The International Journal of Press/Politics*, 17(4). pp. 497–515.

Poster, M. (2006) *Information please: culture and politics in the age of digital machines*. Durham, NC: Duke University Press.

Prior, M. (2013) Media and political polarization. *Annual Review of Political Science*, 16. pp. 101–27.

Rupnik, J. and Zielonka, J. (2013) The state of democracy 20 years on: Domestic and external factors. *East European Politics & Societies*, 27(1). pp. 3–25.

Schudson, M. (2010) News in crisis in the United States: Panic – and beyond. In: Levy, D. and Nielsen, R. (eds.) *The changing business of journalism and its implications for democracy* (pp. 95–107). Oxford: RISJ.

Sparks, C. (2012) The interplay of politics and economics in transitional societies. In: Downey, J. and Mihelj, S. (eds.) *Central and Eastern European Media in comparative perspective: Politics, economy and culture* (pp. 41–61). Farnham, England & Burlington, US: Ashgate.

Starr, P. (2012) An unexpected crisis: The news media in postindustrial democracies. *The International Journal of Press/Politics*, 17(2). pp. 234–42.

Štetka, V. (2013) Media ownership and commercial pressures. Report presented at the *Final MDCEE project conference Media and Democracy CEE in a Comparative Context*. The European Studies Centre, St. Antony's College, University of Oxford, July 9–11.

Trappel, J. and Meier, W. A. (2011) *On media monitoring: The media and their contribution to democracy*. New York: Peter Lang Publishing.

Vihalemm, P., Lauristin, M. and Kõuts, R. (2012) Trends in Estonian media landscape in 2000–2012. *Media Transformations*, 6. pp. 12–63.

Wiik, J. and Andersson, U. (2013) Journalism meets management: Changing leadership in Swedish news organizations. *Journalism Practice*, 7(6). pp. 705–19.

Part II

Media Industry Crises and Transformations

3 European Communication and Information Industries in Times of Crisis
Continuities and Transformations

Laura Bergés Saura and Stylianos Papathanassopoulos

Since the Lehman Brothers bank went bankrupt in 2007, the world crisis has settled at the heart of global capitalism. The financial crisis triggered a process of crisis in the real economy with both political and social consequences. In this chapter we will focus on a part of this system in crisis, the field of communications, understood as a field that encompasses journalism and interacts with the cultural, political and economic fields (Benson and Neveu, 2005). This means our interest is in how, if at all, crisis is transforming the role of media and other information and communication technologies as mediators between different social fields (Bourdieu, 1993), and how the articulations between communicative practices and social evolution are evolving, as Barbero proposed when he asked to move the focus from media to mediations[1] (Barbero, 1987). We will try to "establish and describe the relationships that these events, which we might call discursive events, maintain with other events that pertain to the economic system, the political field or the institutions." (Foucault, 1999, pp. 61f)

More precisely, we are going to focus on some of these discursive events or communicative practices. In effect, in the age of media convergence, we adopt a perspective centred on the production side. Moreover, we will try to identify the main processes that affect information and communication industries in Europe since 2008. Mosco's thesis of structuration, spacialization and commodification (1996) will help us to explore how these industries relate or interact within more general socio-political and economic processes. Therefore, first we present these general processes external to the communication field. Then we explore the changes in the general communication field to reach the final considerations about the articulations or mediations built by media, ICTs and telecommunications in the context of the crisis. To think about this we will use the idea of 'net neutrality,' not just as an issue of Internet speed and architecture but as a concept that can help to think about whether or not the present (re)configuration of information and communication networks, industries and markets is socially and politically neutral.

THE CONTEXT OF CRISIS: WHAT CRISIS?

If we are interested in media and communication industries as fundamental mediators in times of crisis, it is pertinent to examine the nature of the crisis. It is questionable whether it is a short-term crisis, limited to some sectors and some countries challenged by the creative destruction provoked by the consolidation of neoliberal global capitalism, or it is an outcome of the structural and long-term crisis of capitalism itself, and especially of the widely adopted neoliberal model in the last three decades. Is it a crisis of the Anglo-Saxon liberal model and its global expansion or, on the contrary, the definitive defeat of the social market model, after more than twenty years of tension (Albert, 1992)? Any answer to these questions goes beyond the scope of this chapter. Nevertheless, we will try to pinpoint some clues and ideas regarding the continuities and transformations that have taken place since 2008 in Europe. This will also help us to scan the developments in the communicative field.

The first point is related to the exceptionality of the crisis. Certainly, crisis arrived in the US and Europe after decades of continued growth, briefly interrupted by short-term contractions, which has fed confidence in unlimited growth in welfare or affluent societies. But the crisis seems less exceptional if we consider the whole planet progressively integrated into global neoliberal capitalism. In that context, the US and European crisis completes a list until then integrated by peripheral countries. Already in 2001, Loza (2001, pp. 26) closed his record of monetary crisis linked to globalization with the quote: "End of the crisis? Or which is the next?" and in fact, many crises related to financial and natural resources fundamental to global capitalism have been swelling up the list (Figure 3.1). This list should be completed with the environmental crisis, all reflecting the unsustainability of a system based on the continued expansion of consumption and production (cf. Heinberg, 2011; Martínez and Roca, 2000) and related to a growing number of conflicts for natural resources.

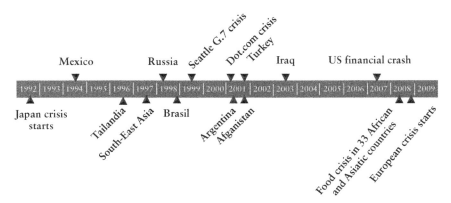

Figure 3.1

Having framed the crises in the problematic process of neoliberal globalization deployment, we are going to focus on what has happened with the main ingredients of this model during the crisis period.

As Strage (1996) pointed out, globalization has meant a retreat of the state or, more exactly, a retreat of the national democratic mechanism to define state politics in favour of big corporations, markets and international economic institutions through which corporate interests act. Liberalized financial markets and big corporate agents in those markets have been one of the key components in this retreat of the state, due to their capacity to influence public policies conditioned by debt and accessibility to financial resources. In this respect, in 2007–2008 the crisis was seen as a crisis of these liberalized financial markets, though six years later, in 2014, there are more continuities than critical transformations within this field of finance. The crisis has shed more light on a financial system that, since the end of the convertibility of the US dollar to gold during the crisis in the 1970s, has been gaining autonomy, complexity and opacity thanks to liberalization and the growth of shadow financial structures[2] (Roubini and Mihm, 2010). Although the crisis forced the introduction of more control, more monitoring of the financial markets and also provoked massive public interventions to rescue financial institutions, few measures to change structural conditions in the financial markets were adopted. At the same time, as the private-sector debt crisis has become a public-sector debt crisis, financial markets and large actors in those markets have kept and even increased their capacity to dictate the economic policies of national governments and international institutions. Ironically, some of the members of this financial system in crisis have been designated to rule over the fiscal policies of Greece, Italy and Spain,[3] while bailout plans funded by the public budget, together with austerity plans, put more pressure on cutbacks in the welfare state.

The crisis also intensifies the restructuring of the international division of labour, characteristic of globalization, which affects communication and information industries. While at a global level this can be seen as continuity, it has caused important changes in Europe, where its hegemonic position is being undermined by the rise of Asia, especially China. As Schiller pointed out (1983), while the US can rely on its financial, military and ICTs advantages to support its position in the new global scenario, the EU has lost many of its competitive advantages in relation to emerging countries, which have labour, financial, energy and industrial advantages. This retreat by Europe is not homogeneous but instead affects those countries with fewer competitive advantages in the global economy. Therefore the crisis is experienced and explained more as a structural transformation in countries with worse economic advancement such as Greece, Portugal, Spain, Italy or even France, and in post-communist countries in Central and Eastern Europe that are still immersed in long-term systemic change. On the contrary, for the more prosperous European countries, the crisis is seen more as a cyclical crash.

Territorial reconfiguration within Europe confirms the existence of a two-speed Europe and crisis has accentuated inequalities between and within countries. Income per capita (Eurostat, 2014) continued to rise in countries with higher standards of living in Luxembourg, Denmark, Sweden, Netherlands, Austria, Finland, Belgium, Germany, France and, non-EU, Norway and Switzerland. In this group of the wealthiest European countries, only the United Kingdom, Ireland and Iceland have experienced a reduction of income per capita. It has also been reducing in Southern countries in the middle of the EU wealth rankings: Italy, Spain, Greece and Portugal. And it has also moved slightly and more irregularly in countries with lower incomes, which remain at the bottom of the lists. In this group, the best results appear in countries linked to the German market: Poland, the Czech Republic and Slovakia (Eurostat, 2014). Thus centre-periphery differences have been reinforced in Europe, reflecting what has happened at a global level.

Socio-economic inequalities also increase at a domestic level, even in countries with a growing GDP (Intermon Oxfam, 2012; OECD, 2014; IMF, 2014), with middle class and young people swelling the ranks of the poor, together with old people, the long-term unemployed and migrants. Feixa and Nofre (2013) link the degradation of standards of living and growth of inequalities with the emergence of social protests. These authors analyze 15M[4] and "outraged" movements in Spain as a symptom of increasing precariousness rather than as a success story of the capacity of ICT to articulate social movements, which is the perspective of many studies in the face of 15M and outraged movements from the perspective of communication studies (BIFI, 2011; Candón and Redondo, 2012).

This situation fits the description of socio-political evolution in the US since the 1980s. Schiller (1983) and Kaplan (2000) point out the increasing social and cultural divisions in those years as a fracture of the national social contract, leading to a new situation of de-territorialized "countries" – understood as groups of people that, independently of where they live, share class, culture, tastes, language, political autonomy or dependence – that brought into crisis the political order and gave rise to new social movements. People excluded from wealth in this new system were considered by Schiller as potentially transforming political actors, though the author also pointed to how these actors find higher barriers to effective political action in this new age, as politics tends to pass through institutions and mechanisms beyond its reach, from markets and corporations to international institutions, lobbying or media.

Twenty years later, in Europe political discontent and activism are evident in those countries most affected by the crisis, where socioeconomic polarization, political frustration and also new forms of political communication and information have led to the emergence of new social movements and political demands. This includes higher levels of conflict on the streets, with new left-wing movements and the re-emergence of right-wing, xenophobic or racist movements. These social movements are challenging the position of parties representing the post-World War II political consensus, gaining positions in countries such as Greece (with Syriza and the opposite fascist Golden Dawn), Italy (Movimento 5 Stelle), Spain (Podemos) or, in another direction, France (Front National) and other right-wing and nationalist parties in many countries. Christian democrats, liberals and social democrats, though, still have a majority in Parliaments and governments across Europe. Among them, crisis seems to have reinforced the position of the (neo)liberal conservative side, while social democrats find more difficulties to propose, defend and apply policies not aligned with the neoliberal order.

THE COMMUNICATION AND INFORMATION INDUSTRIES: CRISIS NOT FOR EVERYONE?

The communication and information industries, like the whole economy, entered the crisis of 2008 after a long-term restructuring process in which they became one of the cornerstones of the new information age. During this long-term process, a number of trends are evident (cf. Becerra and Mastrini, 2010; Becerra, 2011; Hultén et al., 2010; Meier et al., 2007; Trappel et al., 2011): liberalization and privatization of broadcasting and telecommunications; expansion of Internet and ICT activities; consolidation through acquisitions, mergers and alliances, both within and among different sub-industries across the Internet and ICTs, telecommunications, media and content; outsourcing and growth of intra-industry and intra-group markets; internationalization, led by US transnational companies in media and ICTs; and financialization, with growth strongly based on leverage and a strong presence of financial entities (from banks to hedge funds) as shareholders in media companies.

These long-term processes had already placed traditional media industries in crisis, as much from an economic point of view, through the erosion of traditional business models, as from a political standpoint, through the erosion of the central role played by media and professional journalism in organizing and feeding the democratic public spheres (Balčytienė, Raeymaekers and Vartanova, 2011; Barnett, 2002; Davis, 2008). The evolution of communication and information industries since the crisis in 2008 seems to reinforce these previous trends, with different results according to activities, countries and types of companies.

Price Waterhouse (2014) paints a global scenario where, despite the crises, Internet revenues from subscription and advertising continued to grow by between fifty and seventy per cent between 2008 and 2012. Telecommunications, the largest business by revenue, and television have also increased turnover by up to twenty per cent in the same period, five per cent more than video games. In these fields the business evolved more irregularly in different countries. Cinema and radio suffered more from the crisis, and turnover has slightly increased during these years (+6.4 and 2.3 per cent each) at a global level. In contrast, music and books and, especially, newspapers and magazines, which were already activities most affected by the Internet, continued to decline during this crisis period, with the press alone losing up to ten to eleven per cent of its revenues.

Winseck and Yong's (2011) analyses of "network media industries" also show a restructuring process, with ICT firms gaining prominence but with traditional media companies resisting the crisis well "for the most part, however, the traditional media are not in crisis." (2011, p. 6) The authors point out two additional trends in the media industries' evolution before and during the crisis: a "tectonic shift in the centre of gravity of internet use to Asia, notably China, from the United States and Europe" and "the expanding diversity of media and informational forms that are created for reasons other than money and profit." (2011, p. 11f)

The changes in the information and communication industries in Europe during the economic crisis reproduce, to a certain extent, these processes at the global level. Analysis of investments and results of a sample of communications groups operating in Europe (Table 3.1)[5] and reports about communications industries in Europe during the crisis period show five main processes at work: spatial restructuration linked to the global economy; the expansion of new media activities based on telecommunication technologies combined with ICT; the expansion of activities related to fiction, sports and games for mass audiences; the contraction or crisis of national media groups, especially those that are more connected to journalism; and the emergence of new not-for-profit communication and information networks and models linked to new socio-political demands.

Table 3.1 Global players with an outstanding position in Europe: evolution during the crisis (million Euros[1])

Revenues	2013	2012	2011	2010	2009	2008	2007	% change 2007– 2012[2]
Telefónica	57,061	62,356	62,837	60,737	56,731	57,946	56,441	10.5
Vodafone	52,345	57,268	52,888	51,886	46,073	44,663	45,477	49.2
Google	45,062	39,060	27,257	22,149	17,010	14,898	12,125	202.4
News Corporation[3]	n.a.	26,240	24,021	24,760	21,881	22,554	20,938	17.6
Vivendi	22,135	22,577	28,813	28,878	27,132	25,392	21,657	4.2
Bertelsmann	16,356	16,065	15,253	15,065	15,364	16,118	18,758	–14.4
Thomson Reuters	9,568	10,337	9,929	9,873	9,348	8,002	5,331	82.0

Source: Collected by the authors from Annual Reports
1. conversion rates from 2013 to 2007. For Google, News Corp and Thomson Reuters, $/€: 0.753234; 0.778488; 0.719095; 0.755382; 0.719223; 0.683537; 0.730684. For Vodafone, £/€: 1.17774; 1.23378; 1.15264; 1.16671; 1.12327; 1.25890; 1.46211.
2. Variation calculated with data in local currency.
3. In 2013 News Corporation split its audiovisual division into a separate company (21st Century Fox), so for comparative purposes we do not consider this last year.

SPACIALIZATION: TERRITORIAL SHIFTS IN
COMMUNICATION INDUSTRIES

As the evolution of the global economy is challenging Europe's position – with different intensities among countries – in globalized markets, the economic crisis seems to have consolidated similar territorial shifts in the communication field. China, Brazil and some African countries appear as expanding markets for global groups, while in the US and especially Europe, some activities are at a standstill or even dropping, despite still being the main markets.

The larger EU countries (Germany, United Kingdom, France, Italy and Spain) continue to appear among the top ten media markets worldwide (Price Waterhouse, 2014). On the other hand, Southern and Eastern markets, with the exception of Russia and Poland, have lost positions. Eurostat data (2014) on cultural industries' performance within Europe during 2007–2013 are clearly worse in Portugal, Spain, Italy, Greece, the Baltic countries, the Czech Republic, Slovenia and Ireland. In the United Kingdom, the performance of the cultural industries has been better compared to the general economy, while in other countries where the crisis has been shorter and less harsh, performance has been positive. A similar evolution can be seen in the telecommunications market, where the crises have pushed down telecommunications revenues in Europe (ETNO, 2013) despite the continued growth in mobile services. In this case, it is not only the financially troubled countries (e.g. Spain and Italy, Ireland and Greece) that present this trend but even Germany, where the turnover of telecommunication activities decreased between 2007 and 2011 (Eurostat, 2014).

In this scenario, global groups have kept their interests in Europe as it is still a key market, but new investments in the area have been concentrated in countries less affected by the crisis, such as Poland, Germany and Turkey (Annual Reports[6]). However, other emerging economies appear to be more attractive to global information and communication groups, which continued their expansion there, in part compensating for a worsening economic climate in the US and European markets.

China is clearly one of the confirmed emerging markets, though global information and communication groups find barriers to their expansion in a state-controlled market, as shown in investments of the groups analyzed. Despite the growth in the Chinese media and communication markets, both News Corporation and Vivendi have sold their stakes in the country – in television and video games, respectively – replaced by other large US players in alliance with Chinese investment funds and other national companies. Among the big European groups, only Bertelsmann has reinforced its position in China during these years, both with its service division, Arvato[7], offering distribution of mobile devices in collaboration with Chinese agents, and with new agreements with local publishing houses and online marketing-providers. Google's efforts to reproduce in China its dominance of the US and Europe's Internet market have suffered from censorship and protection-ist practices from the government, together with competition from domestic players such as Baidu, the main search engine in the country. At the same time, Chinese mobile and Internet companies are instituting expansionist strategies outside China, with companies such as Xiaomi successfully break-ing into mobile markets in Europe.

The presence of global conglomerates has increased in Latin America, especially in Brazil, with new investments from News Corporation (sports channels in various countries), and Telefónica and Vivendi (mobile services and pay-TV in Brazil). India is another country receiving attention from large groups such as Vodafone and Bertelsmann, which, having sold its TV channels in Greece and the United Kingdom, acquired a publishing group in India. Finally, investments in Africa also increased during the 2007–2013 period, with new acquisitions and new services. News Corporation (TV, films, advertising and audio activities), Vodafone and Vivendi (household and mobile telecommunications) have been the most active groups in Africa. However, Vivendi's high debt in the context of the crisis has forced some divestments, among them the sale of its stakes in Marroc Telekom to Etisalet, a company from the United Arab Emirates, reflecting the decline of some European players in the global arena.

Broadly speaking, although big US and European groups still hold a strong position based on their hegemony in US and European markets, new areas have been emerging. These areas offer new possibilities for interna-tional expansion of US and, to a lesser extent, European groups, but also raise new challenges as new domestic competitors appear, especially in protected economies such as China and, to a lesser extent, in some Latin American countries.

ALGORITHMS, INTERPERSONAL AND GROUP HIGH-VALUE COMMUNICATIONS NETWORKS: EXPANDING MEDIATORS

Expansion of financial markets and of their influence on politics, described as one of the ingredients of globalization reinforced during the crisis, is directly related to an intensive use of information and communication net-works that has not been interrupted by the crisis. At the same time as the European economic relapse in 2011, after some recovery the previous year, a new transatlantic fibre-optic cable was laid between London and New York just to gain milliseconds for high-frequency traders using algorithms for automatized operations[8]. Between 2011 and 2012, Thomson-Reuters acquired a number of companies and patents to reinforce its position as one of the main providers of information and services for financial markets, with technologies including advanced analytic tools automatizing news con-sumption for automatized trade. Companies such as Telefónica, Vodafone and Bertelsmann also take part in the provision of advanced infrastructures, services and content for financial institutions, although US and Canadian companies hold the top positions in this market. In this respect, it is noticeable how, despite all the criticism of US rating agencies such as Moody's and Standard and Poor and their role in the crisis (Rügemer, 2013), efforts by some media groups to create new European agencies have failed.[9]

Attention to high-value content also includes new investments, by Thomson-Reuters, Wolters Kluwer, Google and Bertelsmann, in educational activities and scientific information, which used to be a public or not-for-profit field. Thus while many European states reduce public funds for education and science as part of austerity plans, expansion of information and communication groups promotes liberalization, competitive mechanisms and corporate control in this scientific field, a key space in the definition of conflicts, perceptions and solutions in what Beck described as "risk societies" (1992).

Finally, extended attention to the information and communication needs of business also includes the continued expansion of digital marketing and advertising services during the crisis period, led mainly by US companies. Jordan Edmiston and IAB (2012) report the acceleration of acquisitions by companies such as Google, Facebook and LinkedIn of smaller firms that reinforce their position as providers of services and technologies for advertising and marketing, developing new data collection and analytic technologies.

Thus the crisis has not prevented big information and communication conglomerates, especially the US ones, from being able to afford the expansion of telecommunication infrastructures, ICT services and high-value content directed at industrial consumers, particularly for financial markets. Industrial and financial actors obtain many competitive advantages from these information and communication services, which reinforce not only their economic position but also their political influence. More knowledge, faster connections and economic dimensions continue to broaden the gap between the speed of financial transactions on the one hand and the speed of politics on the other, between the political capacity of these economic actors and that of political institutions and electors. As noted by Duch (2002), the acceleration of time in business through advances in technology "has been a factor directly involved with the increase in wealth and also with the capacity to exercise power (domination) in a way increasingly efficient and omnipresent." (Duch, 2002, p. 231)

MEDIA: TELEVISION, FICTION, SPORTS, MUSIC AND USER-GENERATED CONTENT – CONTINUITIES

In the field of media and content activities directed at household final consumption, the investment strategies of global groups during the crisis confirm some trends that have already been evident during the restructuring of European media markets since the 1990s. If anything, the crisis has increased the pressure on groups to concentrate their strategies in the most profitable business segments, with ICTs consolidating their role as new, powerful mediators in social communications.

Looking at new investments by large media groups between 2008 and 2013, sports, fiction and music appear to be the most attractive content (annual reports). Despite its financial problems, Vivendi invested in football rights, TV-serials production and cinema distribution and acquired free-to-air and pay-TV channels in France. Bertelsmann has directed its attention to new digital services and new platforms for music and books. News Corporation has consolidated its investments in Europe by merging its pay-TV activities, as well as, in Latin America, in football rights and pay-TV platforms.

Large global groups have thus responded to technological change, adapting their business models to new platforms and pay services while also maintaining their position in more traditional and still profitable activities such as free-to-air TV and subscription sports channels. The economic crisis has affected some companies, as in the case of Vivendi, which was forced to make some disinvestments due to its high indebtedness. However, generally there has been a trend towards concentration in the most profitable markets led by the big groups.[10]

As seen, big media, ICT and telecommunication groups concentrate on high-demand contents and services, including diffusion of new technologies offered as additional diversions for family and friends, at a moment when media consumption has apparently gone up (Braun and Cassi, 2012). For example, pay-TV (either cable, satellite or IPTV) in Europe remains healthy and growing and added almost exactly ten million homes between 2011 and 2012, rising from 121 million homes to 131 million in what was one of the worst twelve-month periods economically in the last decade (Rethink, 2012). McDonald and Johnson (2013) attribute the growth of time spent on media consumption to the recession, as it gives people more time and less money to spend outside the home and offers an escape function or a strategy for coping with stress in a recession period.

ICTs and telecommunication companies have taken part in this expansion, introducing some new articulations in the communication field. They do not participate so actively in content creation – although they are increasing investment in audiovisual production (see Chapter 4) – but they have a great influence in organizing content from different sources, introducing new criteria for the selection and gathering of information and content. Together with the fragmentation of audiences provoked by the multiplication of media outlets, the architecture of information and communication services offered on mobile devices and online favours the dispersion of the national public spheres, with communication systems moving from a national mass model to polarized models, with people connecting according to their interests, ideology or emotions (see Chapter 2). Telecommunications and ICTs offer new forms of mediation in political communication (Castells, 2002), based on social networks that provide more ephemeral connections, which can be polarized and dependent on more disparate information created by the media and non-professionals. This offers more pluralism and more voices but also more noise. However, it also seems as if the use of these digital platforms reproduces to a great extent the dynamics of traditional media, with private life, celebrities, sports and mainstream productions (serials, films, music) achieving the highest audiences on the new convergent platforms.

CRISIS FOR NATIONAL MEDIA GROUPS?

While global groups, including European-based groups with global activities, have survived the crisis with good results, even reinforcing their position both in traditional and new markets, national media groups[11] have been most exposed to the crisis as they cannot compensate so easily for losses in one market with benefits in other markets. This has particularly affected the press and public-service broadcasting.

The crisis has had three major effects on national media industries in those countries most hit by the financial crisis, such as Spain, Greece, Portugal and Italy (Fernández and Campos Freire, 2013). Firstly, it has pushed down advertising expenditure, mostly in the press, magazines, and regional and local media. Secondly, it has caused trouble in companies that have based their growth on high levels of indebtedness. And thirdly, as the financial crisis has evolved to become a public debt crisis, it has meant a reduction of public-service broadcasting budgets and of direct and indirect subsidies to private media. Spain and Greece are two clear examples of these phenomena.

In Spain, total advertising spending – below and above the line advertising – dropped thirty-three per cent from 2007 to 2012, but the fall was sixty per cent in the press, fifty-six per cent in magazines and forty-five per cent in television, with regional and local channels the most affected. By contrast, Internet advertising income increased eighty-two per cent in the same period, and personalized mailing has become the main advertising instrument for investment, ahead of television (Bergés and Sabater, 2013). The evolution in advertising revenue has obviously affected the results of media companies, which have responded by cutting costs, in some cases closing operations or reducing the amount of information they provide and the number of newsroom staff they employ. This is the case of the main Spanish newspapers, where the main titles, such as *El País* and *El Mundo*, have carried out severe staff reductions (see Chapter 5).

Together with the fall in advertising, high accumulated debt after years of growth based on leverage also explains the economic constraints in Spanish commercial and public media. Prisa, the main Spanish media group, clearly illustrates this process (Almirón and Segovia, 2012). Debt helped the group to expand from the beginning of the nineties, but from 2008 it forced Prisa to undertake disinvestments, especially in the audiovisual segment, where the emergence of new distribution platforms broke the monopolistic position of the group in the pay-TV market, thus reducing profit forecasts of lenders. Debt pressures led Prisa to close its local channels network (Localia TV), to sell its pay-TV platform to Telefónica and Mediaset, and to merge its free-to-air channels with Mediaset.

Finally, public budget cuts forced by austerity policies have directly affected the Spanish public-service broadcasting system. Public broadcaster RTVE's budget was reduced by twenty-two per cent between 2007 and 2013 (annual reports), while in the public regional system,[12] income has been reduced at least by forty-two per cent,[13] both by the cuts in public funds and a reduction of commercial income. Thus most of the regional PSBs have reduced the amount of channels they offer and are adopting plans to drastically reduce staff, introducing more outsourcing in their operations. The Catalan public broadcaster has merged its children's channel (K3) and its cultural channel (Canal 33) into one. Its commercial revenues have dropped by fifty-eight per cent between 2007 and 2013, while personnel have been reduced by more than six per cent. In the Valencian region, the public-service broadcaster was closed in November 2013 because of a combination of economic problems (fall in revenues, high accumulated indebtedness) and political failings (political interference, lack of newsroom autonomy). Other regional public-service broadcasters face similar problems, added to a fall of audience share.

Greece provides another example of how the crisis is affecting national media systems. The recent fiscal crisis, coupled with the crisis of the economy, brought major losses of advertising revenues for the media industry. On top of this, the austerity package put forth by the so-called Troika – the European Commission (EC), the International Monetary Fund (IMF) and the European Central Bank (ECB), which aims at restoring the Greek economy – looks set to deepen Greek woes.

While the advertising market has been facing collapse since 2007, the public sector has not only diminished its advertising spend but also has postponed many orders for public works. This had a negative knock-on effect on the media, and newspapers in particular, since entrepreneurs in public construction projects were also active in the media field. The owners of TV and radio stations, as well as newspapers, could thus no longer cross-subsidize their media outlets with revenues from public works orders.

Today, Greek media outlets are facing their most difficult period ever, but the print media (newspapers and magazines) are suffering the most. The Greek press has been in a state of permanent crisis since the mid-1990s. Since then, fewer and fewer Greeks read a newspaper on a daily basis (Papathanassopoulos and Mpakounakis, 2010). On the other hand, although only one private channel has closed due to financial problems since 2008, almost all TV and radio stations have been facing severe financial problems due to the collapse of advertising expenditure. However, the closure of the public broadcaster, ERT, on June 11, 2013 was a politically led decision rather than one based on its financial problems. The opposition claimed the government fired ERT's 2,500 employees to prove to Greece's international lenders (the so-called troika) that it was serious about cutting the country's bloated public sector. The troika of international lenders expects 4,000 jobs to go by the end of 2013 (Papathanassopoulos, 2014).

Advertising restrictions, a reduction in newspaper circulations, cuts in public-service broadcasting budgets and restrictions on quality journalism also appear in other countries (see Chapter 5). However, they are not simply a result of the financial crisis. Instead, the crisis appears to act more as an accelerator of trends that have been present in the sector for many years (de Mateo, Bergés and Garnatxe, 2010). Technological convergence, competition by new digital players, a surplus of supply, commercialization tendencies in journalism and the financialization of the media are all features of the media environment, which have become more evident in the context of crisis.

COUNTER-HEGEMONIC FORCES: NEW OWNERSHIP AND FINANCIAL MODELS FOR NEW INFORMATIVE NEEDS

If the crisis seems to have accelerated a long-term process of consolidation, commercialization, inequalities in information access and internationalization, it has also fed some counter-hegemonic forces. As financial, political and media crises persist, new initiatives appear on the margins, articulated with social movements that have grown during the crisis, like 15M, the outraged and anti-capitalists in Spain, the separatist movement in Catalonia and anarchist groups in Greece, among others. The emergence of new counter-hegemonic media also fits in with digitalization, which offers cheaper opportunities to circulate news and information, facilitates co-operation in production, allows the location of financial resources through crowdfunding platforms and provides the plethora of what used to be nanomedia and ephemeral networks with some influence on the mainstream media.

The range of initiatives goes from purely activist media to more professional journalistic projects that try to create more independence through different business and ownership models. In recent years there has been an expansion of media created by not-for-profit associations and by co-operatives of journalists that follow in the tradition of free or social movements' media but have also adapted models involving donations and foundations, which seem to be more resistant to crises.

Social movements that emerged with the crisis have made intensive use of Twitter and Facebook (López, 2013; BIFI, 2011) but they have also used "old" free radio stations, alternative publications and websites, many of them initiated with the previous anti-globalization protests (Bergés, 2013). Most of these initiatives are based on voluntary work and activism, so instability and militant journalism are part of their characteristics. However, the combination of social digital networks with these alternative media has given them more visibility and even more capacity to influence the agenda of hegemonic media. For instance, in the case of 15M protests in Spain, Pinilla (2011) shows how the intense debate circulating in Twitter or Facebook and its capacity to articulate outraged groups and individuals has directed the attention of mainstream newspapers to the movement. Similarly, BIFI's (2011) analysis of Twitter dialogue during the main protests in Spain on May 15, 2010 situates some alternative media (such as Agora News, Periodismo Humano, Kaosenlared, websites of different local camps) as basic nodes in the network woven around 15M.

Other initiatives also try to respond to the social discontent and demands of independent journalism but from a more professional perspective (Table 3.2). In this group there are new-media initiatives, collaborative journalism platforms, observatories created by foundations and single pieces of independent journalism funded by crowdfunding platforms.

Table 3.2 examples of professional non-for-profit journalism linked to social movements

New media initiatives	*Correspondent* (Netherlands): news site, crowdfunded and free-ad. *Eldiario.es*, news site created in 2012. Cooperative of journalists and readers. *La Marea* (Spain) monthly newspaper link to La Marea movement in defence of public services, created by journalists hired from Público, a newspaper disappeared with the crisis. *Periodismo Humano* (Spain). Non-for-profit news site, crowdfunded. *9exili.com and Tmex-La television social*: video platforms created by journalists hired from regional public broadcasters of Valencia and Madrid.
Collaborative journalism	International Consortium for Investigative Journalism project: *Secrecy for Sale: Inside the Global Offshore Money Maze.* Collaborative big data journalism project. Published in 2013, counted on the collaboration of more than 110 journalists in 58 countries.
Transparency digital platforms	*Dónde van mis impuestos* (where do my taxes go), *El indultómetro* (Reprievemeter), *Municipal Civic Observatories* (Spain): platforms that foster public data transparency, produced by non-for-profit foundation and associations.
Crowdfunding journalism	110 journalist projects (book, audiovisual documentaries, free radios, ICTs for independent alternative journalism), have been funded through crowdfunding platforms Verkami and Goteo (Spain), raising more than a million Euros between 2010 and 2012.

Although marginal, these kinds of initiatives are contributing to a more pluralistic but also a more polarized public sphere in which different ideological communities share information but often find it difficult to access a common space for a national public debate. These alternative spaces also include the proliferation of blogs and websites supported by right-wing movements.

CONCLUSIONS

The regression of the crisis, which started with the financial crash in 2008, raises many questions about the nature of the crisis itself. What in the first instance appeared to be a crisis of neoliberal globalization, evolved into a crisis of the European social market economy model and the welfare state. At the same time, if the crisis appeared to be a sign of the unsustainability of a model based on unlimited growth, later developments point towards a polarization between forced economic decline for some countries and social sectors and continued growth for other sectors that enjoy competitive advantages in the neoliberal global order. In this respect, the crisis has strengthened long-term trends associated with the globalisation process, which has broken the economic, social and political consensus agreed after World War II and weakened the position of Europe on the global stage.

A similar evolution can be found in the field of communications, which has been central to the consolidation of this global neoliberal order and is continuing to play a pivotal role in the current situation. The financial crisis has added uncertainty to a sector already hit by technological, regulatory and industrial restructuring. Commercialization of the public sphere, concentration in media markets, competition from ICTs that threatens the traditional business model for professional journalism and a crisis of public-service media are some of the deepening trends linked to the financial crisis.

Consequently, the communication field appears to be emerging as a set of networks that are not neutral, where inequalities of access to useful or high-value information have increased, reinforcing social imbalances and the uncoupling of global finance from national policy-making and the field of formal politics. Social and political mediations built by media, telecoms and ICTs have evolved into a more polarized model in which democratic consensus becomes more difficult. On the one hand, part of this consensus takes place in opaque arenas between corporate players who make intensive and strategic use of information and communication networks. On the other hand, traditional mass media and new digital networks and platforms aimed at a general audience tend to build on an increasingly commercialized public sphere divided by social, economic and political conditions that correspond to a parallel disintegration of national political communities.

However, the intensity of the crisis raises new conflicts that also involve the communication field. New political demands and organizations driven by people feeling excluded from the global neoliberal model question the political consensus among hegemonic parties since World War II. And new communication practices question the traditional role of the core media in this democratic order, whether through mainstream social networks or through independent social movements' media. New competitive, often conflicting, relationships also appear among the hegemonic players – between established and emerging countries, between traditionally hegemonic economic agents and newcomers – as also occurs in the communication field, where new players from the ICT sector unsettle the role assigned to more traditional mass media in the European political model.

NOTES

1. In his book *From Media to Mediations*, Barbero (1987) tried to escape media-centrism to look at the processes – that happen through media but also through other cultural and communicative devices – that link communicative practices of production and reception to the cultural, social and political processes. The concept is based on the idea of social mediation (Martín Serrano, 1977), meaning the diverse practices involved in information management and conscience production, which are consequently involved in the construction and control of perceptions that have an impact on social reproduction and social change.
2. Roubini and Mihn refer to the shadow financial system as the set of tax havens; intra-industrial finances; other kinds of non-bank lenders; hedge funds; broker dealers and other non-regulated financial institutions.
3. In 2011, Luis de Guindos, an advisor at Lehman Brothers in Europe (2006–2008) and responsible for the finance division of Price Waterhouse (2008–2010), became Minister of Economy and Competitiveness in Rajoy's government. Mario Draghi, who was vice-president of Goldman Sachs between 2002 and 2006, when the company helped to hide Greece's public debt, became president of the European Central Bank in 2011. And Mario Monti, who had been a member of the Trilateral Commissions and an assistant at Goldman Sachs, became president of Italy's technocratic government between 2011 and 2013.
4. 15M refers to a social movement that began in Spain with the occupation of main squares in Madrid and Barcelona on 15 May 2011.
5. For the analysis of global groups' performance, we have selected a sample including main media, ICT and telecommunications groups with an outstanding position in Europe markets: Bertelsmann, Vivendi, Thomson-Reuters, News Corporation, Google, Telefónica and Vodafone.
6. We refer to the annual financial statements and annual reports of the sample of companies analyzed (Bertelsmann, Vivendi, Thomson-Reuters, News Corporation, Google, Telefónica and Vodafone) corresponding to 2007–2013. Reports retrieved from corporate websites and SEC filings. http://www.bertelsmann.com/investor-relations/financial-publications/financial-reports/ http://www.vivendi.com/analystes-investisseurs/publications//tax_publication-rapports-annuels/ http://ir.thomsonreuters.com/phoenix.zhtml?c=76540&p=irol-reportsOther http://reports.21cf.com/Report2012/index.html; http://investor.google.com/financial/filings-archives.html http://www.telefonica.com/es/shareholders-investors/html/financial_reports/informesanuales.shtml http://www.vodafone.com/content/index/investors/investor_information/annual_report.html.

7. Arvato is in fact the largest of the group, based on number of employees, and the second-largest based on revenues, after RTL.
8. "New Transatlantic Cable Built to Shave 5 Milliseconds off Stock Trades." http://www.popularmechanics.com/technology/engineering/infrastructure/a-transatlantic-cable-to-shave-5-milliseconds-off-stock-trades. "Cable Across Atlantic Aims to Save Traders Milliseconds." http://www.bloomberg.com/news/2012-03-29/cable-across-atlantic-aims-to-save-traders-milliseconds.html.
9. Bertelsmann Foundation promoted the creation of a not-for-profit agency, which finally did not find enough interested investors. News Corporation also sold its subsidiary Stoxx Ag, a European market indexes-provider, to form a joint venture with CME to develop global financial indexes services.
10. For example, Vivendi acquired Bolloré Group television channels in 2011; the Spanish free-to-air TV market has become almost a duopoly after acquisitions by Mediaset and Planeta (Bertelsmann) of their main competitors; Telefónica bought Prisa's pay-TV platform to concentrate satellite and cable supply.
11. According to Herman and McChesney (1997), among others, information and communication industries comprise a first-tier group of companies with a dominant position in global markets, a second tier composed of big groups dominant in national markets (i.e. Prisa, Lagardère, VNU, Sanoma, ProSieben) and an ensemble of smaller companies acting in regional markets or in a specific segment of activities.
12. Public-service broadcasting in Spain is comprised of the national service (RTVE) and 12 regional public entities that accumulated from 5 to 12.8 per cent shares in their territories. http://www.forta.es/FortaComercial/DatosdeaudienciaShare televisionesautonomicas/tabid/203/Default.aspx#graf).
13. http://fiscalizacion.es/2008/08/23/televisiones-publicas-autonomicas-2/. http://www.lavanguardia.com/comunicacion/20131107/54393842620/cuanto-cuestan-televisiones-autonomicas.html.

REFERENCES

Albert, M. (1992) *Capitalismo contra capitalismo*. Barcelona: Paidós, Estado y sociedad.

Almirón, N. and Segovia, A. (2012) Financialization, economic crisis, and corporate strategies in top media companies: the case of Grupo Prisa. *International Journal of Communication*, 6. pp. 2894–917.

Balčytienė, A., Raeymaekers, K. and Vartanova, E. (2011) Changing Practices of Journalism. In: Trappel, J., Meier, W.A., d'Haenens, L., Steemers, J. and Thomass, B. (eds.) *Media in Europe Today* (pp. 219–33). Bristol: Intellect.

Barnett, S. (2002) Will a Crisis in Journalism Provoke a Crisis in Democracy? *The Political Quarterly*, 73 (4). pp. 400–08. Oxford, Malden: Blackwell Publishers Ltd.

Becerra, M. and Mastrini, G. (2010) Crisis. What Crisis? Argentine Media in View of the 2008 International Financial Crisis. *International Journal of Communication*, 4. pp. 611–29. Los Angeles: University of Southern California.

Becerra, M. (2011) La inmaculada concepción de los medios latinoamericanos en crisis. *Herramientas*, 47. Buenos Aires: Ediciones Herramientas.

Beck, U. (1992) *The Risk Society*. London: Sage.

Benson, R. and Neveu, E. (2005) *Bourdieu and the journalistic field*. Cambridge: Wilwy Polity Press.

Bergés, L. and Sabater, M. (2013) La publicitat. In: *Informe de la Comunicació a Catalunya, 2011–2012*. Barcelona: UAB.

Bergés, L. (2013) 15M, Indignados, #spanishrevolution: counter hegemonic communication experiences to face the crisis in Spain. *Crises, 'Creative Destruction' and the Global Power and Communication Orders*. IAMCR Annual Conference, June, Dublin.

BIFI (Biocomputación y Física de Sistemas Complejos) (2011) *Interacciones entre usuarios 15M*. Universidad de Zaragoza. Retrieved from: http://15m.bifi.es/index.php.

Bourdieu, P. (1993) *The field of cultural production*. New York: Columbia University Press.

Braun, J. and Cassi, A. (2013) *One TV Year in the World 2012 or the multiple TV experience*. Mediametrie-Eurodata TV.

Candón, J. and Redondo, D. (2012) The Internet in social mobilization: the conquest of the public sphere. *Conference on Civil Society and Democracy: Working Group on Democracy of the Austrian Research Association*. Vienna, November 9–10.

Castells, M. (2002) *The Internet Galaxy*. Oxford: Oxford University Press.

Davis, N. (2008) *Flat Earth News: An Award-Winning Reporter Exposes Falsehood, Distortion and Propaganda in the Global Media*. London: Vintage Books.

Duch, L. (2002) *Antropología de la vida cotidiana*. Barcelona: Trotta.

ETNO (2013) *Annual Economic Report 2013*. Brussels: European Telecommunications Network Operators' Association. Retrieved from: https://www.etno.eu/datas/publications/economic-reports/ETNO_Financial_Report_2013_Def-Lands.pdf.

Fernández, F. and Campos Freire, F. (2013) La crisis de los países periféricos europeos. Descapitalización en bolsa de los grupos mediáticos del sur. *Telos. Cuadernos de Comunicación e innovación*, June-September. Madrid: Telefónica.

Feixa, C. and Nofre, J. (eds.) (2013) *#GeneraciónIndignada: Topías y Utopías del 15M*. Lleida, Spain: Milenio.

Heinberg, R. (2011) *The end of growth*. Gabriola Island, British Columbia: New Society Publishers.

Herman, E. and McChesney, R. (1997) *The Global Media: The New Missionaries of Corporate Capitalism*. London and Washington: Cassel.

Hultén, O., Melesko, S. and Tjernström, S. (eds.) (2010) *Media Mergers and the Defence of Pluralism*. Göteborg: Nordicom.

Intermon Oxfam (2012) *Crisis, desigualdad y pobreza. Informe de Intermón Oxfam*, 32, 13 December.

Internet Society (2009) *Internet Futures Scenarios*. Geneva: Internet Society. Retrieved from: http://www.internetsociety.org/sites/default/files/pdf/report-internetfutures-20091006-en.pdf.

Jordan Edmiston Group; IAB (2012) *The social media ecosystem report: Rise of users, intelligence and operating systems*. New York: The Jordan Edmiston Group; IAB. Retrieved from: http://www.iab.net/media/file/JEGIIABSocialMediaReport.pdf.

Kaplan, R. (2000) *An Empire Wilderness: Travels Into America's Future*. New York: Vintage Departures.

López García, G. (2013) Del 11M al #15M. Nuevas tecnologías y movilización social en España. *Revista Faro*, 16. Valparaíso: Universidad de Playa Ancha. Retrieved from: http://www.revistafaro.cl.

Loza, G. (2000) La crisis en Tiempos de la Globalización. *Cuadernos de Futuro*, 3. La Paz: Programa de las Naciones Unidas para el Desarrollo. Retrieved from: http://idh.pnud.bo/d7/sites/default/files/Informes/Cuadernos%20de%20futuro/03%20 Las%20Crisis%20en%20Tiempos%20de%20la%20Globalizacion/Cuaderno3.pdf.

Martín Barbero, J. (1987) *De los medios a las mediaciones*. Barcelona: Gustavo Gili.

Martínez Alier J. and Roca, J. (2000) *Economía ecológica y política ambiental*. México: PNUMA/FCE.

Mateo, R., Bergés, L. and Garnatxe, A. (2010) What Crisis? The Media: Business and Journalism in Times of Crisis. *Triple C. Cognition, communication, co-operation*, 8(2). pp. 251–274.

McDonald, D. and Johnson, B.K. (2013) Is Time Money? Media Expenditures in Economic and Technological Turbulence. *Journal of Broadcasting and Electronic Media*, 57(3). pp. 282–99.

Meier, W.A. and Trappel, J. (eds.) (2007) *Power, Performance & Politics: Media Policy in Europe*. Euromedia Research Group. Baden-Baden: Nomos.

Mosco, V. (1996) *The political economy of communication*. London: Sage.

Navarro, V. and Torres, J. (2012) *Los amos del mundo. Las armas del terrorismo financiero*. Madrid: Espasa.

Papathanassopoulos, S. (2014) The transition to digital television in Greece: Now what? *International Journal of Digital Television*, 5(1). pp. 19–30.

Papathanassopoulos, S. and Mpakounakis, N. (2010) The Athenian press after 1989, Ζητήματα Επικοινωνίας *(Communication Issues)*, 10. pp. 62–70.

Pinilla, A. (2011) La percepción del movimiento 15M en las ediciones digitales de El Mundo y El País. *Tejuelo Didáctica de la lengua y la literatura*, 12. pp. 196–217. Universidad de Extremadura.

PriceWaterhouseCoopers (2013) *Global entertainment and media outlook, 2010–14*. New York: PWC.

Rethink (2012) *The Telcos Strike Back: Pay-TV markets in Europe*. Brockenhurst, Hampshire: Rethink Technology Research.

Roubini, N. and Mihm, S. (2010) *Crisis economics: a crash course in the future of finances*. London: Penguin.

Rügemer, W. (2013) *Las agencias de calificación*. Barcelona: Virus.

Schiller, H. (1983) *El poder informático*. Barcelona: Gustavo Gili.

Strange, S. (1996) *The retreat of the State*. Cambridge: Cambridge University Press.

Trappel, J., Meier, W. A., d'Haenens, L., Steemers, J. and Thomass, B. (eds.) (2011) *Media in Europe Today*. Bristol: Intellect.

Winseck, D. and Yong, D. (2011) *The Political Economies of Media. The Transformation of the Global Media Industries*. London: Bloomsbury Academic.

4 Broadcasting is Dead. Long Live Television

Perspectives from Europe

Jeanette Steemers

INTRODUCTION

The demise of television, and of broadcasting in particular, has long been forecast and debated with particular attention focused on what these changes might mean for audiovisual plurality and diversity in the face of multiple multimedia platforms, interactive opportunities and convergence (Steemers, 1997). Technology, however, is only one factor in the transformation of television as "a medium, an industry, and as a system" (Braun, 2013, p. 432), a transformation that also encompasses longstanding commercialisation and deregulation that has often been at odds with cultural expectations about television's role in society. Watching television as a pastime is unlikely to die any time soon, but the way it is delivered and the systems into which it is embedded are undoubtedly undergoing radical change. For Keilbach and Stauff change is an integral feature of a medium whose 'constant transformation process', has allowed continuous redefinition and reinvention rather than 'stable institutionalization' (2014: 80). Change brings new opportunities for both audiences and industry, but also poses challenges for existing regulatory frameworks and national systems as mostly US-based global gatekeepers and digital intermediaries (content aggregators, search engines, social media and digital stores) emerge to compete with national broadcasters, cable and satellite channel operators, who have focused their activities mainly on the provision of linear television (see Foster, 2012). Online distribution of on-demand television content represents another stage in what many commentators have defined as the post-broadcast/network era of television (Lotz, 2007; Spigel and Olsson, 2004; Turner and Tay, 2009).

This chapter considers the challenge arising from new forms of television distribution within the European Union and whether these challenges constitute a crisis for the industry in terms of sustaining production and maintaining audiences. According to Michalis (2013, p. 38), European television broadcasters have faced three main challenges in recent times: the shift of advertising expenditure from television to the Internet; investment in new digital channels and on-demand services; and the transition towards 'an integrated television-broadband landscape.' These challenges are apparently mirrored in shifts in user behaviour towards multiplatform consumption, which suggests further fragmentation of audiences and revenues, with implications for the funding of European content as revenues are spread more widely, and for the future of traditional broadcast television and public-service media in particular.

Drawing on evidence from industry reports, policy documents and press commentary, this chapter focuses on the impact of digital change on the distribution, production and consumption of European television and the extent to which this might constitute a crisis for the sector. Part One considers changes in the distribution of television content, concentrating on new forms of distribution, the prospects for 'connected TV' and the emergence of new players. Closely connected to distribution, the next sections emphasize trends in reception and production and the extent to which new forms of distribution are already impacting consumption and investment in European content. The final section looks at the role of public-service broadcasters in sustaining content production within the EU and their contribution to the maintenance of a free and universal service that contributes to the democratic and cultural life of society.

TRANSFORMATIONS IN DISTRIBUTION

Some of the most profound changes within the European television landscape appear to be occurring within distribution, the crucial "space in between" production and consumption (Perren, 2013, p. 53) as digital technology integrates socially networked communication with traditional screen media to allow "connected viewing" and interactive exchanges by users across multiple screens. As the distinction between broadcast and broadband reception blurs, the way television is "bought, sold, 'pirated', packaged, policed, redistributed, reimagined, and redefined" (Holt and Sanson, 2014, p. 2) is altered, with implications for market structures as established funding and release models for the most popular content (fiction, films) based on timed releases and revenue-enhancing windowing strategies are disrupted, necessitating innovations in revenue models, new approaches to customer relationships and content (Liu and Picard, 2014, p. 2f). Digitization and an increase in platforms represent a further shift away from the notion of scheduled, appointment-based, universally available generic television channels towards an audiovisual environment that is more engagement-based, on-demand and, depending on the type of service, both more restricted (through the implementation of pay walls) as well as more open (through free online access e.g. YouTube).

For Jenkins et al. (2013), these changes represent a positive cultural shift as users start to personalize and appraise their audiovisual media experiences as part of a more participatory, interactive culture of production and distribution that is both top down and bottom up, involving the adaptation and remixing of content that is then 'spread' by social media within communities and networks as part of a 'networked culture.' According to Hendy (2013, p. 107), this combination of interactivity and a 'long tail' of endless services and content has effected "a profound shift in how we think about the relationship between the communicator and the audience, and between the 'producer' and the 'consumer,'" undermining the idea of broadcasting's unidirectional definition of what is good or true or important in favour of "the Internet's apparently non-hierarchical marketplace of ideas and knowledge and stories". Of course, as the Internet becomes more mature, the dynamics and hierarchical relations of more traditional markets are replicated online, with large corporations endeavouring to colonize online space and organize content and access to their commercial advantage (see Internet Society, 2009). Havens and Lotz (2012, p. 221) point out that "more personally relevant media" might offer gains for consumers, but they also note the potential costs of fragmentation, including the demise of "potentially positive society-making functions" that might occur from sharing a traditional media experience such as broadcast television.

Digital distribution reveals, then, differences between established broadcast models based around the marketing and screening of professionally produced audiovisual artefacts aimed predominantly at mass audiences, which can be measured and sold, and the addition of different economic models based on a more targeted approach to both content and users, focused around engagement rather than ratings (Sanz, 2012, p. 21). One of these online access models, the distribution of pirated content (for example through peer-to-peer file transfer) clearly undermines the closed character of territorially based copyright regimes, which underpin investment in creatively risky products such as drama. (Sanz, 2012, p. 52)

At its most basic, however, the most prominent feature of this new distribution culture in Europe is simply a massive increase in TV-like content centred on sport, serials, celebrities and other forms of popular entertainment. Broadcasters, including the largest European companies are part of this trend, investing in new platforms and integrating their services on all screens in order to maintain reach and relevance across as many platforms as possible in a Create Once, Publish Everywhere (Cope) strategy (Looms, 2014, p. 45). Broadcaster adaptation to the online world includes live streaming of existing channels, on-demand offerings (as catch up, preview or archive TV), additional programme or channel-related content (interviews, behind the scenes, interactive services, games) and original content. Broadcasters have concluded branded channel deals with players like YouTube as well as launching their own online portals. This is also a response to the distribution possibilities promoted by US intermediaries Amazon, YouTube and Netflix, which according to Cunningham and Silver (2013), are emerging as powerful online distribution giants across multiple platforms as they begin to operate as TV-like networks on a global scale by professionalising their content and investing in production. Alongside these branded platforms are another set of hidden but potentially powerful intermediaries that provide the processes of online video distribution, shaping viewing activity through their management of infrastructures and data, which is then used to determine what content consumers can access, where (to support national copyright) and on what terms (Braun, 2013, p. 433; 2014). This constitutes one of the innovations and potentially most controversial aspects of 'new' television viewing and distribution technology as user data is mined from synchronized second-screen devices (phones, tablets) to allow tailored marketing and recommended content that can be pushed back to consumers to capitalize on further commercial opportunities.

In the EU, alongside broadcast, cable and satellite services, online television services include:

- Broadcaster-led catch-up services available online as streaming or download services e.g. the BBC IPlayer (UK), Das Erste Mediathek (ARD Germany), as well as archive services
- Online catch-up services available as extensions to existing pay-TV subscription channels e.g. SkyGo (UK)
- Broadcast-led live TV with supplementary catch-up, on-demand content and PVR functionality involving hybrid services that integrate broadcast and Internet content through set-top boxes e.g. Freeview Plus, BT Vision (UK), Sky Italia (Italy)
- Over the Top (OTT) content aggregators available as video on demand through browsers, apps, set-top boxes and next generation televisions e.g. YouTube (free), Apple I Tunes (transactional VOD), Netflix, Amazon Prime (Subscription VOD).

By 31 August 2014, the EAO's Mavise database (mavise.obs.coe.int) was listing 3,195 on-demand audiovisual services in the European Union, including branded channels on YouTube by established broadcasters. The largest category comprised 1,070 online catch-up TV services, run largely by broadcasters such as Channel 4 (4OD) and the BBC (IPlayer). The second largest category (744 services) consisted of branded channels hosted on 'open' online video-sharing sites, mainly YouTube, followed by 419 VOD film services including various national variations of Amazon Prime Instant Video (UK, Germany), Netflix (Scandinavia, UK and the Netherlands) and the Apple ITunes Store (Europe-wide). The fact that Netflix and Amazon were only available in a limited number of the more advanced markets in September 2014 suggests Europe as a whole was not yet ripe for full commercial exploitation and a pan-European approach to the licensing of rights. In addition to 3,195 on-demand audiovisual services, there are 9,215 channels available in the EU as free-to-air television, cable, satellite and IPTV services (mavise.obs.coe.int).

Yet in spite of the growth in VOD services, the reality of distribution in Europe is more complex than the US, where opportunities for on-demand viewing over the Internet are more advanced. Netflix, for example, was ranked the 25th most visited site in the US in August 2014 (www.alexa.com, an Amazon-owned site), but only 83rd globally. Distribution in Europe is more complex than the US because it covers a fragmented, territory-based advertising and programming market where tastes in programming content tend to be more nationally oriented and where there has never been much interest in pan-European content

(Attentional et al., 2011; Doyle, 2012, p. 13; Ranaivoson, 2010). Within Europe there are huge variations in territory size, language, regulation, culture, income, the rate of adoption for new services, the spread of broadband technologies, the range of what is on offer and the willingness or ability of consumers to pay for content – for example, per capita consumer spending on audiovisual services varies between €8 in Cyprus and €450 in Denmark (Enders, 2013a, p. 11). In this earliest phase of online television, it is the largest markets (particularly the UK) and those smaller, richer markets (Scandinavia, Benelux) where online television distribution models are furthest advanced, but even here, standard television viewing predominates for now (see below).

One further distribution issue for the European television industry relates to regulation at EU level and its place within a more complex distribution environment with tensions between digital distributors who want fewer restrictions on the flow of data on the one hand and content providers who want protection for copyrighted material (Holt, 2014, p. 31). The EU's 2007 Audiovisual Services (AVMS) Directive, which replaced the 1989 Television Without Frontiers Directive, brought less stringent regulation to bear on non-linear, television-like video-on-demand services as opposed to linear television broadcasts that are subject to stricter rules on advertising and the protection of minors, for example. However the Directive is not really designed to deal with hybrid online video sites such as YouTube that mix professional and amateur content as well as filtering and personalisation mechanisms that affect the media's role as editors (Valcke and Ausloos, 2014, p. 37f). Now the European Commission is looking at the potential for delivering audiovisual works online as part of a digital single market (EC, 2011, 2013) in which the digital landscape and its commercial exploitation represent a new cornerstone of the EU's policy (https://ec.europa.eu/digital-agenda/en). In this context, changes in the way content is delivered (push and pull) and the consumption of regulated broadcast content and largely unregulated Internet content on the same platforms raise serious yet unresolved regulatory issues around access regimes (pricing by digital intermediaries); must-carry rules on managed networks; prominence rules for user interfaces and electronic programme guides (EPGs); the protection of intellectual property; the regulation of spectrum for universal delivery (through DTT); and net neutrality, which underpins open Internet access (BBC, 2013a, p. 1f; DCMS, 2013, p. 24; Holt, 2014).

CHANGES IN RECEPTION AND CONSUMPTION

Within the industry and in journalistic reports there is plenty of speculation about the growth of online distribution. With the rise in VOD services, non-linear consumption has indeed increased in Europe, but in 2014 had not yet significantly eroded linear consumption of television (predominantly of generic channels), which continued to rise in many European countries (EBU, 2013; Ofcom, 2013a; Simon, 2012, p. 10). Time-shifted viewing on

PVRs (Personal Video Recorders) continues to grow, but live viewing (as it is broadcast) is still the main way people watch TV. According to the European Broadcasting Union (EBU), linear TV, with a ninety-three per cent share of viewing in the five largest EU markets, remained the most popular means of consuming television content in 2012, with only two per cent and five per cent of viewing dedicated to non-linear consumption online and by PVR respectively (EBU, 2013, p. 25). EU viewers watched television for 3:38 hours per day in 2012, seven minutes more than in 2011 (EBU, 2013, p. 31). Mainstream channels appear to be seemingly resilient in most European markets and the top five generalist channels continue to account for just over half of all television viewing in the Netherlands, Germany, the UK (Ofcom, 2013a, p. 171) and Spain (EGM, 2013).

However, the situation is changing all the time. More recent data on the UK market as part of Ofcom's Digital Day 2014 snapshot of the public's media activities suggest different trends among different generations of viewers. UK TV viewing for all individuals fell unexpectedly in 2013 from 241 minutes to 232 minutes (Ofcom, 2014, p. 10). Moreover, while all adults devoted thirty-seven per cent of their media and communications time to watching television or movies on a TV set, this fell to twenty-four per cent for those aged sixteen to twenty-four (p. 6). It could of course be argued that younger people have always watched less television, but they also spend less of their TV time (fifty per cent) watching live TV than all adults (sixty-nine per cent) and more than double all adult viewing on online viewing (twenty-one per cent) including six per cent of viewing devoted to services like Netflix and Amazon (see Table 4.1). This implies that television viewing, while still attractive, is becoming less attractive as scheduled content on television sets. In some countries this trend is even more pronounced. In Norway, for example, it was reported in April 2014 that twenty-three per cent of Norwegian households (540,000) had a Netflix subscription (http://kampanje.com/archive/2014/04/en-av-fire-har-netflix).

Table 4.1 Time spent viewing audio visual content as part of a 7 day diary – UK 2014

	All Adult Viewing UK	Adults aged 16–24
Viewing of Live TV	69%	50%
Viewing of Recorded TV (DVRs)	16%	16%
Online Viewing divided into:	**10%**	**21%**
- Catch-up services e.g. BBC iPlayer	5%	7%
- Downloaded or streamed services e.g. Netflix, Amazon Prime Instant Video	3%	6%
- Viewing of video clips e.g. YouTube	2%	8%
Physical Media – DVDs/Blu-ray	5%	13%

Source: *Digital Day* Ofcom 2014, p. 64.

Just as linear broadcast television continues to be the most pervasive and robust form of television consumption for the time being, pay television, delivered by satellite or cable, continues to be the most pervasive form of subscription TV. In 2012 there were an estimated 125m pay television subscribers in the EU, generating €31bn in revenues (Bomsel and Rosnay, 2013, p. 27). By contrast, estimated EU revenues in 2012 for the subscription online VOD market (7.3m subscribers) were only €62m in 2012, but estimated to grow threefold to €189m by 2016 (ibid., p. 30). Piracy of the most desirable dramas (US shows *Game of Thrones, Breaking Bad, Mad Men*) is rife, with an estimated 1.6 global illegal downloads of *Game of Thrones* within a four-week period in 2014 (Sweney, 2014). Yet HBO claims piracy fuels publicity around a hit show and fuels legal subscriptions and box-set purchases (ibid.).

With the apparent continued popularity of 'traditional' television and small audiences and revenues for online television in Europe, any crisis in the European television industry appears to be more about the uncertainty of what seems like a transitional intermediate phase in which the public are beginning to watch television on different devices. Any pending industry crisis may therefore be more significant for its long-term effects rather than its short-term ramifications.

TRANSFORMATIONS IN PRODUCTION

Closely aligned to changes in distribution and reception are matters relating to the production of television content within Europe. For organizations like the EBU (2013, p. 22), sustained production of original content is the key to the successful development of new services as well as technological innovation.

In terms of content production, the development of digital technologies has already altered the aesthetics of television, with the introduction of graphics and effects that have impacted the way stories are told (Caldwell, 1995) and allow different types of audiovisual product. Digital technologies have made it easier to shoot and edit video cheaply, fuelling amateur use and blurring the distinction between professional and amateur production, although this type of participation is small set against the totality of television viewership. Amateur and professional producers are uploading material (blogs, video blogs, web series) to participatory platforms like YouTube, uninhibited by editorial guidelines and hierarchies of control, contributing to a participatory culture around TV programming, or producing their own original content (Lewis, 2013). A small number of individual bloggers are hugely successful, racking up thousands of subscribers, sharing advertising revenue with YouTube, generating merchandise sales and creating direct-to-consumer relationships (ibid.). For professional content-producers, television still forms a crucial part of rollout, but more than ever it needs to be aligned with digital distribution and new forms of content and supplementary material on other devices including phones and tablets.

At a broader meso level, however, the increase in capacity generated by new forms of distribution is raising perennial concerns about Europe's international competitiveness as a producer (Doyle, 2012), particularly as increases in capacity fuel demand for more imports. Non-linear video-on-demand services (Netflix, Amazon) offering fiction and films tend to rely more on content sourced from non-European, primarily US suppliers (Attentional et al., 2011, p. 12f), contributing further to the historical dominance of US suppliers in the television content trade (Chalaby, 2012). According to Lange (2011), European channels have sourced up to fifty per cent of their fiction acquisitions from the US, with only eleven per cent sourced from other European countries (Lange, 2011). Occasionally there are pan-European successes such as the thriller drama *The Killing* from public-service broadcaster Danmarks Radio, but these tend to be successful in culturally proximate countries (other Nordic countries) or on minority channels (Jensen, 2014). Drama, however, is hugely significant, because it provides a test of the extent to which European markets can support and market the production of more expensive content beyond national boundaries. Yet even if Europeans have a preference for domestic content, this preference is not absolute, and EC reports that preferences for it are declining among younger adults who access content from a broader range of platforms (Attentional et al., 2011, p. 15).

In a similar vein to the multichannel expansion of the 1980s, content is being heavily recycled on new distribution outlets (Doyle, 2012, p. 13) in the form of low-cost original productions, often based on formats; library material, usually US fiction and films; and repeats. Yet it is this recycling of material on a territory by territory basis that underpins the economics of the European audiovisual business, a market valued at €131billion in 2011, equivalent to twenty per cent of the global audiovisual marketplace (EBU, 2013, p. 7, citing European Audiovisual Observatory Yearbook 2012). According to Enders (2013a, p. 3), territorial licensing of content rights on an exclusive basis forms the 'bedrock' of the European television sector, creating 'an edifice of value' that generates the revenues that allow further investment in European content and so preserving linguistic and cultural diversity. Doyle (2012, p. 16) argues that the outlawing of territoriality would make it harder for content owners to realize the value of their assets. Yet this is what is at stake if the EU creates a single market for digital content through online copyright licensing of multi-territorial and pan-European services (EC, 2011, p. 12; EC, 2013, p. 6).

At this point it is useful to remind ourselves who is still investing in European content. Across Europe it is traditional broadcasters who take on the risk of funding the vast majority of European-originated audiovisual content. European content is most prominent on leading commercial channels and on public service channels, which dedicate between eighty-five to ninety-five per cent of their schedules to European works (Attentional et al., 2011, p. 11). This investment has been reinforced by national advertising economies and the EU's AVMS Directive, which stipulates fifty per cent of broadcasts (excluding news, sports and advertising) should be of European origin. National rules on local content production, tax incentives for production and the maintenance of public-service broadcasting further reinforce domestic production, which is seen as vital for maintaining social cohesion and plurality and for sustaining regional and local identities (Doyle, 2012, p. 10), although evidence for this is rather sparse.

In 2011, the main public and private broadcasters within the EU were reported to be responsible for fifty-six per cent of gross industry revenues, but funded up to ninety per cent of European-originated television content (Attentional et al., 2011, p. 10). According to an e-Media Institute study (2012, p. 16) commissioned by the Association of Commercial Television in Europe, free-to-air and pay-TV accounted for ninety-nine per cent of the €80bn turnover generated by European audiovisual industries (free-to-air, pay, online) in 2010, and forty to fifty per cent of this was reinvested in content acquisition and original production. This included €15.1bn spent by the largest European commercial broadcasting groups in fifteen European markets and estimates of €10bn (excluding news and sport) spent by public-service broadcasters in the top five markets (e-Media, 2012, p. 17; EBU, p. 2013: 2).

In the five largest European markets, public-service broadcasters devoted seventy-one per cent of their programming expenditure to original content (EBU, 2013, p. 8). By comparison, Enders (2013a, p. 5) reports €34.5bn was invested into programming by EU broadcasters in 2009, split between rights acquisitions (€15.9bn, including sport) and original programming commissions (€18.6bn). Of the €18.6bn spent on originations, €2.6bn was spent on news and sports, €8.4bn was spent on in-house productions and €7.6bn on commissions (ibid.). Sustaining these substantial investments in original, first-run European content constitutes a major challenge in the face of audience fragmentation and the lack of any certainty about recouping investment in what have always been risky undertakings.

Continued investment in original content by both public service and commercial broadcasters is therefore dependent on assured revenues, but it is mainstream, advertising-funded and public-service broadcasters who support most production, and it is these revenues that are most under pressure. Italy, Spain, France, Ireland, Poland and the Netherlands experienced a decline in television advertising revenues per head in 2012, just as Germany, Sweden and the UK experienced small increases (Ofcom, 2013a, p. 150), with the UK broadcast TV sector experiencing a further four per cent rise in 2013 (Ofcom, 2014, p. 10). By 2009, EU pay-TV revenues (thirty-two per cent) were matching revenues from advertising; subscription funding is now more important than advertising in France, Sweden, Ireland and the UK (Bomsel and Rosnay, 2013, p. 68f). However, pay-TV revenues in excess of

£18bn in the five largest European markets are not the main source of funding for European original production (Ofcom, 2013a, p. 154). Certainly, revenues from online television and video are rising from a low base, but in 2012, combined revenues derived from advertising, subscription and download-to-own were still small in the UK (£345m), France (£175m), Germany (£100m) and Italy (£56m) compared to a staggering £5.4bn in the US (Ofcom, 2013a, p. 155). According to Ofcom UK, online TV revenue rose forty-one per cent in 2013 to £364m, including £112m in subscription revenues (Netflix, Amazon Prime) (Ofcom, 2014, p. 9). Within this changing environment, broadcasters and channel operators are looking to build on more diverse business models and revenue-earning opportunities (including revenue-sharing with rights-holders and ISPs and through branded content on new platforms), but mainstream sources of revenue from television advertising and pay television still dominate the European market.

The need to raise their profile in key European markets has encouraged some of the US-based VOD intermediaries to invest in first-run content. However, their commitment to invest still falls some way short of investment by European broadcasters (EBU, 2013, p. 21).

YouTube, owned by Google, is the leader in user-generated-content (UGC) and is arguably the only truly global audiovisual network. It has pioneered Original Channels of native content and Partner channels with professional partners. In 2012, Google spent $300m launching Original Channels globally in an attempt to secure content from celebrities, brands and media companies (Lewis, 2013), recognising that it is often professionally produced content that is the most sought after – and most pirated (e-media, 2012, p. 29). In 2012, YouTube launched twenty-one Original Channels in the UK, twelve in Germany and thirteen in France with €25m in funding (Enders, 2013b, p. 32), a small investment compared to the billions invested by the television sector. As a site focused predominantly on short-form low-budget user-generated content, YouTube is unlikely to replace traditional television yet, but it does present a challenge to broadcasters and pay-TV channels through its ability to connect with younger audiences, who are watching less traditional television. Smaller production companies are using YouTube to launch 'channels of the future' and learn about the platform but also look for mainstream success (Burrell, 2014). In 2012, YouTube was estimated to have generated revenues from advertising, sponsorship and promotion of €700m in the EU in 2012, out of $2.9bn globally (Enders, 2013b, p. 32). This is a fraction of the €132bn generated by the EU's AV sector in 2011, including €73bn in broadcaster revenues, €34bn in consumer payments for TV services and only €616m (two per cent) from video-on-demand online (Enders, 2013a, p. 4).

YouTube's performance thus far suggests it is a complementary service to mainstream television. US video-on-demand aggregator Netflix announced in 2013 that it would be spending $2bn a year on content-licensing, but only ten per cent of its content-spending would be on originations (Netflix,

2013). At the start of 2014, it had limited its rollout to the UK, Ireland and the four Nordic nations, suggesting a cautious approach. In February 2013, it launched a heavily promoted $100m remake of the 1990 BBC drama series *House of Cards,* originally a public-service production funded by the British licence-fee payer. Its simultaneous launch of all thirteen episodes of the $34m US horror series *Hemlock Grove* in April 2012 and new episodes of the former Fox sitcom *Arrested Development* suggests ambition to challenge established broadcasters with attractive, high-quality content, but there is no evidence it will become a fully fledged competitor for commissioning European-originated content. According to the EBU (2013, p. 9), Netflix's high-profile investments in production have only served to highlight "what PSM have long known to be true: quality content builds audiences and strengthens their loyalty."

Amazon Prime Instant Video (formerly LoveFilm in the UK) launched fourteen sitcom and children's pilots in April 2013 (Billen, 2013). Production arm Amazon Studios has asked subscribers to evaluate and improve sitcom ideas submitted to it in its search for the next big sitcom (ibid.), thus bypassing traditional broadcasting commissioning structures and allowing users to participate in the development process. However, like Netflix, these production initiatives are focused largely on English-language content and culturally proximate markets in the UK, Ireland and Scandinavia rather than European markets with lower average incomes (EC, 2011, p. 7).

THE ROLE OF PUBLIC SERVICE TELEVISUAL MEDIA

As argued here, the changing distribution and reception of television content have the potential to impact production and the economics of production in this transitional phase of television's continuous development. Yet production in Europe is also closely bound up with the fluctuating fortunes of public-service media (PSM). Throughout, PSM have been the prevailing counter-tendency to the economic and technological logic, which has driven new media developments and the expansion of private television in Europe since the 1980s and 1990s (Donders, Paulwels and Loisen, 2013, p. 12–15). Although there is no single model of PSB/PSM within the European Union, the general PSM approach has concentrated on normative goals associated with informing, educating and entertaining the public in the interests of democratic society. The principles of PSM are grounded on assumptions that diverse ownership, breadth of content and the representation of many opinions are necessary to sustain plurality and diversity (Born and Prosser, 2001). Moving into the twenty-first century, it has been argued that investment in digital technology and the adoption of digital television by PSBs has contributed to the launch of new television services and sustained investment in original content (Moe, 2008; EBU, 2013, p. 4). As part of these developments, public-service broadcasters are significant providers of catch-up TV services and other online services, although further forays into new activities are frequently disputed by commercial rivals who fear that they are being crowded out. (BBC, 2013b, p. 5) In some instances there appear to be concerted moves by some PSM to provide television services for younger consumers on online platforms only. For example, in March 2014 the BBC announced plans to make BBC3 its channel for younger viewers an online only offering. Swiss public television has announced plans to move all of its children's services online, a move already undertaken by Finnish public broadcasting. These types of initiatives may turn out to be a longer term test not only of the audience's willingness to shift its engagement online but also of a continued willingness to engage with content that rests on a public-service ethos. While earlier generations had no choice but to engage with public-service broadcasting, new generations have more opportunities to avoid it entirely, weakening PSM's legitimacy.

The institutional legitimacy of PSM, grounded in technical and financial barriers that prevented a multitude of services in the past and justified a tight regulatory framework, has been undermined by policy decisions that favour deregulation and privatisation as much as technological developments and changes in production and consumption (Steemers, 1997, p. 54). When there are now infinite outlets and sources of material online, the notion of broadcast television is deemed more insecure, as the Internet threatens to "undo the national audience" of PSB through "dispersion, dislocation and disconnection." (Holt and Sanson, 2014, p. 6) Doubts about public-service television have been further deepened by concerns about the sustainability of public funding, particularly in the aftermath of the financial crisis in 2008 and culminating at its worst in the closure of Greek public broadcaster ERT in 2013. Instead of the top-down model practised by both public-service and private broadcasting there are now, it is argued, opportunities for a multitude of organizations and individuals to choose, converse, curate, create and collaborate on many platforms, reinforcing the idea of public media (rather than public-service media), which have the potential to mobilize and facilitate publics in a more engaged and democratic way (Clark and Aufderheide, 2009, p. 6f).

However, the EBU argues that with the expansion of offerings, the role of public-service media in serving the democratic, cultural and social needs of society has become more important (2013, p. 1). Murdock (2004, p. 2) argues for a reinvention of public service through civic initiatives to "provide the basis for new shared cultural space, a digital commons, that can help forge new communal connections and stand against the continual pressure for enclosure coming from commercial interests on the one hand and the new moral essentialism on the other." Hendy (2013, p. 110) points out that even if PSB is losing "whatever normative hold it once had," there is scope for adaptation, filtering and maintaining a "digital public space" that nurtures trust and makes PSBs trusted guides in a sea of online abundance. Evans and McDonald (2014, p. 167) suggest the unpredictability of emerging technologies creates a demand for something that is predictable, consistent, accessible and 'free' in a plentiful media landscape. They maintain that the principles of free and universal access associated with PSB colours the public's approach to digital services, drawing them towards trusted PSB institutions where they expect high quality content for no (or little) direct cost. For Hendy (2013, p. 114), the test of whether PSB is meeting the demands of a new communications environment is the extent to which it allows users to create their own schedules, the degree to which it allows its programme material to be shared and manipulated, and the extent to which it crowd sources by drawing on the contributions of 'ordinary' people.

Where PSM can and do make a difference is in support of local production, the provision of information that counteracts other sources that might cut users off from different and unexpected views, as well as openness and accessibility to all (Harrison and Woods, 2007). Regulation, quotas and tax concessions are one way of promoting indigenous content production, but the most enduring European approach to domestic production has always been through PSM, which in the main tend to produce or commission more original programming than non-PSBs. To illustrate, in 2011 the BBC had the highest share of domestic productions in its schedules (ninety-five per cent), followed by Bulgaria, Germany (all above ninety per cent), France, Spain and Lithuania (all above seventy per cent) (EBU, 2013, p. 22). According to BBC research, these levels of investment by PSBs are beneficial because they fuel positive competition with the commercial sector (BBC, 2013b).

However, there is no certainty about resourcing for public-service media, and in many European countries, they involve institutions that are neither popular nor distinctive, undermining any claims to sustain citizenship and civil society (Lowe and Steemers, 2012). With EU plans to reform the audiovisual landscape, there are concerns about whether access to PSB will be diminished (BBC, 2013a; EBU, 2013). Investment in domestic content and the ability to cater for all segments of society matter, but the terms of access on a growing array of platforms, ease of location and its availability free at the point of use are also important – especially in view of the emergence of globally active digital intermediaries. Financial restraints suggest closer co-operation with third parties and other public institutions to create a public space beyond PSB's own boundaries – pursued by the BBC, for example, as it announced an initiative in March 2014 to forge closer ties with other cultural organizations. Many PSBs do work with independent producers, but beyond these collaborations with professional programme-makers, engagement with users that allows sharing and repurposing that is "interactive, participatory and democratic" (Hendy, 2013, p. 125) is still quite limited. Co-operation with commercial partners, pushed more and more as a policy and strategic option, is more problematic because it carries the risk of diluting public-service principles to satisfy commercial interests.

CONCLUSION

Looking at the prospects for television, it is easy to over-speculate about the promise of new media technologies and disregard older patterns of consumption. Short-term impact is often overestimated and long-term impact is underestimated. In 2014, television is far from dead or in crisis, and for some commentators we are seeing a second golden age of television, particularly in drama, but arguably less of a golden age in the type of 'ordinary' television that has always provided a communal experience and is able to "address and unite a wide audience" (see Schwaab, 2014, p. 21). Linear television remains an important medium across the EU because it still reaches large geographically and temporally bounded audiences. Even though the distinction between linear and non-linear services is likely to become less obvious over time, television as a pastime does not appear to be in crisis, even as it becomes available on more platforms. While it is true that there are radical changes in technological delivery, it cannot be assumed that European publics are all watching television in radically new ways, and many of the structural and economic changes in television predate the appearance of online television with their roots in the privatisation and deregulatory initiatives of the 1980s and 1990s. Growth in connected TVs could change television consumption as both linear and non-linear services become accessible on the same technical interface, but existing pay, free-to-air and publicly funded broadcasters are likely to remain the dominant providers of television and VOD services for some time to come, even as newcomers such as Netflix and Amazon start to gain viewers.

So while there are still strong continuities with the past, there is also evidence of disruption and transformative change, which is discernible even among the "overinflated rhetoric of new media, media revolutions and change" (Lotz, 2013). Television is at the cusp of this disruptive digital era, and while it is unclear what the eventual outcomes will be in Europe, change is likely to emerge in the way that content is produced, circulated and consumed, even if the conventions of digital operation have yet to be firmly established. If a crisis in television is brewing longer term, it is likely to impact those parts of the television industry that are already vulnerable to changing financial circumstances and have failed to adapt their products, marketing and presentation to new platforms and changes in consumption (cf. Picard, 2014, p. 196). This may be the case for public-service broadcasters in some countries, who have insufficient political, financial and, crucially, public support. Moreover, while established television companies may be the largest investors in content, they have lost the absolute ability to control access, with new intermediaries creating and controlling the emerging online distribution infrastructure, including the technologies that deliver personalized content in ways that render the TV industry's metrics "prehistoric." (Airey 2014, p. 71; Picard, 2014, p. 198) The production of high-quality audiovisual content such as drama across a range of both smaller and larger European nations may not be sufficient in the future if the economic model underpinning traditional broadcasting becomes unsustainable and if other players start to determine how and where content is delivered into the home. This returns us to the key issues, which have always been central to the study of television, including the continued focus on corporate power and control (cf. Hermes, 2014).

REFERENCES

Airey, D. (2014) What Television can learn from Yahoo. In: Clapp, Z. (ed). *2024: The Future of Television* (pp. 67–74). London: Premium Publishing.

Attentional, Gide Loyrette Nouel, Headway International, Oliver & Ohlbaum (2011) *Study on the implementation of the provisions of the Audiovisual Media Services Directive concerning the promotion of European works in audiovisual media services.* Retrieved from: http://ec.europa.eu/avpolicy/info_centre/library/studies/index_en.htm#promot

BBC (2013a) *The BBC Response to the European Commission Green Paper "Preparing for a Fully Converged Audiovisual World: Growth, Creation and Values."* London: BBC.

BBC (2013b) *Public and Private Broadcasters Across the World – The Race to the Top.* London: BBC.

Billen, A. (2013) Watch out BBC, we're coming for you: Who will make the TV and films of the future? Netflix, Amazon and YouTube already are. *The Times*, 11 April, p. 5.

Born, G. and Prosser, T. (2001) Culture and Consumerism: Citizenship, Public Service Broadcasting and the BBC's Fair Trading Obligations. *The Modern Law Review*, 64 (5). pp. 657–87.

Bomsel O. and Rosay, C. (2013) *Why territories matter: Vertical restraints and portability in audiovisual media services*, October 2013. Retrieved from: http://www.letsgoconnected.eu/files/Study-Olivier_Bomsel-Why_Territories_Matter-FINAL_14_Oct_2013.pdf.

Burrell, I. (2014) Who needs the BBC? Black comedy starts take the YouTube route to fame. *The Independent on Sunday*, 30 March.

Braun, J. (2013) Going over the Top: Online Television Distribution as Sociotechnical System. *Communication, Culture and Critique*, 6 (3). pp. 432–58.

Braun, J. (2014) Transparent Intermediaries: Building the Infrastructures of Connected Viewing. In: Holt, J. and Sanson, K. (2014) *Connected Viewing* (pp. 124–43). London: Routledge.

Caldwell, J. (1995) *Televisuality: Style, Crisis and Authority in American Television.* New Brunswick: Rutgers University Press.

Chalaby, J.K. (2012) At the origin of a global industry: The TV format trade as an Anglo-American invention. *Media, Culture & Society*, 34(1). pp. 36–52.

Clark J. and Aufderheide, P. (2009) *Public Media 2.0: Dynamic, Engaged Publics.* Washington: Centre for Social Media. Retrieved from: http://cmsimpact.org/sites/default/files/documents/pages/publicmedia2.0.pdf.

Cunningham, S. and Silver, J. (2013) *Screen Distribution and the New King Kongs of the Online World.* Basingstoke: Palgrave. E-book.

DCMS (Department for Culture Media and Sport) (2013) *Connectivity, Content and Consumers*, July 2013. Retrieved from: https://www.gov.uk/government/uploads/system/uploads/attachment_data/file/225783/Connectivity_Content_and_Consumers_2013.pdf.

Donders, K., Pauwels, C. and Loisen, J. (eds.) (2013) *Private Television in Western Europe*. Basingstoke, UK: Palgrave.

Doyle, G. (2012) *Audio-visual Services: International Trade and Cultural Policy*. ADBI Working Paper Series, No. 355, April 2012. Retrieved from: http://adbi.org/files/2012.04.17.wp355.audiovisual.srvc.intl.trade.cultural.policy.pdf.

EBU (European Broadcasting Union) (2013) *EBU reply to the European Commission Green Paper – Preparing for a Fully Converged Audiovisual World: Growth, Creation and Values*, 10 September 2013. Retrieved from: http://www3.ebu.ch/files/live/sites/ebu/files/Knowledge/Initiatives%20-%20Policy/Topical%20Issues/Hybrid/EBU_reply_to_Green_Paper_convergence_final.pdf.

EC (European Commission) (2011) *Green Paper on the online distribution of audiovisual works in the European Union and challenges towards a digital single market*. Brussels, 13.7.2011 COM (2011) 427 final.

EC (2013) *Green Paper Preparing for a Fully Converged Audiovisual World: Growth, Creation and Values*. Brussels, 24.4.2013 COM (2013) 231 final.

EGM (2013) *Resumen general de resulta*. Retrieved from: http://www.aimc.es/-Datos-EGM-Resumen-General-.html.

E-Media Institute (2012) *Creative Media Europe: Audiovisual Content and Online Growth. A study for the Association of Commercial Television in Europe*. March. Retrieved from: http://www.acte.be/library/5/47/CREATIVE-MEDIA-EUROPE-Audiovisual-Content-and-Online-Growth.

Enders Analysis (2013a) *The Value of Territorial Licensing to the EU*, October. Retrieved from: http://www.letsgoconnected.eu/files/Study-Alice_Enders-The_value_of_territorial_licensing-FINAL_11_OCT_2013.pdf.

Enders Analysis LGC2: Progress towards Digital Europe, May. Retrieved from: http://www.letsgoconnected.eu/files/LGC2-Progress_towards_Digital_Europe_14052013.pdf.

Evans, E. and McDonald, P. (2014) Online Distribution of Film and Television in the UK: Behaviour, Taste and Value. In: Holt, J. and Sanson, K. (eds.) *Connected Viewing* (pp.158–79). London: Routledge.

Foster, R. (2012) *News Plurality in a Digital World*. Oxford, Reuters Institute for the Study of Journalism. Retrieved from: https://reutersinstitute.politics.ox.ac.uk/sites/default/files/News%20Plurality%20in%20a%20Digital%20World.pdf.

Harrison, J. and Woods, L. (2007) *European Broadcasting Law and Policy*. Cambridge: Cambridge University Press.

Havens, T. and Lotz, A. (2012) *Understanding Media Industries*. Oxford: Oxford University Press.

Hermes J. (2014) Critical Versus Everyday Perspectives on Television. In: de Valck, M.and Teurlings, J. (eds.) *After the Break: Television Theory Today* (pp. 35–50). Amsterdam: Amsterdam University Press.

Hendy, D. (2013) *Public Service Broadcasting*. Basingstoke, UK: Palgrave Macmillan.

Holt, J. (2014) Regulating Connected Viewing: Media Pipelines and Cloud Policy. In: Holt, J. and Sanson, K. (eds.) *Connected Viewing* (pp. 19–39). London: Routledge.

Holt, J. and Sanson K. (eds.) (2014) *Connected Viewing*. London: Routledge.

Internet Society (2009) *Internet Futures Scenarios*. Retrieved from: http://www. internetsociety.org/sites/default/files/pdf/report-internetfutures-20091006-en.pdf.

Jenkins, H., Ford, S. and Green, J. (2013) *Spreadable Media: Creating Value and Meaning in a Networked Culture*. New York: New York University Press. E-book.

Jensen, P. M. (2014) *Export Patterns and Global Impact of Danish Drama Series*. Conference Presentation, 20 March, Producers and Audiences, University of Lund, Sweden.

Keilbach, J. and Stauff, M. (2013) When old media never stopped being new. In: de Valck, M .and Teurlings, J. (eds) *After the Break: Television Theory Today* (pp. 79–97). Amsterdam: Amsterdam University Press.

Lange, A. (2011) *Challenges for the European TV Industry*. Paper presented at Twenty years of Television without frontiers and beyond, Brussels, 28–29 April.

Lewis, T. (2013) YouTube superstars: the generation taking on TV – and winning. *The Observer, New Review*, 7 April. pp. 8–12.

Liu. Y. L. and Picard, R. G. (2014) *Policy and Marketing Strategies for Digital Media*. London: Routledge.

Looms, P. (2014) Making TV Accessible in the 21st Century. In: Liu Y. L. and Picard, R. G. (eds) *Policy and Marketing Strategies for Digital Media* (pp. 43–59). London: Routledge.

Lotz, A. D. (2007) *The television will be revolutionized*. New York: New York University Press.

Lotz, A. D. *What Old Media Can Teach New Media*. Retrieved from: http://spreadablemedia.org/essays/lotz/#.VFXzX-dXiFo.

Lowe, G. and Steemers, J. (2012) Regaining the Initiative for Public Service Media. In: Lowe, G.F. and Steemers, J. (eds.) *Regaining the Initiative for Public Service Media* (pp. 9–26). Gøteborg: Nordicom.

Michalis, M. (2013) Thirty Years of Private Television in Europe – Trends and Key Moments. In: Donders, K., Pauwels, C. and Loisen, J. (eds.) *Private Television in Western Europe* (pp. 37–55). Basingstoke, UK: Palgrave.

Moe, H. (2008) Public Service Media Online? Regulating Public Broadcasters Services – A comparative analysis. *Television and New Media*, 9 (3). pp. 220–38.

Murdock, G. (2004) Building the Digital Commons: Public Service Broadcasting in the Age of the Internet. *2004 Spry Memorial Lecture*, 18 November. Retrieved from: https://pantherfile.uwm.edu/type/www/116/Theory_OtherTexts/Theory/Murdock_BuildingDigitalCommons.pdf.

Netflix (2013) *Netflix Long Term View*. Retrieved from: http://ir.netflix.com/long-term-view.cfm.

Ofcom (2013a) *International Communications Report*. London: Ofcom.

Ofcom (2013b) *Communications Market Report 2013*. August, London: Ofcom.

Ofcom (2014) *Communications Market Report 2014*. August, London: Ofcom.

Perren, A. (2013) Rethinking Distribution for the Future of Media Industry Studies. *Cinema Journal*, 52 (3). pp. 165–71.

Picard, R. (2014) Digital Media and the Roots of Marketing Strategy. In Liu Y. L. and Picard, R. (eds.) *Policy and Marketing Strategies for Digital Media* (pp. 195–201). New York: Routledge.

Ranaivoson, H. (2010) *Economic Assessment of Digital Trade of Audiovisual Works in the EU*. Study Concerning Multi-territory Licensing for online distribution of audiovisual works in the EU, Stakeholder Workshop, Brussels, 2 June 2010.

Sanz, E. (2012) *JRC Technical Reports: Statistical Ecosystems and Competitiveness Analysis of the Media and Content Industries: European Television in the New*

Media Landscape. European Commission Joint Research Centre, Luxembourg: Publications Office of the European Union.

Schwaab, H. (2014) 'Unreading' Contemporary Television. In: de Valck, M. and Teurlings, J. (eds.) *After the Break: Television Theory Today* (pp. 21–34). Amsterdam: Amsterdam University Press.

Simon, J. P. (2012) *JRC Technical Reports The Dynamics of the Media and Content Sector: A Synthesis*. European Commission Joint Research Centre, Luxembourg: Publications Office of the European Union.

Spigel, L. and Olsson, J. (eds.) (2004) *Television after TV : essays on a medium in transition*. Durham, NC: Duke University Press.

Steemers, J. (1997) Broadcasting is Dead. Long Live Digital Choice: Perspectives from the United Kingdom and Germany. *Convergence*, (1). pp. 51–71.

Sweney, M. (2014) Game of Thrones is world's most-pirated TV show. *The Guardian*. 4 April. Retrieved from: http://www.theguardian.com/tv-and-radio/2014/apr/04/game-of-thrones-most-pirated-tv-show.

Thinkbox (2014) *98.5% of TV was watched on a TV set in 2013*. Retrieved from http://www.thinkbox.tv/98.5-of-tv-was-watched-on-a-tv-set-in-2013.

Turner, G. and Tay, J. (eds.) (2009) *Television studies after TV: understanding television in the post-broadcast era*. New York: Routledge.

Valcke, P. and Ausloos, J. (2014) Television on the Internet. In Y. Liu and R. Picard (eds.), *Policy and Marketing Strategies for Digital Media* (pp. 24–42). New York: Routledge.

5 Crisis of the Commercial Media

*Josef Trappel, Laura Bergés and
Elena Vartanova*

Over much of the last half century, commercial media have been in the driving seat of media development. They not only grew in the numbers of media outlets, they managed to develop into highly profitable businesses. The number of employees grew, together with the profit rate generated by each of them, and they became important economic and political players. Commercial media have been successful in shaping many if not all strands of modern democratic societies, even generating a communication research field known as the "mediatisation debate" (cf. among others Hjarvard, 2013; Mazzoleni and Schulz, 1999; Strömbäck, 2008). Politics, economics, culture, science, sports, religion but also everyday lives are "reconfigured by the increasing reliance on information and communication technologies" (Livingstone, 2009, p. 1), as well as being centrally formed and reshaped by the logics of the media, which are commercial with a few exceptions, notably the public-service media and the non-commercial (third) sector. In Europe, the hegemony of commercial media over non-commercial forms of public communication is historically most pronounced in the field of newspapers and magazines, which were institutionalized as commercial enterprises almost from their beginnings. Later, television and radio underwent a far-reaching process of commercialization, as a result of national and supra-national policy decisions made to allow for commercial operators to exist alongside public-service broadcasters (PSBs). PSBs and their programming strategies stood as an alternative to the free-market (commercial) model. However, from 1970 to the 1980s the dominant position of the non-commercially oriented European public-service broadcasters in the television industry weakened as a result of the technological evolution in cable and satellite television, which called for more deregulation and liberalisation in television (McQuail, 2013, p. 13).

Since the 1990s, media organizations using the Internet as their main means of distribution are strongly commercial in nature as there are no explicit governance rules and no attempts made to institutionalize online media as public-service operations. On the contrary, existing public-service broadcasters are struggling to be politically accepted as contributors and players in this highly contested arena.

Given this hegemony of the commercial media within the entire media landscape, the question arises as to how this very specific type of commercial media manages to cope with crises. Within limits, commercial media are seen as being exposed to market forces and competition. Limits occur whenever commercial media manage to exempt themselves from competition, for example by creating oligopolistic markets or even monopolies or by putting through preferential media policy treatment. Some commercial media formally participate in market competition but enjoy the privilege of affluent owners who cover all deficits for whatever reason – increase owner's social prestige, tax breaks, cross-subsidisation within conglomerates, etc.

These media markets have been affected by crises at least twice over the last fifteen years. One crisis occurred subsequent to the burst of the new economy bubble in the years 2000 and 2001. The other crisis began as a financial market crisis in 2008 and is as yet not entirely over. Both of these crises had severe repercussions on advertising markets, thus affecting commercial media more directly than their non-commercial counterparts.

In this chapter we ask the normative question: In what way are democratic values delivered by commercial media in Europe affected by the crises? By applying findings from crisis theory, various outcomes might be expected. Crises might result in the collapse of existing structures, in our case the shutting down of commercial media enterprises altogether. In their place, new structures might evolve that are better adapted to the critical changes in the environment. Another outcome might be the adaptation of the existing structures to the changed environment with different performance indicators and new ways of delivering services. In our case, this outcome would sustainably change commercial media and their content or, indeed, their programme output according to changes in the media environment. Another possible outcome is that incumbent structures are strong enough to survive times of crises by temporarily living on their own means. In this case, crises suspend, interrupt or modify service delivery only temporarily with a return to business-as-usual thereafter. The latter outcome has been the rule during the long prosperous years from the 1960s up to the late 1990s, which were also interrupted by crises, such as the so-called oil crisis in 1973.

CHARACTERISTICS OF COMMERCIAL MEDIA

According to mainstream neoliberal thinking, commercial media represent the optimal organizational format for mass media. And indeed, commercial media dominate in numbers in Western European countries. Both in large and small states, commercial media far outnumber their public-service and non-commercial counterparts. Newspapers, magazines, private commercial television (including cable and satellite operators) and radio channels together with Internet-based new forms of semi-public communication (user-generated content and social networks) represent the bulk of media companies.

More broadly speaking, journalism and in particular news media organizations are unique types of business because the product – news – is a public good or service, and many scholars emphasize that, unlike other public-goods activities like education or science, media are less protected from market forces (Picard, 2005; Kaye and Quinn, 2010, p. 12). Evidently, the advertising-based commercial business model seriously affected ways of "how market shapes news especially because of the need to maximize either paying audiences or attention to be sold to advertisers." (McQuail, 2013, p. 77) The clash of news and entertainment media, which is especially visible in the European context, partly reflects different social values of the public-service and commercial media.

There are a number of common denominators in commercial media:

- Ownership: Commercial media are privately owned, with a large variety of ownership models, from the traditional family business (many European newspapers) to stock-listed companies or even financial investors. In Germany, for example, the second-largest private television channel, ProSieben Sat1, was owned by financial investors KKR and Permira from 2006 until 2013. In some countries, larger industrial conglomerates are the owners of media companies such as heavy-industry companies Lagardère and Bouygues in France, car manufacturer FIAT in Italy, navy industries in Greece. In the Russian media industry, a few of the biggest owners represent the banking sector such as Rossija or Gazprom banks.
- Revenues: Commercial media operate in dual markets. Income streams are divided into revenues generated by those who consume their content and advertising income. All third options like crowd-funding, donations, foundation-based models etc. are minuscule compared to the two main sources of revenue. Revenues, however, allow for a crucial distinction to be made between commercial media. On a continuum, commercial media might be placed according to their revenue shares generated from the two sources. Highly commercialized media on one extreme of this continuum generate their entire income from advertising. This model was not invented and applied first by Internet-based online media but by private commercial television and radio broadcasters in the 1980s and, in the case of radio, even decades before. In the late 1990s, the commuter press (called "free sheets" by some) adapted this model for daily newspapers, and only lately online media without a so called paywall provide their services in return for advertising money only. On the other extreme of the continuum, the least commercialized media are those who generate all their revenues from readers, listeners or users. Compared to the first category, only very few private media qualify here. Most books and some highly specialized websites behind firm paywalls are among the few examples. The bulk of media organizations is situated in between these two extremes. Traditional newspapers moved

from highly to moderately commercialized, following the recent down-turn in advertising and the loss of classified advertising to Internet-based operators. Magazines are still highly commercialized, again with few exceptions (high-brow cultural and/or critical magazines).

- Profit orientation: Commercial media are by definition profit-oriented. In media economics, "(…) it is assumed that a commercial firm's every decision is taken in order to maximize its profits. The assumption that all firms seek to maximize profits is central to the neoclassical theory of the firm." (Doyle, 2013, p. 5) Some argue that profits generated by media organizations are particularly important in defending and sus-taining their independence from the state and from other vested inter-ests. Robert Picard argues "that financially successful media companies have the resources to serve social needs and be more independent of outside pressures over time than less financially secure firms." (Picard, 2005, p. 339) Profit orientation, however, has repercussions on what commercial media deliver to their audience. With regard to news, John McManus defines commercialization "as any action intended to boost profit that interferes with a journalist's or news organization's best effort to maximize public understanding of those issues and events that shape the community they claim to serve." (McManus, 2009, p. 219)
- Market conduct: Competition is the rule of the game among commercial media. Although this feature gradually applies also to non-commercial media, competition rules are crucial for the market conduct of com-mercial media. Competition in oligopolistic markets such as the media, however, tend to concentrate, with implications for media output. "Con-centration of media ownership can lead to over-representation of certain political opinions or forms of cultural output (those favoured by power-ful media owners, whether on commercial or ideological grounds) and to the exclusion of others. The risk that concentrated media power may create such imbalances – and the accompanying risks for democracy and for social cohesion – represents a key concern for policy-making (…)." (Doyle, 2002, p. 26)

Ownership, revenue generation, profit orientation and market conduct (concentration) taken together circumscribe well the characteristics and understanding of commercial media. It follows that commercial media put emphasis on strategies to generate profit for their owners, to follow the requirements or imperatives of their advertising clients, to survive competi-tion and to twist media concentration in their favour.

COMMERCIAL MEDIA AND DEMOCRATIC VALUES

For this book the authors chose a normative research perspective on the media in times of crises. According to this perspective, media are intended to fulfil certain requirements in order to serve democracies well. The social contract between democracy and the media requires the latter to provide "citizens with the information they need in order to be free and self-governing" (Strömbäck, 2005, p. 332), while democracies – in the form of democratic governments – guarantee and promote individual rights such as freedom of speech, expression and information and foster the independence of media organizations from the state. To elaborate Strömbäck's notion further, media are requested to enhance freedom, diversity, participation, integration, deliberation and self-determination. Media should foster enlightened citizens, the orientation towards a welfare and participative idea of society, and the peaceful comity of nations (for the complete list of values see Chapter 1 of this volume). This is certainly a big order and cannot be delivered by one single media outlet or media company alone. Instead, these values address the entirety of the media system in democratic societies with each media organization delivering its fair share. In this chapter we raise the question: To what extent do commercial media live up to these values in times of crises?

Of course, these democratic values are not the principal and most important objectives of commercial media and might even contradict their internal values. Nonetheless, democratic societies will only function well if all media – including commercial ones – contribute their fair share.

When taking a closer look at this list of values, none of the items is clearly or exclusively confined to a specific type of commercial or non-commercial media. Freedom and diversity are core values and relate, on the one hand, to the independence of the media from the state, and on the other, to the free choice of editorial content by journalists and programme-makers. Commercial media would defend these values as vigorously as non-commercial or public service media. The value of enabling deliberations for enlightened citizens is less clear. Commercial media tend to address consumers of advertised goods rather than enlightened citizens. However, their programme selection and editorial content have inevitable repercussions on public deliberations, for better or worse. The same mechanism applies to the value of orientation towards a welfare and participative idea of society. Commercial media might promote this value to the extent that it is commercially viable but their mission is rather oriented towards consumerism and universal reach. Finally, the value of pursuing peaceful comity of nations is probably the most abstract of all. Commercial media, in particular television, have long expanded beyond national borders, following the model of international public-service television like BBC World or Deutsche Welle. At least equally important, however, than border crossing transmissions are programmes and contents displaying foreign cultures and life styles to a domestic audience. There, commercial television shows fewer ambitions than their public service counterparts with considerably more emphasis on content that entertains rather than informs or educates.

To summarize, highly commercialized media tend to adapt their set of values to marketability. Whenever democratic values overlap with market opportunities, commercial media will adhere to them. Less commercialized media may choose to adhere to more democratic values within limits, however, of profitable business conduct.

COMMERCIAL MEDIA IN CRISIS

As outlined in Chapter 1 of this book, there is no universal definition of crisis in social sciences. Some simply argue that crises occur whenever something of sufficient importance goes wrong. Joseph Schumpeter has criticized this position and pointed out that crises within capitalist systems will occur and return as a cyclical process "of which they are mere incidents." (Schumpeter, 1976, p. 41) Before we apply Schumpeterian thinking to commercial media, we identify the relevant characteristics of crisis for our purposes. Whenever crises occur, the traditional and conventional ways of running businesses or solving problems are no longer an option. Crises in the traditional meaning of the word elicit radical alternatives: survival or death, fortune or misfortune. Agency needs to be decisive and radical. Choices and decisions need to be taken. Crises either bring the end of the story or the beginning of a new story – but nothing in between.

Michel Wieviorka suggests understanding crisis as "a disruption of a system in which uncertainties arise (…)." (2012, p. 97) In the same volume, and with reference to Jürgen Habermas' early writings, John B. Thompson elaborates this understanding further. "A system crisis has to do with the breakdown of system integration: it occurs when the self-regulation mechanisms of a system break down, the medium for coordinating actions fails to fulfill its role, and the system seizes up." (2012, p. 62) Following this understanding, crisis in commercial media systems occurs when their internal mechanisms of self-regulation – the conduct of their main business characteristics – fail or break down altogether. Steve Barnett calls the current state of the (commercial) media a "perfect storm" that is "more destructive than at any time since the beginnings of a free press (…)." (2009, p. 217)

Indeed, there are countless pieces of evidences for this "perfect storm" among European commercial media. We name just a few here.

In its report on the *Evolution of News and the Internet*, the OECD (2010) collected impressive facts. "Between 1997 and 2007 most OECD countries (…) experienced a rapid or certain decline in newspaper employment: Norway (–53%), the Netherlands (–41%), and Germany (–25%)." (OECD 2010, p. 29)

If not quoted otherwise, the following evidence was provided by members of the Euromedia Research Group at the request of the authors of this chapter.

In the Baltic countries, the media crisis forced newspapers to reduce the number of issues published per week and instigate a new wave of 'oligarchization' of the media landscape. International media corporations such as Bonnier (Sweden; sold the quality daily *Diena* in Latvia) and Schibsted (Norway) closed down their businesses in the Baltic, selling their media properties to local oligarchs.

In Belgium, both regions are affected by the crisis. In French-speaking Wallonia the market entry of Tecteo created a duopoly in the daily newspaper market. This new player also has business interests in the cable business as a financial investor. The realignment of the newspaper market resulted in a loss of circulation of some twenty per cent over recent years. Also in Flanders, newspapers were rearranged and merged under a new corporation umbrella, putting at stake some two hundred jobs. In the news magazine market, the Finnish Sanomat Corporation announced its withdrawal from Belgium, putting their titles up for sale.

In Britain, between January 2008 and September 2009 alone, 106 local newspapers (mostly freesheets) closed down (Curran, 2010, p. 465). The circulation of the flagship newspaper *Financial Times* declined from 430.449 in 2006 to 273.047 in March 2013, although the management claims this loss has been overcompensated by digital subscribers (Schlesinger/Doyle, 2013, p. 5). The Telegraph Media Group merged its Sunday and weekly titles in March 2013, resulting in a loss of eighty jobs (ibid., p. 10).

In Finland, the leading daily newspaper *Helsingin Sanomat* lost eighteen per cent of its circulation within four years (2008–2012) and the loss continues. Even more critical is the rapid decline in advertising income, which in the case of newspapers decreased sixteen per cent from 2012 to 2013 and continued to fall in 2014. As a result of the crisis, some thousand journalists have lost their jobs in the five years from 2008 to 2013. Furthermore, the crisis propels ownership concentration as the big regional papers increasingly buy small local papers and the establishing of joint newsrooms for international news by several regional newspapers, even over the competing newspaper chains. In contrast, advertisement-based commercial television was less affected by the crisis as television advertising declined only by some two per cent between 2012–2013.

In France, the press sector has been hard hit by the crisis. The daily *France Soir*, one of Europe's dailies with the largest circulation in the 1950s, was closed in December 2011. In February 2014, the new shareholders of *Libération*, one of the main French dailies and originally co-founded by Jean-Paul Sartre, proposed to transform the journal into "social media" and make its headquarters a cultural location. The sector of the magazine press has also been hard hit by the crisis. The famous magazine *Le Nouvel Observateur* (which owns the *Rue89* news website) was bought in 2014 by the group Le Monde. The group Lagardère is selling ten of its magazines.

In Germany, one of the still prosperous economies in the European Union, two national newspapers were closed down, the *Financial Times Deutschland* in 2012 and the *Frankfurter Rundschau* in 2013, which was taken over by its former competitor. Furthermore, the Internet-only newspaper *Netzeitung* was closed down and all journalists were dismissed in 2009. After taking over the *Berliner Verlag* in 2009, the large publisher DuMontSchauberg integrated its news production (national, foreign and economic news) in Berlin, Cologne, Frankfurt and Halle in 2010.

In Greece, the main source of revenue for commercial media was drastically affected by the crisis that hit the country in 2009. According to Media Services S.A., the company that monitors advertising spent in Greece, the total amount was cut more than half from €2.67 billion 2008 to €1.19 billion in 2013. The consequence was a shake out of titles in the Greece media market, resulting in the closing down of radio and television stations, newspapers, magazines and advertising agencies.

In Italy, in response to a loss of more than €15 million in the first trimester of 2013, the Mondadori group undertook major restructuring, including the closure of four magazines and reshaping of others. Also as a result of the crisis in the publishing sector, the last remaining Italian industry producing paper for newspapers and magazine, Gruppo Burgo, had to close down leaving unemployed its 188 workers in eleven plants across the country.

In Russia, the state has become an important third player in the media market, complementing private and a few non-commercial media organizations. The most popular weekly, *Argumenty I facti*, a long-standing brand from the Soviet period with twenty-six regional offices, was purchased by the Moscow city government.

In Spain, the two leading quality daily newspapers, *El País* and *El Mundo*, dismissed one-quarter and one-third of their journalists in 2012. According to the Federación de Asociaciones de Periodistas de España (2014), about 11,151 Spanish journalists and related workers – 2,365 corresponding to newspapers – lost their jobs between June 2008 and November 2013, and at least 284 media have closed.

In Switzerland, media concentration continues. The market-leading publisher Tamedia took over the main newspaper group in French-speaking Switzerland, Edipresse, in two steps in 2009 and 2013. Furthermore, Tamedia integrates its local competitors in the Zurich region, among them the *Landbote,* in 2013. Within the ten-year period from 2002 and 2012, the number of editorially independent daily newspapers declined from forty-five to twenty-nine, thereby creating monopolistic newspaper markets in most Swiss regions (Meier, 2012, p. 136).

There are exceptions to the rule. The small countries Denmark and Norway are rare examples in Europe where the crisis did not firmly disturb business as usual, apart from a number of free sheets that closed down in Denmark and some readership losses in Norway, with the tabloid paper *Dagbladet* hit worst. In Denmark, observers see the reason in the common self-governed foundation-based ownership of Danish newspapers, which makes them more resistant to crises.

In parallel with market consolidation and concentration, advertising markets change dramatically. Advertising on the Internet surpassed that on television in Denmark in 2008 and in Britain in 2009, according to the Internet Advertising Bureau (Curran, 2010, p. 468). The most striking structural change in advertising, however, is the departure of classified ads from newspapers to the Internet, a process that has been completed in most countries. "Indeed, what is especially ominous for the future of journalism is that some advertising has shifted not from traditional news media to their satellite news web-sites, but has leapfrogged instead to other parts of the Web, which have nothing to do with journalism." (ibid., p. 468) Some former newspaper companies, such as Axel Springer in Germany and Tamedia in Switzerland, have tried to transform their business models by investing in Internet ventures (jobs, real estate, cars, etc.). In the United Kingdom, Des Freedman has shown that the majority of advertising now goes to search, and only twenty per cent each go to display and classified advertising.

> In other words, traditional news groups are strongest in one of the smallest sectors of the market and weakest in the main sector of online advertising. This is not a sound basis on which to compensate for declining revenues nor to seek additional funds for future investment in core services.
>
> (Freedman, 2010, p. 45)

Petros Iosifidis underlines the destructive effect of the combination of two factors. "The worldwide recession of 2008–2009, combined with the rapid growth of Web-based alternatives, caused a serious decline in advertising and circulation, as many newspapers closed or retrenched operations." (2011, p. 54)

Nielsen and Levy summarize the current critical trends as follows: "Commercial legacy news organizations engaged in the business of journalism confront three kinds of challenges today (...): cyclical downturn in advertising; increased competition for attention and advertisements and a new environment due to the rise of a range of new technologies (...); long-term changes of a political, social, and economic character." (2010, p. 4)

With regard to our topic – the crisis of commercial media – the following conclusions can be drawn.

First, some commercial media are more strongly affected by the crisis than others. One difference is due to the degree of commercialization. As a general rule, highly commercialized media are more strongly affected by the advertising displacement onto the Internet than less commercialized media. The bigger the share of advertising relative to the overall revenues, the stronger commercial media are affected. There are, however, exceptions to this rule. On the one hand, commercial television is less affected than the commercial press. Some television advertising (e.g. for mass consumer goods) is difficult to replace by cheaper Internet-based advertising. This provides television with at least a time lag compared to the press. On the other hand, quality newspapers, national and regional, are not among the most commercialized media but they also experienced a severe crisis. This is due to the fact that not only does the commercial business environment (advertising) change but also the structure of demand and the way people use and consume news. Actually, the examples above suggest the combination of both factors, advertising changes and readership changes, create a fundamental crisis, requiring radical agency by incumbent newspapers.

Secondly, commercial media are highly susceptible to changes in profit rates. The current crisis has exposed media owners to lower profits, thereby challenging in particular those owners who are not part of larger corporations or conglomerates. Compared to horizontally integrated media conglomerates, single media owners cannot balance risks resulting from market turmoil. This might drive single owners (such as a family business) out of the market or force them to sell their media company to financial investors or any other larger media group. Examples for this trend can be found easily. In France, for example, the Amaury family, owner of *Le Parisien* and *Aujourd'hui en France*, put its newspaper business up for sale in 2010. In Spain, the Polanco family reduced its engagement in the Prisa group, giving way for US financial investors. Outside Europe, the Graham family, which ran the *Washington Post* since 1877, sold the iconic newspaper to Jeff Bezos (owner of Amazon) in 2013. As a result, big national or even transnational corporations expand their presence in the commercial media market at the expense of single owners, thereby accelerating changes in the institutional structure of the commercial media markets.

Thirdly, the current media crisis leads to more media ownership concentration. This trend is not new and by no means exclusively caused by the media crisis. Media concentration happens as a defining feature of media markets, but the current crisis seems to enhance and accelerate this long-standing trend. Gillian Doyle identifies ownership concentration as a quasi-natural economic process that can be explained by economic theory. "Generally speaking (...) industrial economics attribute expansion – whether horizontal, vertical or diagonal and whether through internal growth or through mergers and takeovers – to two key incentives associated with profit-maximizing behaviour. From the firm's point of view, the main benefits of expansion are that it may increase market power (i.e. the ability to control prices, output, etc.) or it may increase efficiency." (Doyle, 2002, p. 30) Thus the crisis provides another "good reason" to expand ownership concentration for the sake of efficiency gains.

Finally, and going back to Schumpeter's notion of "creative destruction," we ask whether the crisis of the commercial media can be better understood when thinking in cycles. Schumpeter identified new consumers goods as "[t]he fundamental impulse that sets and keeps the capitalist engine in motion." (1976, p. 83) New methods of production and transportation, as well as new markets and new forms of industrial organization that capitalist enterprise creates (ibid.), are responsible both for the creation of new opportunities and the destruction of old structures. Translated into commercial media markets, the 'fundamental impulse' comes from new content (consumer goods) ,which is produced by new methods, transported in new ways and developed by new kinds of media organizations, such as social media like Facebook and Twitter, but also online media such as *eldiario.es* in Spain. Indeed, such cycles might be identified when looking at highly commercialized media. Private commercial television has developed new television genres, such as scripted reality shows, sing-and-dance shows as well as game shows. They did indeed attract audiences and might qualify as new impulses. Moderate or less commercialized media have so far not found convincing responses to the crisis. National and regional newspapers as typical examples of moderately commercialized media have not changed their product output in any considerable form – there has not been any decisive impulse. Experiments, however, have been exercised and are on-going. Decentralized models of newsrooms should help reduce cost for journalism, additional revenues may come from agreements with news aggregators (such as copyright taxes to be paid by Google) and from various forms of pay-walls for online news. Free sheets hardly qualify as they are highly commercialized. Equally, Internet-based online media have so far not managed to develop a moderately or less commercialized model either. Observers even argue there is nothing like a business model for news online at all. "In my view, we are better off admitting what is plainly obvious: there is no business model that can give us the journalism a self-governing society requires." (McChesney, 2013, p. 201)

It might therefore be tentatively concluded that the degree of commercialization is an important predictor for the extent to which crises of commercial media can be understood in terms of Schumpeterian capitalist cycles.

IMPLICATIONS OF THE CRISIS ON VALUES

In the final step of our analysis we try to examine the implications of the critical changes in the commercial media on democratic values.

Freedom as an incumbent core value, both as corporate media freedom from political interference and as individual freedom of expression, seems little affected by the crisis of commercial media. Indeed, crisis-born strengthening of corporate media owners might even enhance corporate media freedom as such large firms are less susceptible to undue intervention. Irrespective of potential gains provided by the Internet at large, individual freedom of expression – which includes both the right to receive and to impart information (European Convention on Human Rights, Art. 10) – is not particularly exerted by commercial media, before and during the crisis. Commercial media are less oriented towards individual freedom as citizens but rather as consumers of goods and services. Nonetheless, if the crisis finally leads to less media choice for citizens, because of the demise of moderate to low commercialized media, then their individual freedom is negatively affected.

Diversity as another core value might be divided into two strands. On the one hand, diversity refers to the amount of different media outlets owned by different persons or groups and thereby delivering external pluralism of views and ideas. In this understanding, the crisis of the commercial media clearly and negatively affects diversity. Accelerated ownership concentration as well as increased corporate ownership do not enhance this important media value. On the other hand, diversity refers to content, which is delivered by the various agents of public communication. The crisis of commercial media has – as shown above – developed some new programme types in the highly commercialized bracket. For moderately and less commercialized media, dismissed journalists, reduced budgets for editorial newsrooms and disappeared newspaper titles have severely affected diversity. With a view to media ownership concentration, Doyle stipulates that "[t]o the extent that diversity of media output is greater 'value' to society than uniformity, then some duplication of media production resources need be seen not as wasteful but as contributing to efficiency." (2002, p. 41)

Furthermore, content diversity is affected by the slump in advertising budgets available to those commercial media that deliver diverse content. "The internet's siphoning off of advertising revenue has also led news organizations to cut back on expensive editorial commitments like investigative reporting and specialist and foreign correspondents." (Freedman, 2010, p. 41)

The democratic value of enlightened citizen must also be differentiated according to the degree of commercialization. While highly commercialized media – with or without crisis – are less interested in the enlightened citizen, some of the moderate or low commercialized media managed to make a business case out of such citizens. As some of these media (mostly newspapers) are traditionally managed by concerned families or even patrons, the crisis might negatively affect this value, as such media are under considerable pressure and in danger of being taken over or closed down altogether. Some examples of such incidents have been quoted above.

The values of participation, integration, deliberation and self-determination are all directed towards the individual reader and viewer of user of media content. Commercial media are primarily oriented towards mass audiences, with the notable exception of highly specialized media in market niches. Nonetheless, these values are important for commercial media to the extent that a viable and profitable business model can be established. This may concern customer-loyalty instruments as well as the acquisition of user-generated content from participating users at low or no cost. Times of crisis come hand in hand with lower financial resources and lower profit rates. Thus less disposable revenue is available for such civic virtues, which may incur additional (and not less) resources. The social-media activities on Facebook and Twitter cost money (newsroom labour) but do not generate immediate financial returns. Although at least moderately commercialized media might be willing to deliver content corresponding to these values, times of crisis are likely to prevent them from investing in such content production.

With regard to the value of orientation towards a welfare and participative idea of society, commercial media do not excel, regardless of whether there are prosperous times or times of crisis. Rather, commercial media are oriented towards market values that do not per se include the notion of a participatory society. Welfare is translated in neoliberal terms as economic success, quite opposite to the understanding of welfare as a common concern. Economic welfare leaves little to no room for civic participation other than in the consumption of goods and services. This value might be even more disregarded in times of crisis as commercial media, struggling for their economic survival, have little capacity to engage in such non-profit ventures.

Finally, the value of the peaceful comity of nations might, at first sight, be considered as suitable for commercial media in times of crisis. International conglomerates operate across national borders, they transfer issues, concerns, formats, etc. from one country to the other and times of crisis enable them to accelerate such trans-border operations. Such transnational corporations are assumed to be better placed to withstand economic crises in one country by cross-subsidizing weaker markets with profits generated in stronger markets. It remains doubtful, however, if such transnational commercial operations enhance the peaceful comity of nations. They rather transnationalize or even globalize some sort of "hybrid culture" or "superculture," as suggested by Colin Sparks (2007, p. 144), with emphasis on finding and creating new markets for labour and for their product (Hesmondhalgh, 2007, p. 238), rather than creating mutual understanding across borders. The crisis evidently accelerates this process but does not alter it in any meaningful way.

CONCLUSIONS

To respond to our research question – In what way are democratic values delivered by commercial media in Europe affected by the crises? – we need to acknowledge that commercial media are highly heterogeneous. And so are the implications of the crisis on the democratic values delivered by them. With regard to democratic values, highly commercialized media did not excel in prosperous times and they are not much different in times of crisis. Apparently, some of these hyper-commercialized media manage to survive quite well, as they do not figure prominently in the list of the most crisis-affected media. Private commercial television, belonging to this group, developed new contents and formats and remains economically rather successful. Their contribution to democratic values is limited, however. At the other end of the spectrum of commercialization, national or regional newspapers that are not part of larger corporations seem to suffer most from the crisis. They are low or moderately commercialized but contribute considerably to democratic values. The crisis is likely to impact not only on their profitability, hence preventing them from investing in value-added activities, but on their economic sustainability. Once such media close down, their contribution to deliver democratic values ceases completely.

Media policy has not reacted to the crisis so far (see Chapter 13 in this volume for details). One could expect that responsible media policy would first establish a policy case and secondly search for solutions. But media policy seems to be characterized by long-term considerations with little room for ad-hoc activities. Instead, in some countries media reform movements have started to discuss the state of the media, but so far with little policy outcome. The US reform movement has started a debate on the notion of media subsidies as a response to the media crisis (Nichols and McChesney, 2010).

The crisis of commercial media, understood in its radical meaning as ultimate diversion, requires radical decisions. While highly commercialized but low value-laden media seem to survive well, their less commercialized counterparts are potential victims of the crisis. Once disappeared, such media cannot be reanimated. Left to the forces of markets and competition, the crisis is likely to diminish democratic values in the field of commercial media. The time for political decisions has come.

REFERENCES

Asociación de la Prensa de Madrid (2014) *Informe Anual de la Profesión Periodística 2013*. Madrid: author.

Barnett, S. (2009) Media ownership policy in a recession: redefining the public interest. *Interactions: Studies in Communication and Culture*, 1(2). pp. 217–32.

Curran, J. (2010) The Future of Journalism. *Journalism Studies*, 11(4). pp. 464–76.

Doyle, G. (2013) *Understanding Media Economics*. Second edition. Los Angeles, London, New Delhi, Singapore, Washington DC: Sage.

Doyle, G. (2002) *Media Ownership: The economics and politics of convergence and concentration in the UK and European media*. London, Thousand Oaks, CA, New Delhi: Sage.

Freedman, D. (2010) The Political Economy of the 'New' News Environment. In: Fenton N. (ed.) *New Media, Old News: Journalism & Democracy in the Digital Age* (pp. 35–50). Los Angeles: Sage.

Hesmondhalgh, D. (2007) *The Cultural Industries*. Second edition. London, Thousand Oaks, CA, New Delhi, Singapore: Sage.

Hjarvard, S. (2013) *The mediatization of culture and society*. London: Routledge.

Iosifidis, P. (2011) *Global Media and Communication Policy*. Hampshire, New York: Palgrave Macmillan.

Kaye J. and Quinn, S. (2010) *Finding Journalism in the Digital Age. Business Models, Strategies, Issues and Trends*. New York: Peter Lang.

Livingstone, S. (2009) On the Mediation of Everything: ICA Presidential Address 2008. *Journal of Communication*, 59(1). pp. 1–18.

Mazzoleni, G. and Schulz, W. (1999) 'Mediatization' of Politics: A Challenge for Democracy? *Political Communication*, 16(3). pp. 247–61.

McChesney, R. (2013) *Digital Disconnect. How Capitalism is Turning the Internet Against Democracy*. New York: New Press.

McManus, J. (2009) The Commercialization of News. In: Wahl-Jorgensen, K. and Hanitzsch, T. (eds.) *Handbook of Journalism Studies* (pp. 218–33). New York, London: Routledge.

McQuail, D. (2013) *Journalism and Society*. London, Thousand Oaks, CA, New Delhi, Singapore: Sage.

Meier, W. A. (2012) Öffentlich und staatlich finanzierte Medien aus schweizerischer Sicht. (*Public and state-financed media from a Swiss perspective*). In: Jarren, O., Künzler, M. and Puppis, M. (eds.) *Medienwandel oder Medienkrise? Folgen für Medienstrukturen und ihre Erforschung* (pp. 127–43). Baden-Baden: Nomos.

Nielsen, R. K. and Levy, D. A. L. (2010) The Changing Business of Journalism and its Implications for Democracy. In: Nielsen, R. K. and Levy, D. A. L. (eds.) *The Changing Business of Journalism and its Implications for Democracy* (pp. 3–15). Oxford: Reuters Institute for the Study of Journalism.

OECD (2010) *The Evolution of News and the Internet: Working Party on the Information Economy*. DSTI/ICCP/IE(2009)14/FINAL. Retrieved from: http://www.oecd.org/internet/ieconomy/45559596.pdf.

Picard, R. (2005) Money, Media, and the Public Interest. In: Overholser, G. and Hall Jamieson, K. (eds.) *The Press* (pp. 337–50). Oxford: Oxford University Press.

Schudson, M. (2010) News in Crisis in the United States: Panic – and Beyond. In: Nielsen, R. K. and Levy, D. A. L. (eds.) *The Changing Business of Journalism and its Implications for Democracy* (pp. 95–106). Oxford: Reuters Institute for the Study of Journalism.

Schumpeter, J. (1976) [1942] *Capitalism, Socialism and Democracy*. Fifth edition. London: Allen and Unwin.

Sparks, C. (2007) *Globalization, Development and the Mass Media*. Los Angeles, London, New Delhi, Singapore: Sage.

Strömbäck, J. (2008) Four Phases of Mediatization: An Analysis of the Mediatization of Politics. *The International Journal of Press/Politics*, 13(3). pp. 228–46.

Strömbäck, J. (2005) In Search of a Standard: four models of democracy and their normative implications for journalism. *Journalism Studies*, 6(3). pp. 331–45.

Part III

Crisis in Journalism Values, Public Communication and Representation

6 Safeguarding Newsroom Autonomy

Tensions Between the Ideal and the Actual

Auksė Balčytienė, Karin Raeymaeckers and Elena Vartanova

INTRODUCTION

The governing notion of democracy moves on ideals of freedom and self-actualization, on principles of pluralism and access to diverse information. Democracy needs freedom and plurality of opinions. And this need defines the conventional role of the media. The democratic media should act as an alert fourth estate that upholds and preserves public dialogues and scrutinizes the uses and abuses of power. As an actor with such a distinctive mission, journalism requires autonomy to control the news flow according to its own norms.

While such a notion of journalistic freedom and autonomy is accepted as a normative ideal to be applied (with different versions of contextual adaptations) in newsrooms, modern-day European media, however, are confronted with novel encounters and even crises. Last decade's news production has been challenged by a number of progressions that have significantly altered these normative ideals of journalistic performance. In most cases, shifts in newsroom thinking are related to technological and managerial factors that, with different implications, influence journalistic professional operations, which have implications for organizational cultures and, consequently, affect newsroom autonomy.

In additional to new technologies and their interactive offers, the capitalist neoliberal ideology and business-inspired thinking appeared to be amongst the strongest drivers of change. Emphasizing economic issues such as profit and efficiency of news organizations has dramatically transformed professional news management and news-making.

The financial crash of 2008, though, has uncovered that much of the rhetoric of the 1980s about market efficiency – which, for the last decades, accompanied neoliberal dogmas of unfettered markets and the cult of privatization and competition – has essentially failed. Voices became widely heard about the crisis in journalism, understood as a decrease in normative ideals of journalism, the professional standards of newsrooms, the established roles of journalists and their autonomy from social institutions and corporate interests. Journalists themselves have also realized that their monopoly in news production and distribution, paralleled by the rise of user-generated content, emerged as one of the threats to their independent professional status, thus making them certain about coming identity crises.

This chapter discusses the effects and consequences these shifts in journalistic and organizational thinking have had on journalistic and newsroom autonomy. It opens the discussion by looking at models that have traditionally been used as valid instruments to safeguard autonomy in European newsrooms. By reviewing historical experiences it questions whether and in what ways the profession of journalism could withstand new pressures arising from current political, managerial, technological or socio-cultural imperatives. It also aims to analyze present crises and shifts of journalism in different European countries through a comparative perspective, referring to examples from older and younger European democracies.

AUTONOMY AS A PROFESSIONAL VALUE: NORMATIVE APPROACH

In the past two centuries, journalism in Europe has lived through several stages, demonstrating rises and falls of different versions of authoritarianism (in eighteenth-century France during the Napoleonic regime), totalitarianism (in the 1930s in Nazi Germany), authoritarian instrumentalism (in the Soviet Union of 1917–1991 and in the communist-ruled countries of Central and Eastern Europe in 1945–1991). Still, in spite of the ideological influences and their various deviations, the traditions of journalism's role and its historically cultivated functions, European journalism has embraced the values of press freedom and free expression and communication as well as its role as an alert "watchdog" – a functioning "fourth estate" (Christians et al., 2009). Journalism gradually became an indispensable part of the European concepts of democracy that, together with the principles of public service, social responsibility, public accountability, critical relationships with elites and several others, also emphasize informed and fair decision-making and journalistic professional solidarity, hence guaranteeing a functioning professional autonomy and freedom (McQuail, 2013). This also puts forward the objective of quality journalism as the core principle of the professional newsroom activity that should be safeguarded by newsroom independence from politics, business goals, public relations, audience demands and pressures, and so forth (Schudson, 1999).

Following the normative line of thinking, journalism as a profession should keep to a certain mission. Media professionals should aim to follow a set of professional standards that frame its specific roles, functions, missions and values. Professional journalism is indispensable for democracy, whereas a functioning democracy appears to be vital for quality journalism (Trappel and Meier, 2011). Ideals and principles of democracy and journalism are codependent. Citizens (and, therefore, democracy) need professional media to help them make informed decisions in crucial times, while democracy is the only political regime that assures and guarantees freedom of expression and safeguards media professionals from censorship. Still, such a normative view and claim of principles-sharing are not without problems. If journalism has powers of enhancing the quality of democracy, why then are there any bad – imperfect, dysfunctional and even corrupt – democracies? As evidenced in Southern European and Central and Eastern European democracies, corrupt politics is reinforced by corrupt journalism. Hence, among the opening questions inquiring about the media's working conditions and its democratic performance qualities should be a question asking what type of contextual setting (i.e. democracy) is necessary in order for the media to perform its agreed-upon normative functions (MDCEE, 2013).

The broadly understood issue of journalism's autonomy in the European academic discourse was widely discussed by Bourdieu, together with the concept of the social "field." Bourdieu considers journalism to be a "weakly autonomous field" (2005, p. 41) with its autonomy depending on an understanding of powers held in the tension between economic and cultural capital. Economic capital in a journalistic field is closely attached to financial issues, predominantly to those of reach, circulation, advertising revenue and marketing, while cultural capital is linked to the production of original stories, uncovering scandal or dishonesty, or influencing the social and political agenda. These two versions of capital may sometimes reinforce each other. However, in the modern media industry, "the imperative in mass circulation, popular news media to sell as many copies as possible, or attract as many 'hits' as possible, tends to weaken the cultural in relation to the requirements of the economic." (Phillips et al., 2010, p. 55)

Taken in a general sense, newsroom autonomy belongs to the core understanding of journalism as an independent social institution of modern democracy. Briefly, newsroom autonomy means the process of agenda-setting inside the newsroom, as well as the selection of topics, sources, opinions, tone and genre, should remain in the hands of the newsroom staff without interference by actors or processes outside the journalistic framework. In all European democracies, autonomy has been safeguarded by various mechanisms, such as the legal provisions for freedom given to media and journalists and legitimated by universally shared approaches to journalism as a public service; by journalism's responsibility and accountability to society; and by its compliance with a number of professional standards supported by society and professionals. In the real work of market-based media organizations, journalists' autonomy has become an important feature of the professionalization concept, in which the idea of newsroom independence has been embedded. Daniel Hallin and Paolo Mancini envision media autonomy along with distinct professional norms and public-service orientation; hence it is outlined as one of the three core dimensions of journalistic professionalization (Hallin and Mancini, 2004, p. 34). The key reason for this is an attempt to justify a greater control, a feeling of some kind of ownership of the artifact produced that journalists should cultivate over their work process. As argued, the autonomy of a journalist is not necessarily that of an individual but is to a significant extent collegial, "the corps of journalists taken as a whole." (Hallin and Mancini, 2004, p. 35) Still, research has identified many influential obstacles that prevent journalists from acquiring full control over the outcome of their production. Among those most often mentioned are the following: the nature of the media industry, in which mass production is the norm; a limited number or an absence of cases of media ownership by journalists; and a rare involvement by journalists in the managerial control of media organizations, as well as others.

It is also obvious that journalists' autonomy may only exist in a society that not only highly values but also protects media from censorship. In the twentieth century, legal measures envisaged all European countries adopting freedom of speech (freedom of media) and the inadmissibility of censorship, not only in their constitutions but also in special legislation on media (Kelly et al., 2008). In addition, a competent, self-regulatory process was considered to be the best solution not only to calls for responsibility and accountability of journalism but also to safeguard professional journalistic autonomy. As Denis McQuail puts it: "'Social responsibility' notions are (...) subordinate to professional autonomy and a freedom to choose goals and standards without any external interference." (2013, p. 55)

Nevertheless, in spite of various actions, real life is somewhat different. Journalists suffer from various pressures on their professional autonomy in their newsroom routines. Numerous examples can be listed from various European countries indicating that contemporary business strategies and their emphasis on predominantly capitalist and neoliberal values of supply and demand seriously distort the view of what professional and quality journalism should be. As a result of the intensification of business-oriented thinking and governing managerial discourse in most European newsrooms, efficiency and profit have become the biggest matters of organizational concern in contemporary news organizations (Starr, 2012; Wiik and Andersson, 2013). Hence more and more journalists object to a lack of control over their work. They do not decide on what topic to cover as news or how to cover it; they are also not free to reveal their own opinions that dispute or otherwise challenge the policy of the employing organization (McQuail, 2013). Mark Deuze lists additional conflicts inside newsroom autonomy including conflicts between journalists and marketers, journalists and editors, and the constant need to upgrade journalistic skills (Deuze, 2005).

EUROPEAN JOURNALISMS AND CHALLENGES THEY ENCOUNTER

With European Union and Council of Europe enlargement in the 1990s, economic and cultural differences inside the European media became even more visible and obvious.[1] The growth and availability of systematic scholarly analysis and informed knowledge about the changeability and variations in European journalism – and particularly of Central and Eastern European journalism and their hybrid character and diverse national colorations (Voltmer, 2013; Hallin and Mancini, 2012) – are among the decisive factors in such a shift of attention. In recent years the attention of scholars has once again shifted – this time to the changes broadly considered by researchers as a major reconfiguration of established democracies through the transformation of citizenship and decreasing public engagement on the one hand (Mancini, 2013; Prior, 2013; LeDuc et al., 2010) and the transformation of media economies and professional journalism on the other. Predominantly the latter circumstance has resulted in decline, crisis and even chaos in the media industry (Doctor, 2010; De Prato, Sanz and Simon, 2014; Levy and Nielsen, 2010).

While the principles and values of freedom, diversity and impartially have been accepted in most European countries as a normative ideal for the news media, their implementation almost from the very early days of modern journalism has been complicated by their contextual conditions and realities, meaning their political cultures and dominating (neoliberal) ideologies. Still, the question of media freedom and independence, of professional journalistic standards and contextual conditions for their implementations, including the autonomy of the newsroom, remains quite relevant in all European countries. For centuries, politics was an area with strong attempts to violate the autonomy of journalists, although with different degrees of success. However, as seen from various cases, principles of objective journalism, based on a reliance on facts and respect for impartiality, have been challenged by the advocacy and instrumental political journalism that dominated European news media in the early days and – paradoxically – became widespread in professional newsroom cultures even in those European countries with the oldest traditions of democracy (Weaver and Willnat, 2012), thus making the sovereignty of professional journalists rather vulnerable. The political factor, in synchronization with economic conditions, is even more dangerous in the younger European democracies. It is quite correct to claim that post-communist transformations of the early 1990s in the CEE took place under economically much weaker conditions. Two decades later, the economic factor is as strong as it was previously, separating the Western and the Central Eastern parts of the same continent. Hence the political thinking of elites in those weaker markets is powerfully shaped by attempts to increase political control of economic capital and resources, and by subsequently engaging media for such purposes.[2] But the CEE media itself is not without sin either. It is prone to heavy manipulation, populism, sensationalism and political consumerism (Gross, 2014). In general, all such locally maintained and complex relations between the key elite groups seriously affect the professionalization of CEE journalism, particularly its independence, which is seen through media-freedom indicators being much lower in CEE countries if compared to those in Western Europe.

Economic conditions have always been a decisive factor in ensuring successful media operations. However, in the past few decades new criteria and indicators, specifically those of cost efficiency, return on investment, revenue streams for media managers and owners became the most visible markers of the success of media organizations, reducing the importance of journalistic professional values and the ways to safeguard them (Wiik and Andersson, 2013). Since the last century alone, as a result of liberalization and privatization, many of the ideals of the previously dominant logic of the social contract were marginalized or entirely disregarded in the policies of Western European democracies as well. In many European States the activities that were previously supervised by the government, such as education or health care, were taken over by the guidance and logic of the market. As Starr (2012) shows when explaining the background to the news media crisis, the primary mistake under such thinking and its submission in the media field was its ignorance of the fact that journalistic product such as news is a public good and public goods tend to be systematically under-produced in purely market-driven circumstances.

One of the recent threats considered to lead to newsroom autonomy crisis came from technological developments and the rise of the Internet and social networks that have challenged journalistic activity, as well as newsroom processes and the shifting relationships between journalists, news organizations and their audiences (Pavlik, 2001). Today the activities of new, more open and often amateur journalists differ from traditional professionals' work in a number of areas, including the existence of editorial control, production of news outside the traditional newsrooms, and delivery of the content interactively and at greater speed (Fenton, 2010, p. 6). Therefore the challenges the technological advancements pose for journalism should be considered to have long-term effects and serious consequences, the most significant being reduced news cycles and the increasing pressures on journalists; diversification of sources and thus challenges of offering audiences direct access to news; changing news agendas and shifting control levels on the professional side; lack of resources in media organizations to meet all needs of the new audience; institutionalization of copy-paste journalism, as well as many others.

All things considered, it comes as no surprise that due to these developments, the concept of newsroom autonomy as an essential part of the idea of professional journalism has called for new understanding and conceptualization. Can autonomy be an answer to contemporary challenges that European journalists encounter? Which are the core factors that most strongly influence performance of journalism in different countries?

SAFEGUARDING AUTONOMY: HISTORICAL PATHWAYS, TRADITIONS AND MECHANISMS

Various models, traditions and instruments have been developed to sustain newsroom autonomy in Europe. Although the efficiency of those measures and initiatives is closely intertwined with cultural conditions and traditions in different countries (Hallin and Mancini, 2004), some of the measures might be regarded as fit for all media. Among those safeguarding mechanisms found across various countries in Europe are newsroom charters, the trusts (foundations), the shareowner status of journalists and also newsroom ombudsman positions.

Newsroom charters – or editorial policy documents that secure the newsroom staff – are still widely used in different countries. The content of those documents, however, differs widely. In most cases, variations depend on a degree of enforcement towards actors outside the newsroom.[3] Newsroom charters that define the relationship between the newsroom and the other partners or policy levels in the media company are more common practice in the countries of Northern Europe. Still, exceptions are found also in Southern European countries, for example at *El Mundo* in Spain and the French magazine *Le Nouvel Observateur*. A key element in those charters is the consultation procedure between management and the newsroom to solve conflicts in a strict setting. This type of consultation procedure is well established in Sweden.[4] In Germany, the first wave of newsroom charters could be seen in 1969 when different regional and local newspapers worked out a model to secure the independent relationship between media owners and newsrooms. Later, other prestigious media with national distribution joined in the seventies (*Süddeutsche Zeitung* and *Frankfurter Allgemeine Zeitung*); since 1993 the *Tageszeitung* also joined. After several years of consultation between journalists and media owners in the Netherlands, a collective contract was agreed upon in 1977 stating that newsroom charters were necessary in all media (Model-statuut voor hoofdredactie en redactie, 1977). In Belgium, newsroom charters are a relatively new phenomenon with the charter of the magazine *Humo*, dating back to 1978, an exception in the magazine market. The first newspaper (1990) with a newsroom charter in Flanders was the progressive and previously clearly left-wing title *De Morgen*.[5] All in all, this model is a minimal interpretation of the conditions that every contract between media management and newsroom should include. On behalf of autonomy of the newsroom the newsroom charter clarifies the position of the different parties involved; it states who is responsible and for what actions.[6]

Still, in spite of various attempts to secure the working conditions of journalists, histories of mainly Western European journalism confirm that there were moments when the newsroom charter did not provide sufficient protection. It failed to prevent further concentration or the dismissal of editors-in-chief, and it did not guarantee that newsrooms were consulted in the appointment of a new editor-in-chief (Brakman, 1999). The most recent criticism of charters rests on its instructions for the editor-in-chief and manager as having a mutual responsibility for managerial aspects. A shift proposed in the new thinking would be the suggestion that the advertising policy should be excluded from this mutual agreement (and the logic that the news production also has business essentials) to make sure the editor-in-chief gives priority to journalistic motivations over commercial goals.

While newsroom charters often are designed to maintain newsroom autonomy in a shorter time perspective, the trusts (foundations) aim at the preservation of the ideological branding of a medium in a longer time perspective. Since 1936, the Scott Trust Ltd. has guaranteed the English newspaper *The Guardian*.[7] Securing ideological branding was also a priority concern of the founders of the Dutch title *Het Parool*, a newspaper that, after being an underground paper during World War II, remained in the post-war market.[8] Also a different Dutch newspaper, *De Volkskrant*, established such a structure.[9] We observe the same strategy to launch trusts to secure autonomy in the Swedish newspaper market at a moment when the concentration process bundles different titles, previously ideologically secured by some major family shareholders. Some of these trusts control the full ownership of the media involved but there are also examples of different shareholders' majority or minority positions, thus providing a very complex ownership structure intertwined with trust elements (Hadenius, 1993). Finally, the French newspaper *Le Monde* also has a trust that is not related to the systems of journalists' shareholders structures.[10] The first example of a trust in the Belgian media market is the *Raad Het Laatste Nieuws*, established in 1955 (Prevenier, 2010) and inspired by the model of the Scott Trust.[11] An alternative interpretation of trusts is to be found in the example of the *Frankfurter Allgemeine Zeitung*, a right-wing conservative quality German newspaper founded in 1949.[12]

Other reliable instruments to safeguard newsroom autonomy are attempts by journalists or journalists' associations to acquire shares of their companies, or create newsroom ombudsman positions. Acquiring shares would require a large financial investment and therefore is rare. An interesting example is the French newspaper *Le Monde*.[13] In the German magazine market, the example of *Der Spiegel* is a good illustration of journalistic shareholdership. Founded in 1947 by Rudolf Augstein, journalists and collaborators control half of the shares and also have a return on investment (profit shares) at the end of their career.

Across the CEE countries, variations are found in all the above types of instruments that historically emerged as a product of the process of journalism professionalization in the West. As can be seen in most cases, these were implemented as policy attempts and ignored local contextual conditions (journalistic and organizational practices), and thus their outcomes are only of a symbolic significance in terms of professionalization of journalism across the CEE (Harro-Loit et al., 2012).

All in all, these instruments are increasingly under strain through different external and internal mechanisms caused by the most recent developments in the European mediascape.

PRESENT CHALLENGES TO NEWSROOM AUTONOMY

Pressures on journalists' autonomy are recognized by media worldwide and have been traditionally opposed in European newsrooms by various instruments analyzed above. Still, the type and degree of application of these instruments appears to vary greatly across Europe. The opportunities for journalists to make independent decisions differ, depending on contextual conditions and on the influences that in certain cases may acquire the status of central and determining importance in a selected country. These factors may also be assessed as having an external or internal impact and effects (see Figure 6.1).

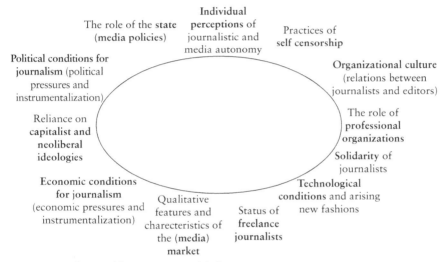

Figure 6.1 Changeable pressures and influences on newsroom autonomy.

Generally, the protection of the autonomy of an individual journalist seems to be an all-European problem. It might be defined by:

- The type of media organizations, for instance news vs. entertainment media, press vs. broadcasting, quality vs. popular/sensational media
- The national media contexts created by different cultural and political traditions (McQuail, 2013).

Debates about constraints on newsroom autonomy have a long tradition. Forces that influence and restrain journalists' autonomy at their place of work include owners, advertisers, public relations, job routines, social environment and audience. Recent studies have also identified innovations and, more broadly, technology as an influential factor in putting pressure on editorial autonomy, although not all of these influences need to be regarded as being negative (Deuze, 2005, p. 449). Halliki Harro-Loit and Epp Lauk add to this list the position of journalists inside the newsroom, areas of reporting and "individual sensitivity and ability to understand the concept of autonomy" (Harro-Loit and Lauk, 2012).

Many actors try to influence the newsroom practice from outside, and these pressures should be considered as being external. There also exist many processes situated within the journalistic field, and these might be considered internal pressures. Pressures that come from technological developments might produce multiple effects, representing influences both from outside (audiences, amateur journalists, news sources) or from inside (new speed of work routine and news production, becoming multi-skilled, competition with colleagues).

Major groups of external actors concerned with media coverage are commercial actors who are striving for media attention for their products beyond the borders of the commercial messages and political actors (politics or civic society), whose messages want to sustain or protest a specific policy. Their attempts at influence are often subtle (Gandy, 1982) since journalists are reluctant to use identifiable PR material (Wintour, 1972; Fengler and Russ-Mohl, 2008). As British journalist Nick Davies argues, the more subtle attempts to direct the media agenda, however, do have impact and journalists are eager to use this type of material (Davies, 2009). The rise of the public-relations professionals in recent decades has meant journalists were faced with a greater volume of PR information than even before. This is not just a rise in the amount of information journalists use in materials that are either initiated by PR or in which PR has been used (Fenton, 2010, p. 94f). It is also proven by studies, which show that around forty per cent of journalistic articles contain PR material, whereas around fifty per cent of print stories are informed by PR (Lewis et al., 2008, p. 20). Similar evidence from other national contexts, especially from CEE countries, is numerous (Harro-Loit and Lauk, 2012).

Political actors – parties, politicians, even business actors seeking political influence – also try to influence the media agenda and get their message in the media content. In many European contexts, journalists consider these actors as interesting partners to get scoops or inside information, as well as powerful partners in the news-making process. And many scholars pointed to journalists' dependence on their sources from the political field who might be considered to be major holders of power in the news production process who pressure the news agenda for their own sakes.

On the other hand, political instrumentalization of journalism – particularly media instrumentalization in Central and Eastern Europe, Russia[14] and Southern European regions in the context of absence (or failures) of mechanisms to protect newsrooms and journalistic professional independence – has become a visible trend (Bajomi-Lazar, 2014). Such features as political clientelism – or state paternalism, as Karol Jakubowicz emphasizes – often reveal themselves in "the situation when politics pervades and influences many political systems" (Jakubowicz, 2007, p. 304), thus making journalists' newsroom autonomy quite vulnerable.

External pressures are often considered to come from corporate ownership and marketing departments of media organizations, and this reflects the central conflict in the nature of media being simultaneously an institute of democracy and a commercial enterprise. Therefore media owners and managers approach journalists as dependent on their work on the logic of business. Indeed, the situation in European countries varies. In their survey of journalists in 1992, Donsbach and Patterson revealed that about one-third of Italian journalists and less than ten per cent of German journalists said they survived "pressures from management" on "the job" they did (quoted in Hallin and Mancini, 2004, p. 35). In post-communist countries, pressures from owners are described as even more aggressive and threatening, since the professional will of journalists might be bargained for a simple need defined as "the wish of journalists to eat." (Harro-Loit and Lauk, 2012)

However, these pressures are not quite obvious everywhere, and, as Humphreys states,

> there is little evidence of any direct external influences on the UK media, though general commercial pressures adversely influence the quality of news. The main area of potential direct influence is proprietorial guidance relayed via the internal management structure, but the actual extent of this is disputed. (2011, p. 323)

Recent examples of economic crises in newsrooms produced by external economic forces involve financial cuts, journalists laid off, journalists having to do more with fewer resources, an increase in freelancing, and newsroom mergers and transformation into converging environment (Fenton, 2010, p. 41). One of the recent influences of the new media rise over the newsroom became the increasing presence of non-professional or 'citizen' journalists who are able to disrupt or change professional journalism and autonomy under conditions where readers could have greater impacts on news (ibid., p. 10 & 14).

On the other hand, the internal pressures on journalistic autonomy relate to organizational structures (Lowrey et al., 2011) and organizational cultures, especially traditions and values maintained in the newsrooms and society as a whole (Hallin and Mancini, 2004). Deadlines, increasing workload, working in a converged newsroom for multiple distribution platforms, cuts in staff and budgets (Gandy, 1982; Davies, 2009) have a major impact on the autonomy of journalists.

Pressures of sources have a mixed nature, since for many journalists, news sources are an external factor linked to either professional news-providers (news agencies, other media) or to personal contacts. However, decisions about news selection are often made in workplaces under strong pressures of time, high speed of news supply and rolling deadlines. Results provided in the Cardiff University research study show that only twelve to twenty per cent of stories were generated by reporters themselves, while the rest were based on external sources. Moreover, it became clear from the research that even when journalists initiated stories themselves, they had no time to use more than one source (Fenton, 2010; Davies, 2009).

Gender inequality still plays a role inside European newsrooms, and this is proven by the fact that men are more frequently employed with a permanent contract than women. New requirements of digital technological skills also create instability and pressures for older journalists, especially female ones (Lee-Wright in Fenton, 2010).

Technological impacts include pressures arising from integrated newsrooms and their impacts on news media production, journalists' professional standards and ethics, and journalistic cultures. New pressures also arise from the new demands for more technologically based skills, for abilities to work in the convergent, multi-platform and multi-channel media environment. This has decreased the role of the permanent newsroom staff compared to a more mobile but less expensive work force of freelancers. Various studies of journalists in Europe reveal great variations among media professionals. Freelancing appears to be a popular activity among Western Europeans, and a relatively large number of journalists in all European countries are employed under temporary contract agreements or other atypical work relations.

As the survey of European journalists also demonstrated, recent changes in the structure of traditional newsrooms under the pressures of digitalization resulted in more cost-efficient models that merge, in a single newsroom, the editorial activities and the business operations with the new media. Integrated newsrooms, which account for more than forty per cent of the total number of European media companies and the diffusion of non-dependent work relations, increasingly require the emergence of eclectic job profiles that are found mostly among freelancers. The survey has indicated that in a number of European countries such as France, the UK and Romania, newsrooms are more inclined to heterogeneity than others such as Sweden, Poland or Spain. This new eclecticism, in fact, transforms the professional routines to the point that journalists lose their active involvement with the production of independent texts. The interviews with the BBC News web journalists reflected their frustration to act as no more than sub-editors reformatting copy. In some journalists' minds, the new conditions of working with the mass of facts and eyewitness reports "reduce them to butchers supplying a sausage machine." (Lee-Wright in Fenton, 2010, p. 81)

CONCLUSIONS

It still seems that economy is a very strong determinant of a healthy media climate, particularly its freedom and independence. According to the

Freedom House data, in most European countries (with only few exceptions among younger European democracies such as Hungary) higher GDP scores correlate with higher media freedom and democratization results. But economy, of course, is not the only issue that positively shapes media operations. As argued here, Europe's older democracies have preserved specific conditions for the better functioning of their media. In spite of various financial uncertainties, different Western countries are still portrayed as being politically and economically stable. Western democracies are famous for their journalism cultures, strongly influenced by the idea of the public sphere as offering a critical forum of debate, they also have established various media policy provisions, for example by securing financial support mechanisms (subsidies, VAT exemptions, public funding) for their media. And, finally, these countries manifest high degrees of professional solidarity among their journalists, which, as revealed through historical experience and the practices of charter and foundations design, still appears to be a very helpful and socially engaging instrument to safeguard autonomy and hence create much better professional working conditions than the media currently have in the younger European democracies. In the CEE countries, it seems, journalism is still struggling with specific cultural and historical legacies and urgent circumstantial pressures, among which influences from political and business elites seem to be the most frustrating and threatening. CEE journalism's quality is also fashioned by various socio-cultural particularities, such as self-interest supremacy and stronger expressions of particularism, and, thus, weaker engagement in public matters and weaker public-service orientation in those societies. Such qualities of the general societal culture also strongly influence perceptions of journalists' freedom and autonomy and distress the media's democratic performance.

All in all, the rise of market-inspired imperatives, specifically the ones leading to supremacy of managerial thinking, to business strategies and to reliance on capitalist and neoliberal ideologies, might seriously jeopardize normative ideals, principles and visions of democracy. Promotion of the logic of competition and financialization, which have formed the main dynamic in European economies for the past century, had resulted in various societal shifts. These affected distributions of wealth and, consequently, challenged social well-being conditions across all European countries. Different types of fluctuations and uncertainties were also registered in other social fields, predominantly in the political, where the increasing passivity of the electorate and the anti-democratic behaviours of the European elites were registered. Likewise, a number of dangerous shifts were echoed in the field of media, suggesting business-like thinking, managerial discourses and effectiveness logic as governing strategies of its professional, everyday operations. When journalistic ideals are being risked, informed and engaged decision-making and thus democracy might be endangered, too. Although such a shift in the newsrooms appears to be an all-European issue, its effects and consequences might be especially threatening in the younger European democracies.

NOTES

1. In spite of the still dominant voices of the CEE region's relative homogeneity, a group of scholars emerged who emphasize the importance of looking at CEE transformations as incorporating multilateral – pre-communist, communist and post-communist – attributes and legacies found in their political cultures (Gross and Jakubowicz, 2012). In succeeding arguments, the historical perspective sounds particularly significant, emphasizing that the communist decades in those countries were in many ways as diverse as those of the new democracies turned out to be. The communist-ruled states in Central, Eastern and Southern (Balkan) Europe resembled various ways of life and of self-organization and, quite analogously, today's Central and Eastern Europe is nothing more nor less than a heterogeneous constituency of political and media cultures where the patterns of today's politics (dominating discourses, policy choices, regime stability) and economic development correlate with patterns of politics and institutional choices in the region made in the critical times of the past century (Ekiert and Ziblatt, 2013).

2. For example, in Romania and Hungary, the dominant culture of political and media elites has led to state 'politization,' defined as the capture of the state by various political powers and interests. In such operations, the media are viewed as instrumental players, actors who have a mission of skillfully managing public opinion. Thus the subsequent occupation and colonization of their logics and operations by political or business interests seem to be an everyday reality and vitally important for elites in those countries. In the case of Hungary, for example, the government tends to keep its media under great pressure, whereas in other CEE States (Romania, Bulgaria, Latvia), oligarchs instrumentalize media organizations, ensuring positive political coverage that should lead to political and economic gains (Bajomi-Lazar, 2014; Stetka, 2013).

3. A good example is provided in the charter of the French newspaper *Libération*. Next to the expressed intention to provide qualitative and fact-checked information on a daily basis, the charter also stresses the branding of the title as free and independent. The ethical guidelines for the journalists limit the possibilities for external pressure. Journalists cannot have side jobs that interfere with their objectivity and independence and the rules provide very detailed description. The charter sets out rules for non-acceptance of reimbursement of travelling costs as paid by external actors unless the editor-in-chief approved it. Also the individual influence of the journalists themselves is restricted.

4. In Swedish news media they refer to the name *samråd*, which is defined as "common deliberation." Although, strictly speaking, this arrangement is not a part of the newsroom charters, the existence of this mechanism is important. Since 1969, this *samråd* procedure is set down unanimously in the collective employment contracts between editors and newsroom staff for all Swedish media. When conflicts occur, a committee with an equal amount of representatives of both contracting parties assembles to search for a compromise approved by a majority of the representatives. It is formally stated that this procedure cannot be used (misused) to communicate already made decisions to the newsroom. Nevertheless the deliberation system offers no real leverage for the newsroom representatives to defend their autonomy. Moreover, it is possible that editors sideline the *samråd* procedure for those cases where they consider

the economic prosperity of their media threatened (Fischer, Molenveld, Petzke and Wolter, 1975).

5. Since the title was taken over by a large media group, De Persgroep, a group with a more liberal ideological branding, it defines the ideological profile of the title while also stresses newsroom autonomy. However it did not prevent serious conflicts between newsroom and management, and the position of the management proved to be the stronger one. Other Belgian examples (*L'Echo*, *De Tijd*, *La Dernière Heure*, *La Libre Belgique*) have worked out some arrangements when the titles were acquired by a larger group, thus trying to secure the ideological and content-branding. Also for these examples, we observe that it was not a guarantee to sustain autonomy when appointing or dismissing editors-in-chief. The management proved to be the stronger actor (Vanheerentals, 2006).

6. The editor-in-chief is the one who is responsible and journalists act autonomously, while the media owners are obliged to discuss measures that have an impact on the identity of the media brand with the editor-in-chief. Measures that have an impact have been identified: changes in content and layout, dismissal or appointment of the editor-in-chief, or plans for cross-participation or collaboration with other media. The basic model suggests a procedure to solve conflicts within the newsroom by an elected editorial committee. This committee can act as intermediary between management and editor-in-chief vs. newsroom staff. And as a third element in the statute, there is the obligation to define the newsroom editorial baseline. Since there is a close connection with the identity of the medium, the model newsroom charter only offers overall guidelines such as respect for the freedom of information and the right to be informed.

7. The title first appeared in 1821 and Charles Prestwich Scott, who has been editor-in-chief since 1872, acquired the title as owner in 1907. The new trust explicitly defines its goal and ambitions: "to secure the financial and editorial independence of *The Guardian* in perpetuity as a quality national newspaper without party affiliation; remaining faithful to liberal tradition; as a profit-seeking enterprise managed in an efficient and cost-effective manner." Up till today, the Scott Trust is the holder of the ideological profile and has full ownership of the title (Guardian Media Group PLC, 2010).

8. The underground experience stressed the importance of autonomy of newsrooms, since commercial arguments in many newsrooms converted into publication under German rule. Stichting Het Parool acquired the ownership, although this was degraded over different waves in the concentration of the Dutch market. When the Belgian media group De Persgroep took over different Dutch titles, amongst them *Het Parool*, a new foundation (Stiftung) was created, Stichting Het Nieuwe Parool.

9. The title originally was founded in 1921 in close relationship with the Catholic party and labour union in the Netherlands. In the 1960s, a more independent position was put forward while the stronger relationship with the traditional political actors was broken up. In the concentration wave, the title was joined to the same group as *Het Parool* and ideologically made a left shift. In 1985, *De Volkskrant* strove for more autonomy and some shareholders transferred their shares into Stichtung De Volkskrant (Musschoot, 2010).

10. This trust is related to the readers of the newspapers who in 1985, concerned about the financial troubles their newspaper was facing, raised money to invest in a *société anonyme*. Their shares were raised over the years. Today approximately

12,000 readers have invested in the SA (*Société des lecteurs du Monde*, 2012a). Although this vehicle is registered on the French stock exchange, there are limitations for the shareholders. Their shareholdership has to be approved by the board of directors. (*Société des lecteurs du Monde*, 2012b).

11. Family owners of that liberal title wanted to guarantee the ideological branding and the foundation (Stiftung) had a board of trustees of famous liberal politicians and representatives of liberal civic society. Stiftung is still active today and besides the members of the board, also invites the CEO of the media group De Persgroep and the editor-in-chief of the newspaper as observers. The former left-wing title *De Morgen* (today a more progressive brand rather than ideologically left), which was bought by De Persgroep, established a trust as owner of the brand to safeguard the autonomy in case of new ownership. This trust does not have a representative on the Board of Directors of the larger media group and thus has little influence. In the media group Corelio we observe the "vzw Redactie," an organization that is open for all journalists. This organization was established by journalists in the bankruptcy process of the group in 1976. The vzw Redactie is one of the shareholders of the Krantenfonds N.V., which has a place on the Board of Directors of the group.

12. The industrial entrepreneur Haffner, together with some friends amongst whom was the professor of Economics Erich Welter, created an association of investors that moulded into a Fazit-Stiftung in 1959. This Stiftung controls the majority (56.3 per cent) of the shares of the *Frankfurter Allgemeine Zeitung*. In the Charter is a remarkable article that orders all benefits originating from the newspaper to be used for investment on behalf of public interest. The Publizistikwissenschaft (Media Studies/Communication Sciences) is mentioned as an important field to invest in. (Röper, 1997b, p. 374).

13. Due to post-war regulations, French newspapers that kept appearing after November 1942 were abolished. The post-war government was in search of new actors who were willing to invest in media and the technical equipment of the former French title *Le Temps*, which was acquired by a new investor who launched the title *Le Monde*. One of the leading journalistic names in that epoch was Hubert Beuve-Méry who, after a series of disputes with the management, stepped aside in 1951. This was the starting point for the newsroom staff to protest and demand the establishment of a *Société des rédacteurs* that would have impact on the nomination of newsroom management staff and, more precisely, the editor-in-chief. The idea was realized and the new *Société des rédacteurs* also acquired shares to weight the decisions of management (Fauvet, 1977; Fischer, Molenveld, Petzke & Wolter, 1975). Over the years the *Société* managed to obtain more shares and increasing impact. Today the position of the journalists is strong enough to influence decisions that have impact on the branding of the newspapers and they can have a voice in the decisions that might occur in a concentration scenario. Their power is important since they have a decisive voice in the nomination of the director of the company, a job that combines the responsibilities of editor-in-chief, editor and member of the board of directors. This combination risks overpowering one person and many conflicts were to be attributed to this unbalanced situation. Although the strong position of the *Société des rédacteurs* has positively contributed to the quality branding of the newspaper, the financial situation has not been boosted. Although the *Société* was the major shareholder until 2011, its position was reduced to one-third of the shares due to the arrival of new

owners, Pierre Bergé, Matthieu Pigasse and Xavier Niel, who invested more than €110 million, or more than 60 per cent of existing shares. This operation was approved by a large majority of the SRM (*Société des rédacteurs du Monde*) since specific measures to safeguard journalistic autonomy were guaranteed. Nevertheless, this historical shift took away the economic ownership, or the majority of the economic ownership, from the journalists.

14. The character and degree of political instrumentalization and influences over the media among the mentioned countries, however, cannot be likened, paralleled and directly compared. This applies especially to the CEE countries and Russia. As witnessed in times of the current geopolitical turmoil in the Eastern Europe, journalists on the Russian side and journalists on the side of the EU's Central and Eastern European countries report about it from different ideological perspectives.

REFERENCES

Bajomi-Lazar, P. (2014) *Party colonization of the media in Central and Eastern Europe*. Budapest: CEU Press.

Bourdieu, P. (2005) The political field, the social science field and the journalistic field. In: Benson, R. and Neveu, E. (eds.) *Bourdieu and the Journalistic Field* (pp. 29–47). Cambridge: Polity.

Brakman, I. (1999) Het redactiestatuut: houvast voor journalistieke onafhankelijkheid. *Mediaforum*, (13). pp. 338–339.

Christians, C., Glasser, T., McQuail, D., Nordenstreng, K. and White, R. (2009) *Normative theories of the media: Journalism in democratic societies*. Urbana, IL: University of Illinois Press.

Davies, N. (2009) *Flat earth news*. London: Vintage Books.

De Prato, G., Sanz, E. and Simon, J.P. (eds.) (2014) *Digital media worlds: The new economy of media*. Hampshire, New York: Palgrave MacMillan.

Deuze, M. (2005) Professional ideals and ideology of journalists reconsidered. *Journalism*, (6). pp. 442–64.

Doctor, K. (2010) *Newsonomics: Twelve new trends that will shape the news you get*. New York: St. Martin's Press.

Ekiert, G. and Ziblatt, D. (2013) Democracy in Central and Eastern Europe one hundred years on. *East European Politics and Societies*, 27(1). pp. 90–107.

Fauvet, J. (1977, March 25) Le souci de l'indépendance. *Le Monde*.

Fenton, N. (2010) *New media, old news: Journalism and democracy in the digital age*. London: Sage.

Fengler, S. and Russ-Mohl, S. (2008) Journalists and the information-attention markets: towards an economic theory of journalism. *Journalism*, 9(6). pp. 667–90.

Fischer, H., Molenveld, R., Petzke, I. and Wolter, H. W. (1975) *Innere Pressefreiheit in Europa*. Baden-Baden: Nomos Verlagsgesellschaft.

Gandy, O. H. (1982) *Beyond agenda setting: Information subsidies and public policy*. Norwood, NJ.: Ablex Publishing.

Gross, P. and Jakubowicz, K. (2012) *Media transformations in the post-communist world: Eastern Europe's tortured path to change*. Plymouth, US: Lexington Press.

Gross, P. (2014) The devolution of media evolutions in Eastern Europe: The Romanian case. Paper presented at the 7th *CEECOM conference in Wroclaw, Poland*, June 14–16, 2014.

Guardian Media Group PLC (2010) *Formation of the trust.* Retrieved from: http://www.gmgplc.co.uk/the-scott-trust/history/formation-of-the-trust.

Hadenius, S. (1993) *Concentration of ownership in the Swedish newspaper market.* Düsseldorf: European Institute for the Media.

Hallin, D. and Mancini, P. (2004) *Comparing media systems: Three models of media and politics.* Cambridge: Cambridge University Press.

Hallin, D. and Mancini, P. (2012) *Comparing media systems beyond the Western world.* Cambridge: Cambridge University Press.

Harro-Loit, H. and Lauk, E. (2012) Journalists' professional autonomy: Europe-wide comparison. Paper presented at the seminar Journalists' professional autonomy and journalism ethics, University of Jyvaskyla, June 14.

Harro-Loit, H., Lauk, E., Kuutti, H. and Loit, U. (2012) Professional autonomy in journalism as a factor for safeguarding freedom of expression: A comparative perspective. Media Freedom and Independence in 14 European countries: A Comparative Perspective. Retrieved from: http://www.mediadem.eliamep.gr/wp-content/uploads/2012/09/D3.1.pdf.

Humphreys, P. (2011) UK News Media and Democracy: Professional Autonomy and its Limits. In: Trappel, J., Nieminen, H. and Nord, L. W. (eds.) *The Media for Democracy Monitor: A Cross National Study of Leading News Media* (pp. 319–45). Gothenburg: Nordicom.

Jakubowicz, K. (2007) *Rude awakening: Social and media change in Central and Eastern Europe.* Cresskill, NJ: Hampton Press.

Kelly, M., Mazzoleni, G. and McQuail, D. (2008) *The media in Europe.* London: Sage.

Krantenfonds NV (2012). Wat is het Krantenfonds? Retrieved from: http://www.krantenfonds.be/index.php/wat-doen-we.

LeDuc, L., Niemi, R. G. and Norris, P. (2010) *Comparing democracies 3: Elections and voting in the 21st century.* London: Sage.

Levy, D. A. L. and Nielsen, R. K. (2010). *The changing business of journalism and its implications for democracy.* Oxford: RISJ.

Lewis, J., Williams, A., Franklyn, B., Thomas, J. and Mosdell, N. (2008) *The quality and independence of British journalism.* Cardiff: Cardiff University.

Lowrey, W., Parrot, S. and Meade, S. (2011) When blogs become organizations. *Journalism,* 12(3). pp. 243–59.

Mancini, P. (2013) Media fragmentation, party system, and democracy. *The International Journal of Press/Politics,* 18(1). pp. 43–60.

McQuail, D. (2013) *Journalism and society.* London: Sage.

MDCEE (2013) *Media and democracy in Central and Eastern Europe* (project design). Retrieved from: http://mde.politics.ox.ac.uk/index.php/research.

Musschoot, I. (2010) *Stichtingen van Europese kranten: vergelijkende analyse.* Report for *Raad Het Laatste Nieuws.*

Pavlik, J. (2001) *Journalism and new media.* New York: Columbia University Press.

Phillips, A., Couldry, N. and Freedman, D. (2010) *An ethical deficit? Accountability, norms, and the material conditions of contemporary journalism.* In: N. Fenton (ed.) *New media, old news: Journalism and democracy in the digital age* (pp. 51–69). London: Sage.

Prevenier, W. (2006) *Raad Het Laatste Nieuws: een terugblik.* Asse/Kobbegem: *Raad Het Laatste Nieuws* vzw.

Prior, M. (2013) Media and political polarization. *Annual Review of Political Science,* 16. pp. 101–27.

Schudson, M. (2008) The public journalism and its problems. In: Graber, D., McQuail, D. and Norris, P. (eds.) *The politics of news, the news of politics* (pp. 132–149). Washington, DC: CQ Press.

Starr, P. (2012) An unexpected crisis: The news media in postindustrial democracies. *The International Journal of Press/Politics*, 17(2). pp. 234–42.

Stetka, V. (2013) Media ownership and commercial pressures. Report presented at the *Final MDCEE project conference Media and Democracy: CEE in a Comparative Context*. The European Studies Centre, St. Antony's College, University of Oxford, July 9–11.

Trappel, J. and Meier, W. A. (2011) *On media monitoring: The media and their contribution to democracy*. New York: Peter Lang Publishing.

Trappel, J., Nieminen, H. and Nord, L. (2011) *The media for democracy monitor: A cross-national study of leading news media*. Goteborg: Nordicom.

Vanheerentals, L. (2006) Het ene redactiestatuut is het andere niet. *De Journalist*, 90. pp. 10–11.

Voltmer, K. (2013) *The media in transitional democracies*. Cambridge: Polity Press.

Weaver D. H. and Willnat, L. (2012) *The global journalist in the 21st century*. London: Routledge.

Wiik, J. and Andersson, U. (2013) Journalism meets management: Changing leadership in Swedish news organizations. *Journalism Practice*, 7(6). pp. 705–19.

Wintour, C. (1972) *Pressures on the press: An editor looks at Fleet Street*. London: Andre Deutsch.

7 Crisis of the News

The Framing of the Euro Crisis and the 'Greek Problem'

Leen d'Haenens, Willem Joris and Stylianos Papathanassopoulos

INTRODUCTION

The crisis in the media is undeniably linked to the crisis in society, thus producing a considerable challenge to European integration, the European institutions, the Eurozone and a common currency. This chapter deals with the representation of the Euro crisis in the news coverage since its emergence in 2008. The Euro crisis has had a huge impact on the global economy. In Europe, while there is no doubt that the populations of the hardest-hit countries – those of the South – have been suffering the most, northern countries are increasingly feeling its direct effects as well. For a majority of citizens the news media are the pre-eminent source of information on this complex matter. Not only do the mass media select the issues they report on, they also choose the ways in which to do so. Research into these mechanisms is relevant since issue coverage is bound to have a tangible effect on public opinion and public reactions to the responses of policy-makers. This chapter presents two newspaper coverage studies with differing scopes, methodologies and periods of analysis. The first study identifies the framing and metaphors in Euro-crisis coverage with an emphasis on North-Western Europe (i.e. the Low Countries), while the second study focuses on coverage of the Greek financial crisis by international quality newspapers.

THE EURO CRISIS AND THE GREEK FISCAL CRISIS

The news media are fundamental to democratic governance and play the role of crucial buffers in the articulation of issues of common concern in the European public sphere (Papathanassopoulos and Negrine, 2011). Through their coverage they tend "to dominate the European public sphere" (Zografova, Bakalova and Mizova, 2012), while playing a significant role in agenda-setting and creating images of society (Schudson, 2008; Aalberg and Curran, 2012). European institutions undoubtedly make important decisions and adopt directives and policies that directly affect citizens. But the question is how to cover a European crisis when one never reports on Europe as a whole or when Europe seems to present the well-known 'communication deficit'? Since the 2007 crisis in the US, there has been a growing interest in the media research field with respect to the role of the media in the global crisis, given that the news media play a critical role in covering and commenting on social and political crises, natural disasters and financial recession (Cottle, 2009; Chakravartty and Downing, 2010).

Broadly speaking, the media coverage of the economy is important for at least three reasons. Firstly, because it can affect the public agenda. Secondly, because it may influence, in certain circumstances, public attitudes towards existing or proposed policies, especially with respect to the economy (Carroll and McCombs, 2003). Thirdly, it may also affect citizens' behaviour in various sectors of the economy, such as consumer behaviour, financial activities, professional and investment decisions, and their commercial transactions, etc. (Kollmeyer, 2004).

The substantial sovereign debt problems in European countries and a widespread lack of trust in European leadership have hugely affected the global economy (De Grauwe, 2010). It goes without saying that in Europe, the populations of the hardest-hit countries – that is, those of the South, starting with Greece – have been suffering the most from this crisis. But Northern European countries are also increasingly feeling its direct impact. Typically, in a crisis situation, people start looking for information about causes and effects more than they usually do (Coombs and Holladay, 2004). For a majority of citizens the media are the main source of information on the euro crisis. People rely on them to make sense of a subject that is characterized by a fair degree of complexity. In other words, and as always, the media shape the perception of events of many millions of Europeans through the information made available and the way it is accessed (Scheufele and Tewksbury, 2007).

Coverage of the economy does not usually get extensive coverage in comparison to news related to domestic and foreign policy, societal issues (for example, unemployment, health, pensions, education, etc.), and human-interest stories (Kollmeyer, 2004). Not only do the media select the topics they report on, they also are sole judge of the way they will cover them when it comes to angle, intensity, tone, etc. Therefore research into these mechanisms is needed since coverage of the current financial crisis will have a tangible effect on public opinion. Moreover, as de Vreese (2003) has noted, the European financial issues are largely covered from a national perspective.

The media coverage of the Greek and Euro crises is influenced by factors that are related to the coverage of the economy and the depth of the financial crisis. Moreover, a financial crisis is considered as a negative outcome per se, and subsequently the related topics get extensive coverage in contrast to any other financial news story. Additionally, the financial crisis affects the media since the former usually brings major losses of advertising revenues for the media industry. In other words, the EU is a difficult topic for media coverage, especially under conditions of crisis.

In the Greek crisis, the news media were invited to refer to complex technical and political issues with various possible implications for the economy as well as democracy, while in practice, journalists seemed to have a limited knowledge regarding the scope and the dimensions of the crisis. Furthermore, the coverage of the Greek crisis or the Euro crisis may affect financial markets and generate fear among citizens who are worried about the future of their deposits or bonds (Tzogopoulos, 2013). Or, as Hahn and Jaursch (2012, p. 98) have pointed out, "[T]his business journalistic storytelling became 're-Grecized.'" That is why, other than measuring these effects, a content analysis of the news coverage of the debt crisis is required.

This chapter focuses on two studies pertaining to news coverage of the financial crisis in Europe. The first study primarily identifies the frames and metaphors embedded in the coverage of the Euro crisis, while the second one looks at newspaper coverage of the Greek financial crisis, highlighting the respective perceptions of roles and responsibilities among major actors such as the main EU countries, the Eurozone and Greece. These studies differ in their methodologies, and they scrutinize different countries and different time periods. However, the roles and responsibilities of the key actors of the Euro crisis (e.g., European leaders, countries or institutions) in the second study are also an important component in the construction of the frames in the first study of this chapter. After all, both studies analyze the perception of the financial crisis in European newspapers.

Research procedures and results will be presented separately. We shall first look at the framing of the Euro crisis in Flemish and Dutch newspapers, then at the positions of newspapers in France, Germany, Spain and the UK regarding the Greek fiscal crisis. Before going any further, let us briefly discuss the context of the crisis.

The Greek crisis started in October 2009 when the newly elected government came into power and announced a budgetary deficit that proved much greater than generally assumed (12.5 per cent vs. 3.9 per cent) (Hui and Chung, 2011). The debt crisis was mainly blamed on Greece's government and its 'feckless politicians.' However, Greece was not the only Eurozone Member State with a debt problem. While Greece may have been the most problematic case, Ireland, Portugal, Spain, Italy and Cyprus also resorted to harsh austerity measures (Tzogopoulos, 2013). The Greek debt crisis runs parallel with the crisis of the Eurozone as a whole, which also suffers from its failure to regulate financial markets and the fragility of European institutions.

Coverage of international affairs varies over time. In tranquil times, relatively little attention is paid to foreign news as national audiences mostly follow domestic issues. In more turbulent times, international affairs become more pressing and their visibility in news coverage increases (Tzogopoulos, 2013). Research confirms that the more an event concerns 'elite' countries, the likelier it is to become news (Galtung and Ruge, 1965). This is obviously the case for the Euro crisis, especially for Greece. Had the country not been a member of the Eurozone, attention to the debt crisis would have been much lower (Tzogopoulos, 2013). Of course, economic and political developments in the other, so-called PIIGS countries were extensively discussed in the European press. But in sharp contrast with the treatment of other EU countries, rather stereotypical stories of Greek corruption, overspending and bureaucracy were a dime a dozen in the European press (Tzogopoulos, 2013). Although the two studies presented in this chapter differ in scope, there is a large degree of overlap between the Euro and Greek crises in terms of coverage. Overall, and not surprisingly, Greece was depicted as primarily suffering from the Euro crisis (Joris and d'Haenens, 2013a; 2013b).

The following research questions are investigated in both studies covered in this chapter.

Across different types of newspapers rooted in different country contexts, and depending on metaphorical references and frames, various sets of interpretations and expectations can be triggered in the readers' minds.

RQ – STUDY 1: What are the dominant frames in the newspaper coverage of the Euro crisis in Dutch-speaking Belgium and the Netherlands?

RQ – STUDY 2: How (i.e. focus and tone) is the Greek crisis presented by quality newspapers in the larger EU countries?

Specifically, Study 2 assesses whether or not Greece was perceived as a country that deserved help and whether or not the Greek problem was seen as part of a larger problem within the EU or the eurozone. Furthermore, the study looks into the portrayal of the EU as Greece's saviour or as a deeply divided conglomerate of states. Lastly, attention is paid to the policy implications of the Greek problem as well as the prominent actors in the news stories.

THE EURO CRISIS IN FRAMES AND METAPHORS: THEORETICAL VIEWS AND PREVIOUS RESEARCH

The news-framing approach is central to our study of the Euro crisis, based on Entman's widely accepted definition (1993, p. 52): to frame is to "select some aspects of a perceived reality and make them more salient in a communicating context, in such a way to promote a particular problem definition, causal interpretation, moral evaluation, and/or treatment recommendation." Functions of framing are adopted in reasoning devices – that is, underlying, latent components in the text to be discovered by careful reading. Such devices can be manifest, but a central assumption of framing theory is that while a reasoning device may not be spelled out in a news article, it may still be evoked by the frame message as part of the reader's processing and interpretation of the text (Van Gorp, 2005). Besides reasoning devices, this study also looks at framing devices – clearly perceptible elements in a text or in specific linguistic structures, such as metaphors (e.g., the Euro crisis represented as a 'tsunami,' as some sort of disease, etc.), catchphrases and historical examples from which lessons can be drawn (e.g., the Euro crisis compared with the run-up to WWII) (Gamson and Modigliani, 1989). Together, reasoning and framing devices form a frame package.

STUDY 1: THE EURO CRISIS IN FRAMES AND METAPHORS

Metaphorical language is instrumental in the construction of frames in news reporting (see also Millar and Beck, 2004). Moreover, metaphors are essential to the development of thought – they structure thought and define our perception of reality (Lakoff and Johnson, 1980; Lakoff and Turner, 1989). One gains insight into a new and complex situation thanks to a metaphor's reference to another event. Research has shown that use of metaphors is strongly related to the evolution of a crisis. In crisis situations, the use and power of metaphorical language increase, while they decline in more serene times (De Landtsheer, 2009). Of course, intensive use of a metaphor weakens it, as its original meaning tends to become lost.

In a 2013 cross-country study on the use of frames and metaphors in connection with the Euro crisis (co-ordinated by the Reuters Institute for the Study of Journalism), dominant frames with a metaphor at their core were analyzed in ten EU countries: Belgium, Finland, France, Germany, Greece, Italy, The Netherlands, Poland, Spain and the UK (Joris, Puustinen, Sobieraj and d'Haenens, 2015). In each country four newspapers were analyzed: the leading financial business paper, two quality newspapers and the leading popular newspaper or tabloid. In total, 10,492 news articles were analyzed. In each article, the first two metaphors were identified. These metaphors were mainly found in the headline or the lead of the articles, which usually summarized the content of the entire article. The metaphors, as part of the framing devices, were axially clustered into mutually exclusive frame packages (Corbin and Strauss, 2008). Our inventory also included the reasoning devices, from causes of the crisis to possible solutions. Finally, the cross-country study highlighted five dominant frame packages with a metaphor at the core of each frame: war, disease, natural disaster, construction and game.

STUDY 1: PROCEDURE

The relative occurrences of the news frames identified in the cross-country study (Joris, d'Haenens and Van Gorp, 2014) were examined in six Flemish and Dutch newspapers: the financial business newspapers *De Tijd* (FL) and *Het Financieele Dagblad* (NL), the quality newspapers *De Standaard* (FL) and *NRC Handelsblad* (NL), and the popular newspapers *Het Laatste Nieuws* (FL) and *de Telegraaf* (NL). The news stories analyzed were published between 2010 and 2012 within eleven two-week periods centring around major events related to the Euro crisis (see Table 7.1). All articles using the 'Euro' and 'crisis' keywords were selected. In total 1,073 articles were analyzed.

Table 7.1 Description of the periods under study – Study 1 and Study 2

	Period	Dates	Description of event
Study 1	1	4–18 Feb 2010	EU summit of 11–12 February 2010 related to role of European governments and IMF in any intervention
	2	25 Apr – 9 May 2010	Eurozone members and IMF agreement for 100bn euro intervention for Greece
	3	9–23 Dec 2010	EU contract change of 16 December 2010
	4	29 Jul – 12 Aug 2011	ECB asks Italy for more austerity measures
	5	28 Sep – 12 Oct 2011	Greek general strike against austerity measures
	6	20 Oct – 3 Nov 2011	EU Summit of 26–27 October boosting stability fund, extending new aid, and requiring banks to raise new capital
	7	5–19 Nov 2011	Berlusconi's resignation/Monti's appointment and French austerity measures
	8	20–30 Nov 2011	European Commission Green Paper on stability bonds and proposal to bring national budgets under EC control
	9	16–30 May 2012	EU summit of 23 May to boost growth and balance austerity
	10	21 Jun – 5 Jul 2012	Spain formally requests assistance and EU summit on debt crisis
	11	8–22 Jul 2012	Merkel affirmation of need for adherence to budget targets and European monitoring
Study 2	1	21 Mar – 10 May 2010	Debate support mechanism of the EU and IMF
	2	29 Oct – 14 Dec 2012	Negotiations between Greece and troika leading to Medium Term Fiscal Strategy 2013–2016

In order to determine the relative occurrence of each of the news frames and to enable us to compare the newspapers/countries involved, a quantitative content analysis was required. Therefore, the coder indicated whether or not a frame package was present in a given article. In other words, for each article the coder had to determine whether each of the five dominant frames was present by giving a simple yes/no answer. This study did not consider the frequency of a news frame per news article. For instance, a single metaphor referring to war might activate the complete war frame with all related reasoning devices. If several frame elements arose in an article, this was likely to increase the salience of the underlying frame package.

For each article (N = 1,073) the following variables were coded: newspaper name, date of publication, article size and the presence of any of the five frames (0 = absent; 1 = present). Training led to high scores in intercoder reliability (Krippendorff's Alpha), on a sample of ten per cent of the articles (n = 108). Overall, the results were very good for all frames: war (α = .81), disease (α = .92), natural disaster (α = .90), construction (α = .72) and game (α = .72).

STUDY 1: RESULTS

Overall, the Belgian newspapers (54.8%, n = 588) published more articles about the Euro crisis compared to the Dutch newspapers (45.2%, n = 485). Additionally, most articles were published in quality newspapers (43.3%, n = 465), followed by financial business newspapers (42.8%, n = 459). Fewer articles about the Euro crisis were found in the popular newspapers (13.9%, n = 149). In our sample, most articles were published in 2011 (53.3%, n = 572). The numbers of articles in 2010 (23.4%, n = 251) and 2012 (23.3%, n = 250) remained stable.

Articles were mainly medium-sized (44.0%), but there also were a size-able number of short news stories (i.e. less than 500 words) (36.8%). Long articles (more than 1,000 words) were less recurrent in the sample (19.2%). Article length varied significantly across newspapers, $F(2,1070) = 35.056$; $p < .001$. Average article length (1 = less than 500 words, 2 = between 500 and 1,000 words, 3 = more than 1,000 words) was higher in quality newspapers (*Mean* = 2.03), followed by the business newspapers (*Mean* = 1.70). Popular newspapers had the shortest news stories about the debt crisis (*Mean* = 1.58).

In order to determine the prevalence of each of these frames with a view to comparing the newspapers and countries involved, a content analysis was required. All five frame packages were found in the Flemish and Dutch newspapers. The war frame (47.1%) recurred the most, followed by the disease (32.2%) and construction frames (26.4%). The natural disaster (18.9%) and game frames (13.7%) were less present. One in five articles (21.2%) – mostly short news items – did not feature any of the five frame packages. Research (among others, d'Haenens, 2005) already indicated that short articles feature fewer news frames. This finding is again confirmed in the present study, $F(2,1070) = 69,720$; $p < .001$. In a very small number of mostly long articles (0.6%), the five frames occurred together. In other words, some articles included elements from several frames.

Average number of frames per article did not differ significantly between countries ($t(1042,394) = -1,215$; $p = .225$). The Netherlands (*Mean* = 1.42) only had a slightly higher average number of dominant frames per article compared to Belgium (*Mean* = 1.35). Furthermore, the prevalence of the five frames was slightly different between Belgium and The Netherlands. In both countries the dominant frame was the war frame, followed by the disease and construction frames. The fourth-ranking frame was natural disaster in Belgium and game in The Netherlands. The war $(t(1036,257) = 2,497; p < .05)$ and natural disaster $(t(1065,928) = 2.502; p < .05)$ frames had a significantly higher occurrences in Belgian newspapers, while the presence of disease $(t(1012,029) = -2.102; p < .05)$, construction $(t(998,564) = -2.364; p < .05)$ and game $(t(889,437) = -4.126; p < .001)$ frames was significantly higher in Dutch papers. Dominant frames in the Belgian and Dutch articles on the Euro crisis are shown in Figure 7.1.

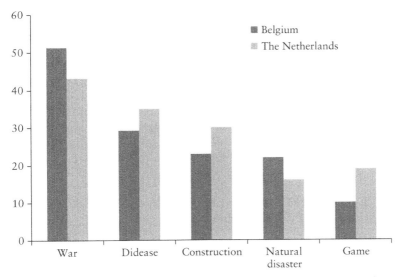

Figure 7.1 Presence of the dominant frames of the euro crisis (in %) – Study 1.

The relative occurrences of the five frames were similar in all three newspaper types (financial, quality and popular newspapers), the dominant frame being the war frame, followed by disease, construction, natural disaster and game. Additionally, no significant differences in presence were found across newspaper types, except for the natural disaster frame, which occurred significantly more in financial newspapers, $F(2,1070) = 3.299; p < .05$. However, a significant difference across newspapers was found in the numbers of frame packages per article, $F(2,1070) = 3.692; p < .05$. Most packages were present in quality newspapers (*Mean* = 1.44), followed by financial (*Mean* = 1.39) and popular newspapers (*Mean* = 1.17). However, articles in popular newspapers were usually shorter than those in quality newspapers and financial newspapers. Hence, controlling for article length, it appears there was no significant difference in frame numbers across newspaper types $(F(2,1069) = 2.182; p = .113)$.

Presence of the five frames over the entire interval of time under scrutiny is one thing. Quite another is the question of whether there is any variation in such presence. And in fact, the war, disease and construction frames peaked in the first two periods and then slightly decreased, except during specific events. The war frame had a new peak throughout the fifth period. Since this fifth period centred around a general strike against austerity measures being enforced in Greece, the prominence of war references is hardly surprising. The disease and construction frames were dominant in the ninth period, during which there was a summit on growth (as opposed to a focus on austerity measures). An explanation for the increase might be that the diagnosis for the illness had changed and another cure was being recommended (disease frame) or that the structure of the Euro was being analyzed anew, which entailed a renovation viewpoint where the EU was concerned (construction frame). The natural disaster and game frames remained fairly stable, except on the occasion of a major EU summit in the sixth period (20 October – 3 November 2011). Research by Joris et al. (2013) points out that news coverage of the Euro crisis peaked at the end of 2011, especially in October and November.

Overall, use of metaphorical language was higher at the start of the Euro crisis, a likely attempt to help readers comprehend a new and unclear situation. Furthermore, the numbers of metaphors or frames increased at the most critical times and decreased when things quieted down.

STUDY 2: INTERNATIONAL NEWSPAPERS AND THE GREEK FISCAL CRISIS

Besides use of frames, the tone of the coverage is central in presenting the issue. Hence the attention paid, among other things, to the tone adopted by newspapers in four major European countries in their coverage of the Greek crisis. In terms of solidarity or lack thereof within the Eurozone, the ways in which they portrayed the crisis indicates whether Greece was perceived as deserving of help, whether it was thought the EU should come up with a bailout plan, etc. Thus this study gives an inkling of the way major Eurozone countries – although each different in strength – may view an economically weak party such as Greece.

STUDY 2: PROCEDURE

This part looks at the ways selected newspapers in the four largest EU countries (France, Germany, Spain and the UK) viewed the Greek fiscal crisis in two different periods. In the first period there was an intense debate in Greece as to whether the country should apply for assistance under the EU support mechanism or seek the IMF's help (21 March to 10 May 2010). The second period is the phase during which exhaustive talks between the Greek government and the Troika led to the Medium Term Fiscal Strategy 2013–2016 (29 October – 14 December 2012). The multi-bill was submitted to the Greek Parliament on November 5 as part of an urgency procedure.

It was passed on 7 November with 153 votes from the Nea Democratia (Conservative party) and PASOK (Socialist party) parliamentary groups, even though all members were not in agreement. The parliamentary verdict gave rise to fiery debate as the package of new measures imposed on Greek society had far-reaching consequences for the labour and pension rights of citizens. The comparative analysis of the above-mentioned periods is based on the assumption that the international image of a small country such as Greece is quite fragile. Hence our central question: When and how did the crisis affect the country image abroad?

The research sample included eight quality newspapers in the four EU countries under scrutiny: *Le Monde* and *Libération*, *Frankfurter Allgemeine Zeitung*, *Süddeutsche Zeitung* (in 2010), and *Die Welt* (in 2012), *El Mundo* and *El Pais*, *The Daily Telegraph* and *The Guardian*, respectively. The sample relates to the two crisis periods under study (21 March – 10 May 2010 and 29 October – 14 December 2012). In addition we looked at the web editions of the above newspapers, analyzing 864 items on Greece and the financial crisis. The unit of analysis was any newspaper article (presented as news) focusing on the Greek economic crisis and the Euro area.

STUDY 2: RESULTS

The dire situation in which Greece found itself seems to have been a thought-provoking subject for the newspapers in our sample. In all four countries there were numerous articles about the Greek crisis. In our sample (N = 864), most articles were published in Germany (39.2%, n = 339), followed by France (21.1%, n = 182) and the UK (20.0%, n = 173). Fewer articles were found in the Spanish press (19.7%, n = 170). Most pieces were written in 2010 (53.7%, n = 464). The second period (2012) yielded 400 articles (46.3%, n = 400).

In both periods, the German newspapers were the most attentive to the Greek crisis, while it was in the UK that publications on this topic increased the most. Between the two periods, interest for the topic clearly waned in the Spanish and German press, while in France, news items ran at about the same level. In 2012, Spain was the country with the least media coverage of the Greek recession – a potential explanation being that the Spanish financial crisis was at its peak in 2012. See in Figure 7.2 the number of articles per country for both periods.

The length of the articles devoted to Greece was mostly short. A significant difference between the four countries was noticed ($X^2(3)$ = 15.214; p < .01). The German press tended to produce longer articles on the Greek crisis, while its French and Spanish counterparts mostly favoured short items. In 2010, the recession and Greece's subsequent ill fame were mainly highlighted through simple stories as well as longer background articles. In 2012, background articles (37.5%) remained at the same levels, but

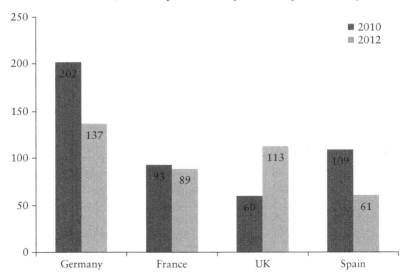

Figure 7.2 Number of articles per country for both periods (in *n*) – Study 2.

editorials dramatically increased (from 0.4% in 2010 to 17.5% in 2012). A small increase was apparent in opinion articles as well (from 14.9% to 18.8%). In both periods, commentaries had a significant presence, which indicates that beyond the simple exposition of 'facts,' the press considered the recession as worthy of in-depth interpretation.

The general tone towards Greece was slightly negative (M = 1.92; SD = .547, based on a three-point scale with one as negative, two as neutral and three as positive). Most articles were neutral or unclear in tone (69.6%). However, more negative articles (19.0%) were identified in the coverage of the Greek crisis than positive ones (11.5%). Sentiment towards Greece differed significantly across countries ($F(3,860)$ = 7.438; p < .001). The UK was most negative about the Greek debt problems, followed by Spain and Germany, while France was significantly more positive. Between the two periods under study, a significant difference was found as well ($t(840,110)$ = –3.907; p < .001). Overall the general tone of the articles was more negative in 2010 than in 2012.

This finding was also confirmed by answers to the question as to whether Greece was portrayed as deserving of external help. There were positive assessments, although they were limited. Comparing the two periods, a contraction of negativity was noticed, giving way mainly to voices of neutrality. In 2010, the negative views (51.5%) outnumbered the positive ones (28.4%), indicating Greece was seen as rather less than deserving of the help of its European partners or other third parties, while in 2012, portrayals were more positive (21.5%) than negative (11.8%).

In our introduction we noted that Greece was not the only nation to blame for the debt crisis. Our results show that the newspapers mostly described the Greek problem as part of a much larger one involving all of the Eurozone or EU (65.0%). The number of articles placing the cause of the Greek crisis squarely with the European Union was higher in 2010 (67.9%) than in 2012 (61.8%). This is in line with the findings of Study 1, which indicate Greece's debt problem was viewed as part of the Euro crisis as a whole.

Since Greece's problem was viewed as being part of a larger, pan-European issue, one might expect the EU to be among its main rescuers. At the beginning of the financial crisis the international press failed to plainly state whether Greece should find its salvation within the EU. The newspapers were almost equally divided on this, with over one half (53.5%) of the articles answering in the affirmative while almost as many either offered no opinion or rejected outright the EU rescue scenario (46.6%). In 2012, while expenses to Greece such as loan repayment were skyrocketing without visible results, journalists became even more cautious about the EU stepping in. Negative or ambivalent approaches to the issue were on the increase (52.8%).

This study also aimed to analyze whether the EU was portrayed as a strong coalition of nations or a loose group with differing or even conflicting interests. The international press depicted the European Union as a coalition mostly based on consensus (84.4%). In both periods, coverage of European affairs mostly gave the impression that there was little disagreement among EU Member States. Even more impressive, as time went by this image became stronger in the news stories under scrutiny. In 2010, 78.9% of the articles described the EU as a solid coalition. In 2012, the figure had shot up to 90.8%.

The Greek debt crisis led to a large number of policy measures. A majority of articles (63.5%) referred to positive or negative policy implications such as the multi-billion Euro austerity packages, accompanied by higher taxes and higher unemployment to tackle Greece's fiscal imbalances. Additionally, the fiscal crisis was interlinked to the common currency and the participation of Greece in the Eurozone since the country had to comply with the terms of the Stability Pact. In 2010 (65.3%), more articles mentioned policy measures than in 2012 (61.5%), but they also pointed out the need of a new potential 'haircut' of the Greek debt as well as the societal impact of the subsequent austerity measures on the Greek people.

Finally, the prominent actors in the Greek crisis were identified. In 2010, German Chancellor Angela Merkel (28.9%) was everywhere in related news items, followed by Greek Prime Minister George Papandreou (20.0%). In 2012, Merkel's towering presence faded (7.3%) while Greek Prime Minister Antonis Samaras rose to prominence (9.8%).

CONCLUSIONS

The news coverage of the Euro crisis has produced highly mediated portrayals of Europe, its institutions, its Member States and its common currency.

The Euro crisis put a lot of pressure on politicians and policy-makers faced with difficult decisions described as a choice between austerity and stimulus. Although Study 1 and Study 2 differed in scope and methods, some general conclusions can be drawn. Mostly, the newspapers covered the Euro crisis by painting a picture of chaos, uncertainty and fear. Much was made of the image of bankrupt Greece and a rather unhealthy EU, as shown by the length of the news stories. Extended press coverage of the Greek problem evidenced the severity of the financial crisis. Judging from both studies, the press in the countries under study published a large number of articles about the debt crisis.

Five dominant frame packages were identified in the press coverage of the Low Countries: war, disease, construction, natural disaster and game, in order of importance. The war frame proved to be the most frequently used frame. Consequently, the crisis is perceived as a problem caused by the financial markets or the European leaders, who are chiefly self-interested. In contrast, two other frequently used frames, disease and natural disaster, are framed in our culture as phenomena occurring without anyone's specific responsibility. These frames suggest no one is guilty for the Euro crisis as it arrived unpredictably. When the construction frame is resorted to, the audience might be afraid the Euro zone will collapse, referring to a domino effect. Furthermore, as the game frame, which normalizes the severity of the Euro crisis, is the least frequently used frame, we may suggest the crisis is mainly covered as a threatening problem for European society. At the beginning of the debt crisis, the occurrence of the five dominant news frames was higher, indicative of an attempt to bring real clarity to this new and complex situation.

Furthermore, tone of coverage was more negative towards Greece in 2010 than in 2012, with a higher number of articles opining that the country did not deserve external help. In terms of Eurozone solidarity, it was encouraging that the tone became more positive in 2012. The number of articles portraying the country as deserving of help increased in the second study period as well. However, as the crisis evolved and support did not lead to satisfactory results, the perceived role of the EU as a Greece's saviour lost favour, although a positive trend was observed in that a consensus grew over the notion of a joint approach towards solving 'the Greek problem.' Overall, while the costs for Greece were mounting with no end in sight, the dominant view was that the European Union still must support the Greek government to avoid even worse problems.

Finally, although the position of the Belgian and Dutch newspapers towards the Greek crisis was not analyzed in this chapter, we might expect the Dutch press to favour the UK's austerity stance, in line with the Dutch government's position on the matter. The Belgian newspapers, on the contrary, would probably take mitigating circumstances into account and opt for stimulus programs in an approach not unlike that of France.

In all, this study did not show a shared representation of the unfolding financial crisis across countries, newspapers and periods through the lenses of the newspapers under study. Divergence in the country-specific frames and tones or in the understanding of the complex causes of the crisis, responsibilities of a wide variety of relevant players as well as different approaches to address the crisis – what went wrong, who's to blame and why – points in the direction of a fragmented, domestic public sphere rather than illustrating a single European public sphere. Attention towards the financial crisis also differs greatly across newspaper types. Business and quality newspapers aimed at the political and financial elites clearly devote more attention to the crisis than the popular press. This divergence or dissonance in the representations of the Euro crisis in the newspaper coverage also implies a high potential for different identifications with the European project and European integration.

REFERENCES

Aalberg, T. and Curran, J. (2012) *How Media Inform Democracy: A Comparative Approach*. London: Routledge.

Carroll, C.E. and McCombs, M. (2003) Agenda-setting effects of business news on the public's images and opinions about major corporations. *Corporate Reputation Review*, 6 (1). pp. 36–46.

Chakravartty, P. and. Downing, J.D.H. (2010) Media, technology, and the global financial crisis. *International Journal of Communication*, 4. pp. 693–95.

Coombs, W.T. and Holladay, S.J. (2004) Reasoned action in crisis communication: An attribution theory-based approach to crisis management. In: Millar, D.P. and Heath, R.L. (eds.) *Responding to Crisis Communication Approach to Crisis Communication* (pp. 95–115). Hillsdale, NJ: Lawrence Erlbaum Associates.

Corbin, J. and Strauss, A.L. (2008) *Basics of Qualitative Research*. Thousand Oaks, CA: Sage.

Cottle, S. (2009) *Global Crisis Reporting: Journalism in the Global Age*. Maidenhead, UK: Open University Press.

De Grauwe, P. (2010) Crisis in the Eurozone and how to deal with it. *CEPS Policy Briefs*, 204. pp. 1–5.

De Landtsheer, C. (2009) Collecting Political Meaning from the Count of Metaphor. In: Musolff, A. and Zinken, J. (eds.) *Metaphor and Discourses*. London: Routledge.

De Vreese, C.H. (2003) *Framing Europe: Television News and European Integration*. Amsterdam: Aksant.

d'Haenens, L. (2005) Euro-vision: the portrayal of Europe in the quality press. *Gazette: The International Journal of Communication Studies*, 67(5). pp. 419–40.

Entman, R.M. (1993) Framing: Toward clarification of a fractured paradigm. *Journal of Communication*, 43. pp. 51–58.

Galtung, J. and Ruge, M.H. (1965) The structure of foreign news. *Journal of Peace Research*, 2 (1). pp. 64–91.

Gamson, W.A. and Modigliani, A. (1989) Media discourse and public opinion on nuclear power: A constructionist approach. *American Journal of Sociology*, 95(1). pp. 1–37.

Hahn, O. and Jaursch, J. (2012) Telling the Greek story of Europe and the bull trap: How U.S. correspondents attribute news value to a topic-oriented country's status within the Eurozone's debt crisis. *Journal of Applied Journalism and Media Studies*, 1 (1). pp. 97–113.

Hui, C-H. and Chung, T-K. (2011) Crash Risk of the euro in the Sovereign Debt Crisis of 2009–2010. Journal of Banking & Finance, 35. pp. 2945–55.

Joris, W. and d'Haenens, L. (2013a) *The Euro Crisis, Media Coverage, and Perceptions of Europe within the EU*. Report on Belgium. Oxford: Reuters Institute for the Study of Journalism. Retrieved from: https://reutersinstitute.politics.ox.ac.uk/fileadmin/documents/discussion/National_Report_Belgium.pdf.

Joris, W. and d'Haenens, L. (2013b) *The Euro Crisis, Media Coverage, and Perceptions of Europe within the EU*. Report on the Netherlands. Oxford: Reuters Institute for the Study of Journalism. Retrieved from: https://reutersinstitute.politics.ox.ac.uk/fileadmin/documents/discussion/National_Report_The_Netherlands.pdf

Joris, W., d'Haenens, L., Van Gorp, B. and Vercruysse, T. (2013) De eurocrisis in het nieuws. Een framinganalyse van de verslaggeving in Vlaamse kranten. *Tijdschrift voor Communicatiewetenschap*, 41(2). pp. 162–83.

Joris, W., Puustinen, L., Sobieraj, K. and d'Haenens, L. (2015) The battle for the Euro: Metaphors and frames in the Euro crisis news. In: Picard, R. (ed.) *The Euro Crisis in the media. Journalistic coverage of economic crisis and European Institutions*. Oxford: Oxford University Press.

Kollmeyer, C.J. (2004) Corporate interests: How the news media portray the economy. *Social Problems*, 51 (3). pp. 432–52.

Lakoff, G. and Johnson, M. (1980) *Metaphors We Live by*. Chicago: University of Chicago Press.

Lakoff, G. and Turner, M. (1989) *More than Cool Reason: A Field Guide to Poetic Metaphor*. Chicago: University of Chicago Press.

Millar, F.E. and Beck, D.B. (2004) Metaphors of crisis. In: Millar, D.P. and. Heath, R.L. (eds.) *Responding to Crisis. A Rhetorical Approach to Crisis Communication*. Hillsdale, NJ: Lawrence Erlbaum Associates.

Papathanassopoulos, S. and Negrine, R. (2011) *European Media: Structures, Politics and Identity*. Cambridge: Polity.

Scheufele, D.A. and Tewksbury, D. (2007) Framing, agenda setting, and priming: The evolution of three media effects models. *Journal of Communication*, 57. pp. 9–20.

Schudson, M. (2008) *Why Democracies Need An Unlovable Press*. Cambridge: Polity Press.

Tzogopoulos, G. (2013) *The Greek Crisis in the Media: Stereotyping in the International Press*. Farnham, UK: Ashgate Publishing.

Van Gorp, B. (2005) Where is the frame? Victims and intruders in the Belgian press coverage of the asylum issues. *European Journal of Communication*, 20. pp. 485–508.

Zografova, Y., Bakalova, D. and Mizova, B. (2012) Media reporting patterns in Europe: The cases of construction of the EU and Reform Treaty. *Javnost – The Public*, 19 (1). pp. 67–84.

8 Gender and Media in Times of Crises

Claudia Padovani and Karen Ross

INTRODUCTION

Much of the discussion about the current financial crisis and, more broadly, the political and cultural crises in Europe largely ignores issues of gender and of media. At the same time, the media have the potential to act as a force for good in shaping the agenda around potential resolutions, even as they are experiencing their own sectoral crises. Issues of gender and equality are then added to this mix.

Although critical junctures are considered by some to offer opportunities for radical change, including the potential to advance equality between women and men, little effort has been made to reflect on the role and responsibility of the media in favouring such transformations, neither within the media sector itself nor in society at large. Looking at contemporary Europe, we ask two fundamental questions: Are the media implementing gender-aware approaches in addressing these crises, including the ones occurring in their own sector, and what does the current situation of women's presence and roles in European media organizations suggest as far as challenges and opportunities towards better gender equality in the region? In this chapter, we interrogate the findings of a research project conducted in twenty-eight European countries, set out within the context of a broader reflection on why the media should promote gender equality in times of crisis and on a redefinition of the institutional role of the media in democratic societies.

FRAMING CRISIS, MEDIA AND GENDER

As long ago as 1976, Edgar Morin suggested the widespread and vague use of the term 'crisis,' with its associations to many areas of human experience – crisis of society, humanity, civilization and so on – prevented a proper understanding of real social problems. If everything were more or less a crisis, then the meaning of the term became devalued, and the very notion of crisis as an extreme and highly damaging social phenomenon was itself in crisis. Morin also recalled how, in ancient Greece, "*krisis*" signified *"le moment decisive, dans l'evolution d'un processus incertain, qui permet le diagnostic*" (the decisive moment in the evolution of an uncertain process, which allows diagnosis), while today it is mostly used to indicate "indecision." (Morin, 1976, p. 149; see also Koselleck and Richter, 2006) In this chapter, we would like to revive the original meaning of the term, and look at the nexus between media, crisis and gender in Europe today as a decisive moment in media transformation and a meaningful way of discussing institutional media crisis in its relation to democratic norms and values, as suggested in Chapter 1.

Current media changes and challenges can be positioned in the context of plural critical junctures, hence our interest in considering if the media are actually recognized and invited to play a meaningful role, as social actors and stakeholders, in framing and possibly overcoming such crises. More specifically, we look at if and how the media are implementing gender-aware approaches in addressing these crises, including the ones occurring in their own sector. We elaborate the crisis concept as we develop our argument. We start from a specific focus on the ongoing economic and financial crisis and its implications for women and men. We then discuss the interrelations between crisis and media beyond the financial situation to include gender equality as one element of media crisis and a sustained challenge to media's role in fostering democratic values. We conclude by describing the realities of gender employment and inequalities in decision-making in media industries across Europe. The 'diagnosis' concerning gender inequalities in the media is informed by the findings of one particular research project but influenced by decades of research on the broader topic. And it is used as a starting point to suggest ways forward to enable women and men to achieve their potential and to assist in addressing specific aspects of media and crisis while reasserting the media's role in fostering and promoting democratic values. Our final aim is to open up a space for thinking about the gender dimension of media institutions' crises and how improving gender equality can be seen as a means to overcoming multiple societal crises.

THE GENDER DIMENSION OF THE ECONOMIC CRISIS

Several reports have been produced over the past few years, by EU institutions such as the Parliament and Commission as well as by NGOs such as the European Women's Lobby and the scholarly community, to consider the gender implications of the current economic and financial crisis. These reports respond to the fact that "despite the growing debate over the causes of the crisis, less attention is paid to its material impacts, and very little to gender considerations." (Vertova, 2012, p. 123)

Many contributions point to the need for the adoption of a gender-sensitive perspective to assess the impact of the on-going crisis on gender equity and enhancing women's rights and potential (Antonopoulos, 2009;

EWL and Oxfam, 2010; EWL, 2012; European Parliament, 2011; European Commission, 2012).

What emerges from these reports is that, contrary to expectations, the current economic crisis is affecting women more than men because of its depth and duration. Whilst financial markets now appear calmer in comparison to a couple of years ago, industrial outputs in Europe are 10.8 per cent below their 2008 peak and the expected EU GDP in 2013 constituted a 0.2 per cent decrease following a contraction of 0.4 per cent in the previous year. This situation inhibits the private investment, crucial to recovery, which has seen a drop of 14.5 per cent between 2007 and 2011.

The situation has also had a significant impact on employment rates (unemployment in the first half of 2014 was averaging 10.7 per cent, ranging from 4.3 per cent in Austria to 26.1 per cent in Spain), real wages (with declines of up to 12 per cent in Greece and Lithuania) and household incomes (Library of the European Parliament, 2013). Men seem to have been more severely affected in the early years of the crisis and this can be partly explained by the structure of EU labour markets, with the immediate effects of job losses and redundancies hitting male-dominated sectors such as manufacturing and construction.

However, as the crisis deepened, so have inequalities in the workplace, particularly affecting temporary workers, young people and low-skilled workers, many of whom are women. Moreover, subsequent anti-crisis measures have moved towards fiscal consolidation because of pressures to restore public finance. As a consequence, while women still earn less than men with an average EU-pay gap of 16.5 per cent in 2010 (partly explained by the specificities of the sectors where they are employed and partly by the roles attributed to women in different cultures), economists expect female unemployment to worsen because the sectors in which they are a majority of the workforce – health and social care, education and public services – are now being particularly affected by the recession.

Indeed, women are not only vulnerable as employees in the public and third sectors but also because they are the primary beneficiaries of the services these sectors provide. Cuts in spending on care and social services are having a disproportionate effect on women as care-giving is again forced into the private sphere of unpaid work. Finally, these adverse trends in women's experiences are accompanied by rising levels of domestic violence against them as the crisis puts pressure and strain on families and relationships (Antonopoulos, 2009; EWL and Oxfam, 2010; WSL, 2012).

Overall, then, the financial crisis is worsening the conditions of women's lives and their potential and actual participation in the labour market, forcing them back into 'traditional' roles of unwaged care-giver and family support. Precarious working conditions, increasing discrimination in the labour market with subsequent shifts to informal (unpaid) work, rising levels of poverty, reduced access to services and rising levels of domestic violence, accompanied by cuts in vital support services, are all highly visible signs of the deep recession taking place across Europe (EWL and Oxfam, 2010; EWL, 2012).

As a result, much of the progress that had been achieved in terms of gender equity in different sectors and levels of society has now stalled and risks being eroded (European Parliament, 2011; 2012). Similarly, gender stereotypes that position women within a narrow range of public and private roles are once again playing a role in constraining the promotion of women's rights and their empowerment, which are, on the contrary, crucial to economic and societal recovery. From the view of many commentators, the media are seen as key players in the production and reproduction of negative gender 'norms' (Elston, 2010; Vertova, 2012).

CRISIS OR CRISES?

Interestingly, most discussions and reports assume crisis as a non-problematic concept. They mostly refer to the economic crisis or the crisis centred around public finance and sovereign debt issues resulting from the financial crisis that erupted between 2007 and 2008, when the sub-prime mortgage debacle in the United States had a disastrous and global impact with different consequences for Western economies and those of other parts of the world.

Where attempts to conceptualize the crisis are made, they mainly acknowledge the time factor characterizing an economic crisis, structured around phases: the first one related to the 2008 credit crunch and the financial-services sector, and the subsequent, still on-going phase with austerity policies adopted by individual countries to respond to public indebtedness, often resulting from public finance disasters that occurred during the previous phase. As a study invited by the European Parliament notes: "The victims of unemployment during the first wave of the recession may fare better in subsequent phases, while those who were initially 'insulated' may find themselves exposed." (2011, p. 10f)

One of the few attempts to contextualize the crisis more broadly is offered by Oxfam International, in a paper titled "Gender Perspectives on the *Global* Economic Crisis." "The current crisis, which originated in the financial economies of the North, does not exist in isolation, and needs to be understood as the latest element in a complex web of sudden onset shocks and longer-term traumas that affect individuals and their families in developing countries (…)" (Oxfam 2010, p. 3), as it has become clear, for European families as well.

Similarly, Antonopoulos states: "[T]he global economic downturn has exacerbated effects from other crises manifest in food insecurity, poverty, and increasing inequality." (2009, p. 1) It seems that only when the European situation is put in the broader global context a more sophisticated understanding of the challenges emerging from multi-dimensional crises can be offered. However, hardly any attempt has been made to connect, at a conceptual as well as at empirical level, the different decisive moments with which we are now confronted.

Citizens' detachment from politics and governing institutions has become an issue of growing concern as it may undermine the very foundations of democratic life. Global and European security are put at risk by several factors, including environmental[1] and geopolitical issues, such as energy, water and resource control. Moreover, socio-economic inequalities[2] are growing and causing social unrest in many regions, as witnessed by developments after the Arab Spring and ongoing conflicts across Europe, the Middle East and Africa.

In this context the crisis of democracy, the crisis of capitalism and the crisis of civilization itself appear as recurrent yet separated themes in public and media discourse. While Morin cautions against the casual use of the term, we nonetheless need to recognize that "crisis is a structuring concept" and "by labeling a situation as one of crisis, one declares the presence of a threat to the prevailing order." (Raboy and Dagenais, 1992, p. 5)

In this context we need to highlight the role of the media in relation to existing crises and to be fully aware of how powerful the media are as agents of social communication by which crises are framed and made meaningful to the public. The media are crucial in shaping our understanding of ongoing recession dynamics as well as the multiple and interlinked 'uncertain processes' taking place in the political, institutional, cultural and social realms. This is because journalists and media outlets claim to reflect the public's concerns as well as disseminate political responses to the crises. At the same time, we also need to consider the critical situations media organizations themselves are experiencing, not only in their attempts to respond to technological, commercial and political challenges but also in their effort to maintain a democratic function in fostering values such as truthfulness, freedom and responsibility but also inclusion, diversity and participation of all citizens, women and men.

In the words of Ogrizek and Guillery: "Crisis is confusion, a trial, a break, an opportunity. All of this is true." (1999: xiii) The media can therefore be seen as both part of the problem but also, more positively, part of the solution. But can we see them acting as meaningful agents in addressing the challenges deriving from critical uncertainties and in supporting necessary decisions?

MEDIA AND/IN CRISIS AND GENDER

The media, as a sector, scarcely appear in the documents and reports we mention above, which have dealt with the gendered implications of the current recession. When they are cited, they tend to be seen as elements of an immediate response to specific aspects of the economic crisis[3] and what tends to be highlighted is their complicity in perpetuating gender stereotypes, thus undermining the achievements that have already been made and restricting further progress, including working towards gender equality.

More generally, the media do not seem to be considered as relevant stakeholders, nor understood as an economic sector in their own right, in spite of the many crises they are experiencing. They are in crisis as institutions and epistemic agents in their national contexts; they are challenged in their democratic functions by corporate logics; they are exposed to pressure by the technological and social transformations that characterize the new digital and convergent media environment; and the economic crisis is having a profound impact on media outlets, with structures disintegrating and growing unemployment in the sector even as new initiatives, mostly online operations, are being created.

Furthermore, we argue the complex relationship between crises, media and gender, and the ways in which each impact on the others, has not been adequately appreciated. Nor has attention been paid to the long-term crisis in the sector, which is exemplified by persistent gender inequalities in media content, operations, employment and decision-making structures. In Morin's terms, we can regard media outlets and their gender-(un)aware operations, as the the evolution of an uncertain process, which makes it possible today, on the basis of numerous accounts, to identify the nature of an illness by examining the symptoms (the diagnostic). Such symptoms have been described and analysed through decades of research and monitoring efforts, upon which we now set the scene, today, for a decisive moment[4].

Worldwide collaboration in the four iterations of the Global Media Monitoring Project since 1995 have revealed persistent inequalities over time, together with the very slow pace of change in women's visibility in the news. Their presence in the genre, both as producers and subjects of news, has increased from seventeen per cent in the mid-'90s to twenty-four per cent in 2010 (GMMP, 2010). Stereotypical and disrespectful representations, particularly in advertising, have been at the core of a number of reports, including recent statements by the EU Commission ("Breaking Gender Stereotypes in the Media," 2012).

In 1991 and 2001, the International Federation of Journalists (IFJ) conducted surveys among journalists' unions in thirty-nine nations to determine women' status in newsrooms and their membership and leadership in unions. The 2001 report for IFJ (Peters, 2001) noted that in Europe, women represented forty per cent of the journalists in newsrooms, but only held three per cent of the decision-making posts. The glass-ceiling effect in European newsrooms has been documented by any number of European case studies (see, for example, Capecchi, 2006) and by transnational investigations (IWMF, 2011), showing an ongoing trend of discrimination towards women in media organizations, where their occupation of merely one-third of top managerial positions seems to constitute a gendered 'rule' across regions and cultures.

These findings and statistics are clear symptoms of a crisis in the media, namely that of the sector's inability to fully perform its democratic role in giving voice to all sections of society, both men and women, and to foster societal transformations that would favour pluralism, diversity and gender equity, especially in times of crises. We highlight the fact that this specific component of media crisis is seldom mentioned when discussing the challenges faced by the media in relation to the decline of traditional forms of consumption and the switch to online content and platforms.

We also argue this lack of attention is all the more problematic since gender equality has long been recognized as a core component of sustainable and innovative knowledge societies, particularly through the adoption of gender-equality plans and guidelines (EU Strategy for equality between women and men 2010–2015). Suggestions have been made to implement mainstreaming gender across policy domains, to integrate gender-equality promotion in crisis-relieving policy-making, to address sectoral segregation and strengthen the position of women in political and corporate sectors, and to enhance women's participation in decision-making[5]. But what does the current situation of women's presence and roles in European media organizations suggest as far as challenges and opportunities for change in times of crises? Are European media outlets, both public-service broadcasters and private organizations, recognizing the decisive moment of crisis and promoting gender equality, thus attempting to overcome this crisis?

CRISIS AND CONTROL: GENDER AND POWER IN EUROPE'S MEDIA INDUSTRY

Part of the 'benefit' of a world in crisis is that it forces us to consider radical alternatives to the status quo, ways of being, doing and thinking that could produce better and more equitable outcomes for all. But in order to imagine the unimaginable, we must first understand the reality on the ground. We argue that so far, there has been little theoretical or empirical consideration of the ways in which crisis, media and gender work as forces on and with each other.

One way to begin to understand something of how this particular set of dynamics play out is to look at the ways in which women experience the media industry as an employer and the potential impact a crisis culture can have on their career development. We explore this through a discussion of a recent, EU-funded project that was led by the authors and was undertaken during 2012–13.[6] The work identified the extent to which women were involved in the decision-making apparatus of some of Europe's major media institutions, including all the public-service broadcasters across the EU28 (thirty-nine in total), together with sixty large-scale private companies.

We also interviewed sixty-three women media practitioners across the nations surveyed. The project aimed to assess the extent to which one of the key aspirations of the Beijing Platform for Action – Section J.2: to increase the participation and access of women to expression and decision-making in and through the media and new technologies of communication – was being achieved. It also explored the existence of gender-equality policies and action plans in the same ninety-nine organizations.

Lastly, the project included a media monitoring aspect in which popular TV channels were monitored in each country, with a focus on the extent to which women and men were selected to appear in a variety of fact-based and entertainment shows and where decisions on who to include were taken by programme and production teams. The visibility of women as media practitioners, including as journalists, presenters and hosts, was also monitored. Given the importance of the media in framing world events, including the global crisis and the ongoing and well-documented inequalities that exist between women and men (and within and between other groups), a study that brought together media and gender under the same spotlight was extremely timely.

The remainder of this chapter considers the primary findings of the study and draws conclusions about the impact of crisis management on women's potential as change agents, arguing the irresistible push towards the safe and familiar, which is a routine response to crisis, too often results in a reluctance to break the traditional mould of male managers. This means the distinctive contributions and perspectives women bring to the decision-making and problem-solving process, given what is already known about gender-based differences in management styles, are considerably reduced, with the consequence that crisis conditions are extended when they could have been alleviated.

FINDINGS[7]

The principal finding from the first part of the study, the survey of ninety-nine organizations, shows the continued under-representation of women in decision-making positions, despite the increasing numbers of women graduating from media programmes and entering the industry. Out of 3,376 senior positions that were coded from the total sample, comprising both employees and board members, 1,037 were occupied by women (thirty per cent). At the most senior level, such as CEO or President, this percentage decreases to sixteen per cent. Just over one in five (twenty-one per cent) Chief Operating Officer positions, such as Director-General or Editor-in-Chief, were occupied by women (EIGE, 2013, Section 2, p. 26).

Public-service broadcasters were more likely to recruit women to senior positions than private companies. As far as gender-equality plans, diversity policies and codes are concerned, just under half the organizations in the survey have some kind of equality policy that at least mentions gender, although less than one in five organizations have a policy explicitly focused on gender (Section 2, p. 37). A similar number have formal mechanisms in place to monitor their gender and/or equality policies and nine organizations have an Equality or Diversity Department. In terms of practical measures, the most frequently mentioned measure is related to sexual harassment, although even then, fewer than twenty-five per cent of organizations mentioned this, followed by a dignity at work policy (nineteen per cent) and a maternity leave policy (seventeen per cent) (Section 2, p. 40). Only six organizations support structured training programmes for women, although slightly more (nine per cent) provide equality-awareness training for staff. In terms of sectoral differences, public-service broadcasters were significantly more likely to have formal gender and equality structures than private-sector organizations.

Interestingly, there was no clear correlation between the existence of gender-equality policies and high numbers of women in senior positions. We suggest this is because workplace culture, informed by a particular leadership approach, exerts a strong influence on the extent to which equality issues are taken seriously. Some organizations have high numbers of women in decision-making roles but very little evidence of a gender-equality framework, and we have no way of knowing how or even whether women's senior status carries real authority or whether more cynical management strategies are in play that provide the veneer of equality but power still resides in male hands at the very top of organizations.

At one level, more women in senior positions, regardless of their actual power or authority, can only be seen as a good thing as it suggests a movement in the right direction and that women are at least in a position to be able to take advantage of promotion opportunities when they arise. However, the testimonies of many of the women who were interviewed for the project suggests that even when they do attain senior positions, they are always in a minority, they are easily picked off and they often have to conform to 'male' ways of working in order to survive, let alone thrive. The following two comments exemplify the frustration many women articulated about their working lives.

> If you are surrounded by men, you tend to take their standards, rules and agendas for granted. And believe me, they would be different in mixed teams.
>
> –Katharina

> If a woman is really determined to cross the border into "male" areas … she must adjust at least partly to the rules of the men's club.
>
> –Erzebet

What most women identified as both the problem and the solution was the commitment (or not) at the top of their organizations to pursue a gender-equal workplace. If we accept that most working environments are created and sustained by the leadership team at the top, then the importance they give to equality issues will determine the cascading commitment, or otherwise, down the chain of command, including the place of equality within the broader human-resources framework. Without the existence of robust gender-equality policies and practices that are embedded as an integral part of an organization's human resources policy and are regularly monitored and actioned when failures or breaches are identified, then women are always vulnerable to discrimination and unequal treatment.

Women are mostly overlooked for promotion for reasons other than their competence, including their gender (discrimination on grounds of sex) and their perceived inability to take on new opportunities because of their domestic and/or family responsibilities (discrimination on grounds of family or caring role). Sometimes women do choose to prioritise family over career but this is often because workplace cultures make it impossible to achieve a work-life balance, which benefits both the individual and the employer.

Very little attention has been paid so far in investigating not only the existence but also the active and sustained implementation and monitoring of equality policies, including those focused on gender. Whilst there have been numerous reports and guidance about fairer representation in terms of media content, there has been much less work focused on issues of employment and promotion. This study has identified, again, a systemic problem of the under-valuing of what women can contribute to enhancing the prospects and growth of the European media industry at a time of crisis. Disavowing the talents and experiences of half the workforce does not seem like sensible management practice and, as several recent studies have shown, companies that do recruit and promote women into senior positions also tend to be the ones that are prospering (BiS, 2011; CED, 2012; McKinsey & Co., 2012).

CONCLUSIONS

Earlier in this chapter, we suggested much of the discussion about the current financial crisis and, more broadly, political and cultural crises in Europe largely ignore issues of both gender and media. At the same time, we argued the media have the potential to act as a force for good in shaping the agenda around potential resolutions, even as they are experiencing their own sectoral crises. One positive feature of critical junctures is the opportunity – because there is nothing to lose – to think more creatively about change.

When applied to the media sector, this thinking could indeed produce a less risk-averse management approach, which takes a chance on recruiting and promoting more women as potential agents for change. Unfortunately, from the findings of our own recent study, this does not appear to be the route the European media industry has followed nor seems likely to follow in the future. At the national, regional and global level, policies and guidance abound on how to improve and enhance women's representation in decision-making across all sectors, within cultural, economic, judicial and political structures.

The problem has been known for decades and there already exist a range of actions that could be taken to address the problem. The study discussed in this chapter adds specific data and knowledge from the European context, including specifying more indicators as benchmarks to guide future political action and media operations[8]. But instead of seeing the current *krisis* as an opportunity to rethink the existing business models and imagine something better able to respond to the complexities of critical times, most organizations – as much the media sector as other economic sectors – seem to be involved in a process of retrenchment, less rather than more willing to develop alternative strategies or encourage new voices to be heard. There seems little will to make change happen despite the palpable failures of the business-as-usual model.

In difficult times, it is tempting to take a risk-averse strategy and maintain the status quo, but we argue that now is in fact the best time to make the kinds of radical change that will empower women, which many have advocated, as the old ways of doing things are clearly not working. While more women in decision-making positions in media industries (or indeed any industry), alongside better and more balanced gender representation in media content, cannot and should not be seen as the only solution to the current media institutional crisis, women's continued marginalization from the apparatus of power is, we argue, definitely part of the problem. Gender equality should not be seen as an issue only for the 'good times' but rather a core component and a baseline for decisive moments towards ideating and implementing policies and programs to overcome European societal crises.

If the media are part of the problem, then implementing principles of inclusion of diverse voices, balance and fairness in perspectives, and participation of women and men alike in their very operations may be part of the solution. This may indeed be a concrete move to facilitate and foster a redefinition of the institutional role the media are to perform in democratic societies.

NOTES

1. See the latest International Panel on Climate Change report "Climate Change 2013: The Physical Science Basis," released in September 2013. Available at http://www.ipcc.ch/report/ar5/wg1/#.Ukf89xa563A.
2. See Piketty, 2014; Rosenvallon and Goldhammer, 2013.
3. As in the European Parliament's study titled "Gender aspects of the economic downturn and financial crisis" where, in discussing the need to support couples and single parents to navigate the recession in the UK, reference is made to the need to "Encourage men to make more use of their entitlements to parental leave and other working-time adjustments … and of flexible working options available at their workplace … [R]esearch shows that for (interventions) to be effective action is needed on multiple fronts: information campaigns in the *media* and by social partners at the workplace targeted at men and their employers." (2011, p. 120).
4. Also restated by the recently launched UNESCO Global Alliance for Media and Gender: to act today, more promptly and effectively than in the past, to guarantee gender equality in and through the media. See http://www.unesco.org/new/en/

communication-and-information/crosscutting-priorities/gender-and-media/
global-forum-on-media-and-gender/homepage/.

5. A Directive establishing a procedural quota, proposed by the European Commission in 2012 and voted by the European Parliament in November 2013, is currently being discussed by the Council of the EU.

6. Study on Area J of the Beijing Platform for Action: Women and the Media in the European Union (EIGE/2012/OPER/07).

7. Data in this section refer to the final Report of the study, *Advancing gender equality in decision-making in media organizations*, available at http:// eige.europa.eu/content/document/advancing-gender-equality-in-decision-making-in-media-organisations-report.

8. It is worth mentioning the policy relevance of a research project, like the one discussed in this chapter, conducted in the context of the Council of the European Union that took place in June 2013, on behalf of the Irish Presidency of the Union and the European Institute for Gender Equality. A primary aim of the study was to identify a set of key indicators through which media organizations could be benchmarked to identify the extent to which they were pursuing a gender-equal agenda in the workplace. As a consequence of the findings, three indicators were indeed developed, one relating to the proportion of women in senior positions, one relating to the proportion of women on company boards and the final one relating to the existence of gender-equality policies and actions, including mechanisms for monitoring, implementation and action (EIGE, 2013, p. 49). These indicators were subsequently taken up and formally adopted by the European Council. Though it is not quite clear how they will be implemented, by whom and when, it is important to highlight how policy-making in this area is nowadays informed and supported by a plurality of studies and sound empirical evidence. These need to be expanded and updated, but certainly constitute fundamental knowledge resources to address media crisis from a gender perspective while offering the possibility for a triangulation among such diverse stakeholders as governments, academia, media industries and professionals.

REFERENCES

Antonopoulos, R. (2009) *The current economic and financial crisis: a gender perspective*. Working papers, The Levy Economics Institute, No. 562. Retrieved from: http://www.econstor.eu/dspace/bitstream/10419/31580/1/605411867.pdf.

Bettio, F. et al. (2012) *The impact of the economic crisis on the situation of women and men and on gender equality policies*. Brussels: ENEGE.

BiS (Department for Business, Innovation and Skills) (2011) *Women on Boards*. London: BiS.

Capecchi, S. (ed.) (2006) *Inchiesta*: trimestrale di ricerca e pratica sociale, numero monografico su Donne e Media, No. 153, Anno XXXV, Edizioni Dedalo, Bologna, luglio–settembre 2006.

CED (Committee for Economic Development) (2012) *Fulfilling the Promise: How More Women on Corporate Boards Would Make America and American Companies More Competitive*. Washington DC: CED.

Council of the European Union (2011) *Council conclusions on the European Pact for gender equality for the period 2011–2020*. Retrieved from: http://www.consilium. europa.eu/uedocs/cms_data/docs/pressdata/en/lsa/119628.pdf.

EIGE (2013) *Advancing gender equality in decision-making in media organizations*. Retrieved from: http://eige.europa.eu/content/document/advancing-gender-equality-in-decision-making-in-media-organisations-report.

Elson, D. (2010) Gender and the global economic crisis in developing countries: a framework for analysis. *Gender & Development*, 18(2). pp. 201–12.

European Commission (2010) *Strategy for equality between women and men 2010–2015*. Retrieved from: http://ec.europa.eu/justice/gender-equality/files/strategy_equality_women_men_en.pdf.

European Parliament (2010) *Gender aspects of the economic downturn and financial crisis on welfare systems*. Retrieved from: http://www.europarl.europa.eu/RegData/etudes/etudes/join/2013/474396/IPOL-FEMM_ET(2013)474396_EN.pdf.

European Parliament (2012) Directive of the European Parliament and of the Council on improving the gender balance among non-executive directors of companies listed on stock exchanges and related measures.

European Parliament (2012) Draft report on the impact of the economic crisis on gender equality and women's rights (2012/2301(INI)). Committee on Women's Rights and Gender Equality.

European Parliament (2012) *Gender Quotas in Management Boards*. Retrieved from: http://www.europarl.europa.eu/RegData/etudes/note/join/2012/462429/IPOL-FEMM_NT(2012)462429_EN.pdf.

European Parliament resolution of 17 June 2010 on gender aspects of the economic downturn and financial crisis (2009/2204(INI)).

EWL (European Women's Lobby) (2012) *The price of austerity. The impact on women's rights and gender equality in Europe*. Brussels: EWL.

EWL and OXFAM International (2010) *Women's poverty and social exclusion in the European Union at a time of recession: An invisible crisis? A genderworks paper*. Brussels: EWL and Oxfam.

GMMP (2010) *Global Media Monitoring Project* reports. World Association of Christian Communication (WACC). Retrieved from: http://www.whomakesthenews.org/images/reports_2010/global/gmmp_global_report_en.pdf.

Koselleck, R. and Richter, M. (2006) Crisis. *Journal of the History of Ideas*, 67(2). pp. 357–400.

IWMF (2011) *Global Report on the Status of Women in the News Media*. Retrieved from: http://iwmf.org/pdfs/IWMF-Global-Report.pdf.

LSE (2013) *Research Project and related publications*. Retrieved from: http://www.lse.ac.uk/media@lse/research/The-Euro-Crisis-in-the-Press.aspx.

Lyberaki, A. (2011) *Gender aspects of the economic downturn and financial crisis*. EP, Policy Department C, Brussels.

McKinsey & Company (2012) *Women Matter 2012: Making the Breakthrough*. McKinsey & Co. Retrieved from: http://www.mckinsey.com/client_service/organization/latest_thinking/women_matter.

Morin, E. (1976) Pour une crisologie. *Communications*. pp. 149–63.

Ogrizek, J.M. and Guillery, M. (1999) *Communicating in crisis: A theoretical and practical guide to crisis management*. Piscataway, NJ: Aldine Transaction.

Oxfam International and European Women's Lobby (2010) *Women's poverty and social exclusion in the European Union at a time of recession: An invisible crisis?* Retrieved from: http://www.womenlobby.org/publications/reports/article/an-invisible-crisis-2010.

Pearson, R. and Sweetman, C. (eds) (2011) *Gender and the Economic Crisis*. London: Oxfam.

Périvier, H., Cochard, M. and Cornilleau, G. (2011) *Gender effects of the crisis on labor market in six European countries, OECD meeting, June 2011*. Retrieved from: http://www.oecd.org/eco/labour/48215665.pdf.

Peters, B. (2001) *Equality and Quality: Setting Standards for Women in Journalism*. Brussels: IFJ.

Piketty, T. (2014) *Capital in the XXI century*. Massachusetts: Harvard University Press.

Rosenvallon, P. and Goldhammer, A. (2013) *The society of equals*. Massachusetts: Harvard University Press.

Vertova, G. (2012) Women on the verge of a nervous breakdown: The gender impact of the crisis. In: Papadopoulos, E. and Sakellaridis, G. (eds.) *The political economy of public debt and austerity in the EU*. Athens: Nisson Publications.

9   A Crisis in Political Communication?

*Stylianos Papathanassopoulos and
Ralph Negrine*

There is no crisis in political communication or at least, not if we understand the phrase to mean something akin to an absence of communication about public affairs. If anything, one could argue there is a surfeit of political and public communication via websites, blogs, Twitter, Facebook, Buzzfeed and other sources. In which case, one may ask: Where and what is the crisis? In the introduction to this volume, it was suggested that "the current media change qualifies as an institutional media crisis" because, and in part, the media's role in nation-building has itself eroded. It follows, therefore, that one can write of an "institutional media crisis."

This is not the place to return to the themes that are developed more fully in Chapter 1. The purpose of this chapter is to address the question of whether or not there is a crisis in or of political communication. In their much referenced piece on the crisis of public communication, Blumler and Gurevitch argued:

> the deepening of the current crisis of civic communication can be best explained precisely in systemic terms, that is, in terms of developments in the relationships between politicians and journalists, between the institutions of politics and of the media, viewed in the context of the socio-political environment, i.e. in the context of the relationship of these institutions with an increasingly disaffected and fragmented audience/public/citizenry. (1995, p. 8)

In outlining the broad contours of the crisis in terms of a "systemic crisis," they highlighted the ways in which changes that were taking place within the institutions and in their key relationships could lead to significant and serious consequences. Indeed, parts of their discussion, written over twenty years ago, are as relevant today as they were then and, more importantly perhaps, remind us of the ongoing concern with continuity and change in the process, content and consequences of political communication. One of those continuing themes is that of civic disengagement or, more precisely, the lack of civic engagement and the growing disenchantment with politics and those in politics. Their work, after all, was about "the crisis of communication *for citizenship*" (emphasis ours). For example, they approvingly quote Weaver (p. 3) on these themes:

Regardless of which side seems to be more in control of the campaign agenda, if this agenda is perceived as mostly controlled by politicians and the press without much real input from the public, then increasing alienation and cynicism is likely to occur.

Or, in their section on "widespread projection of an image of the 'turned-off' citizen," Blumler and Gurevitch note:

the news media are thus continually projecting the *systematically influential* perception that the respect of many voters for their political leaders and institutions has been plummeting. Indeed, the media could be said to be constructing for audience members how they are, and therefore *should be*, regarding their politicians and institutions. (1995, p. 212. emphasis in original)

Given these matters were lively issues over twenty years ago, it is appropriate to ask: In what ways have things got so much worse as to occasion another round of soul-searching? The post-mortem on the 2014 European Parliament election has highlighted the low turnout – an average of 43.9 per cent across the EU28 – and disconnection and cynicism on the part of the citizenry, as well as the turn to populist parties and political parties. Yet, as we have indicated above, these concerns are fairly longstanding ones. What makes it possible – if that is the case – to see the current situation as a deeper crisis than the one described by Blumler and Gurevitch some twenty years ago?

One problem is that it is hard not to be swept along with the broad themes in the crisis of public communication approach, even though there is a real danger that in focusing on the crisis in/of political communication – however configured – we are exaggerating the place of the media in that crisis and underestimating the crisis of political institutions. Or possibly, vice versa: underestimating the place of the media in generating the crisis and overestimating the crisis of political institutions.

As regards the media themselves, there is certainly a crisis to the extent that a structural adjustment is taking place and the old is being displaced by the new. For example, printed newspapers are in decline and competition for established broadcasters is eroding their audience share. Yet, and despite these changes, access to established media via the Internet is breathing some life into the old media. A similar argument could be made for those political institutions that are centrally involved in the systemic crisis Blumler and Gurevitch discuss, the political parties. Their combined share of the vote has certainly declined over the last five decades, as has their membership (Hartleb, 2012, p. 17f). But they are still there, feverishly adjusting to a very different socio-political environment. Even in the 2014 European Parliament elections, the established parties gathered significant number of votes despite the explosion in the number of populist and anti-politics parties elected.

If we are to follow Blumler and Gurevitch and their idea of a systemic crisis, we may need to explore in greater depth those elements of the political communication system that could produce that crisis. As Blumler and Gurevitch put it:

> if we look at a political communication system, what we (still) see are two sets of institutions – political and media organizations – which are involved in the course of message preparation in much "horizontal" interaction with each other, while, on the "vertical" axis, they are separately and jointly engaged in disseminating and processing information and ideas to and from the mass citizenry. (1995, p. 12)

On the other hand, the proliferation of news media has led to media fragmentation and audience segmentation and this has also affected democracy too. Mancini (2013, p. 49–51) points out four possible consequences. These are increasing social and political polarization, new forms of political socialization, more complex processes of social and political negotiation, new forms of public scrutiny.

If there is a crisis of sorts it may be, say, a crisis of representative democracy and, in a secondary way, of the traditional organizations of representation (the media) that, in turn, feed into – and feed off – it. Or, possibly, the other way round: a crisis of media that exacerbates a crisis in the polity. It may also be a matter of the public being detached from the on-going machinations of the two institutions that are so central to the political communication process. Or, and this is a possibility also, it may not be a crisis after all but merely something akin to a recalibration of relationships for a different political and communication environment, shifting from the twentieth to the twenty-first century. There are many possibilities.

The aim of this chapter is to explore whether we can discuss the theme of a crisis of political communication in the European context, also bearing in mind that the nature of political communication in Europe varies across nation states and sometimes in very significant ways. (cf. Kun and Nielsen, 2013) We begin by setting out some of the changes that have been commonly experienced across most European countries. These relate, in general terms, to changes in the nature of media systems and to the public participation in the political process.

CHANGING MEDIA, CHANGING POLITICS, CHANGING POLITICAL COMMUNICATION?

Changes at the Level of Media

This refers to changes in the media environment but also to changes in the ways in which media work, especially in their vertical roles as disseminators of information.

In most European countries, as in other developed countries, the media are not simply a channel for transmitting messages but also an autonomous mediator in society. As Mazzoleni and Schulz (1999, p. 249) noted, the media are not mere passive channels for political communicators and political content. "Rather, the media are organizations with their own aims and rules that do not necessarily coincide with, and indeed often clash with, those of political communicators." Work on the mediatisation of politics – see, for example, http://mediatization-of-politics.com/defining-mediatization/ – confirms this and the centrality of communication to governance.

One must also include here the processes of commercialization that privilege 'media logic' over 'political logic' (Mazzoleni, 1987) with the effect of forcing those in politics to become aware of the needs of the media and, in many cases, mixing politics with their personal lives in an effort to seek popular support. In Russia, President Putin seeks to present himself as a kind of 'father of the nation.' In Italy, Silvio Berlusconi appeared as the longest-serving prime minister of the country after World War II and continues to dominate tabloid coverage even as a 'retired' politician, while in France, President François Hollande has lost credibility for both his policies and his personal life. In Germany, ex-Chancellor Gerhard Schröder became known as the media chancellor, whereas the present Chancellor Angela Merkel is known as the iron lady. In the Netherlands, the late populist politician Pim Fortuyn increased his popularity using the magnifying glass of television for his adversarial tone, style and culture.

By and large, politicians all over Europe are constantly under pressure to adapt to new media developments in their attempt to improve their communication strategies. It is not a coincidence that during every presidential campaign, European media and campaign consultants as well as political executives travel to the US to see and study the Republican and Democratic strategies at close range since media logic has strongly influenced the behaviour of party politicians. In the same way, American political consultants are very often employed in European national election contests (Papathanassopoulos et al., 2007). In effect, we are currently experiencing a rationalization of persuasion where the intent on the part of political actors as a broad category is to find and utilise "effective means of persuasion based on research on audiences and the organization of systematic campaigns." (Mayhew, 1997, p. 190) The obvious risk here is that in pursuing these strategies – in talking at people – we all experience what Manin called "audience democracies" (ibid.).

But just as the media have grown in importance as mediators of politics, they have been convulsed by technological changes that have created a more complex media landscape. The Internet has grown in dominance whilst newspaper sales have declined, although the reach of newspapers via their online versions has sometimes compensated for the decline in print (see Chapter 5).

Television, however, continues to be a surprisingly popular medium for the consumption of news and information. According to a recent eleven-nation research study, television remains the dominant medium for news consumption (Papathanassopoulos et al., 2013). In the same vein, a recent Eurobarometer survey found that in most European countries, television remains a pre-eminent medium not only for entertainment but also for accessing political news with the other means of communication jostling for position (Eurobarometer, 2013; Reuters Institute, 2013).

In general, and this applies to both print and broadcast news brands (e.g. legacy media), the level of trust in them is considerable and is one of the reasons for their continuing appeal among consumers of news. But as more and more people use the Internet to access news, it is hardly surprising that political actors will gradually devote less resources to traditional forms of political communication – especially to television – as they have to deal with the challenge of the Internet (see also Reuters Institute, 2013). In effect, it has become commonplace to find political actors all over the Internet and on websites, Twitter, Facebook and other platforms. The question is, however, if they use it as the main means of political communication in their political and campaign strategy or just as complementary means of communication, popular to the younger generation, which is by and large uninterested in political news (Reuters Institute, 2013).

With so many different ways to communicate politics and to access politics, it would be hard to argue that there is a crisis in political communication, if that is understood in terms of simple quantity and practices. If the crisis – if there is one – is to be explored, it must be done through analysis of the quality of the information, both as a value in itself but also as an end product of the relationship between media and politics. Put differently, in respect of the 'horizontal' and 'vertical' axis outlined in the Blumler and Gurevitch systemic model (see above) there may be significant changes to take note of.

What we do know of the horizontal axis is that it can no longer be described as comprising two sets of actors who are, most of the time, friendly and complicit in their relationships. On the one hand, political actors have become much more professional in their dealings with the media to the extent that they seek to dominate the relationship and the news agenda. This was something that was already evident in the 1990s as Blumler and Gurevitch were only too aware. They wrote:

> Today they [the oppressive social structures of mass society] are reflected especially in the professionalization of politics and associated attempts to manage and control public communication for manipulative purposes, with the resulting alienation of many citizens. (1995, p. 221)

The response to this has undoubtedly been the emergence of a much more belligerent and questioning media system. This is not necessarily a bad thing. To take one example to which we shall return: It is now commonplace to note that broadcasters are often hyper-adversarial in their interviewing techniques when confronting politicians. Leaving aside whether or not this is true of all broadcasters and at all times, one could legitimately argue that hyper-adversarialism is actually a good thing. In other words, the current state of political broadcasting and political communication as far as the public is concerned is rather healthy and much healthier than it was in the past. Frank Esser has described this shift in the nature of journalism from the late 1960s towards what he calls "critical professionalism." (Esser, 2013, p. 169) With increasing professionalization, "the news media assume a more autonomous, proactive role within core processes of representative democracy – those of responsibility and accountability." (ibid., p. 170)

A similar set of conclusions are arrived in Fink and Schudson's work on the changing nature of news over the last fifty years. Whilst their work is essentially about changes in the US, there are trends there that one could easily spot in the European context, which is something they acknowledge. What they describe, then, are changes that have taken journalism away from a comfortable and complicit relationship with political actors in the 1960s to a much more complex relationship and a much more difficult relationship. "Every measure shows that that comfortable and cooperative journalistic world is gone." (Fink and Schudson, 2014, p. 17) Brants et al.'s (2010) study of politicians and journalists suggests their relationship is no longer symbiotic – or mainly or only so – it is one of "mutual mistrust," which is why this should be so relevant to this chapter. First, they argue, there is the development from a party democracy to an "audience democracy." Second, they point to "the rise of a more market-driven news order." Third, "the public is beginning to challenge the Enlightenment ideal of rational discourse and as the *vox populi* to demand a voice." (2010, p. 29f)

A summary of these points would be that the public feels it has been outside the loop of political communication for far too long and it no longer believes (and behaves) as if it thinks those in power know or have all the answers. Nor can they deal with all the problems they (we?) confront. Although tensions between governments, politicians and the news media are "as old as democracy itself" (Barnett, 2002, p. 400), the suggestion is that the nature of the current tensions are qualitatively different.

According to Mancini, due to an increased social and political polarization, the news media, especially the niche media and blogs, do not play the function of social integration and they do not foster the so called objective, middle way approach. On the contrary, media choices increasingly reflect partisan considerations. In this context, according to Mancini,

> Media outlets may progressively substitute political parties and other traditional organizations of political socialization; they may join the already existing ones and/or give space to new forms of social aggregations. At the time of the mass audience, it was clear that news media were replacing political parties as the main sources of information and instruments of political socialization. Now the situation is different:

the news media outlets are becoming political actors. Different media outlets and single media figures (anchormen, TV stars) enter the field of politics with either their own organizations or with an organization that they construct thanks to the Internet. (2013, p. 51)

CHANGES AT THE LEVEL OF THE POLITICAL PARTY

At the level of the political party, there have been vast changes as well. The transformation of parties into electoral professional political parties is an example. The consequences are a different approach to the practice of political communication, political advocacy and political engagement. Much of this is common across Europe where political parties have witnessed a decline in their membership and a changed relationship between voter and public. At the turn of the twenty-first century, the average ratio of party membership to the electorate across (old and new) European democracies hovered at around five per cent (van Biezen, Mair and Poguntke, 2012; Mair and van Biezen, 2001). In 1980, by contrast, an average of almost ten per cent of the electorates of the older democracies were affiliated to a political party, while at the beginning of the 1960s, the average party membership ratio stood at almost fifteen per cent (Katz et al., 1992). In other words, parties in contemporary European democracies are no longer able to engage citizens as they once used to. Amidst talk of "audience democracies" (Manin, 1997), these processes of disengagement and detachment are serious since they disconnect the public from those who seek to represent them, and vice versa.

Voters, it seems, are no longer making political decisions only on the basis of traditional allegiances (e.g. class, religion) and are more prepared to switch votes, and hence more open to persuasion. This has major implications for the political process. The recent financial crisis (2007 onwards) has had a major impact on voters' allegiances. Although the financial crash has impacted on all, those in the Eurozone have experienced its consequences differently from those who are not members of the Eurozone.

More specifically, citizens in Greece, Spain and Portugal may have a different experience of the financial crisis and the politics of austerity than, say, citizens in the UK, who have faced a different type of austerity. In effect, the political system in some Southern European countries, such as Greece and Italy, underwent dramatic changes following the scandals and the judicial inquiries that have caused the death or near death of traditional parties and the arrest of prominent politicians.

The rise of populist parties is another major consequence of these developments. In Sweden, traditional political stability has to a certain extent been challenged by a more volatile public opinion. In the Netherlands, ideology and religion are less of a dominant factor in voter choices and party membership has fallen to one of the lowest in Europe (Papathanassopoulos et al., 2007). Moreover, the number of floating voters has grown at every election and the numbers who have been 'turned-off' politics has also increased.

Political parties must therefore turn their attention to how they can communicate with the public/voters, how they can get their messages across, how they can persuade and mobilize voters. Furthermore, in a situation where citizens have become less supportive of political parties, less trusting of the political system and more likely to abstain, there is likely to be a greater incentive to employ those skilled in the arts of communication and marketing – the professional consultants, communicators and organizers – to help the political parties position themselves in the minds of the citizen/voter. "This raises serious questions concerning the viability of party democracy, which necessitates that parties provide a meaningful, substantive link between rulers and ruled." (Sartori, 1976, p. 25) After all, the viability of this link depends, to a substantial degree, on the viability of parties as organizations with an active membership. (ibid., p. 207)

This has led to considerable organizational change, ranging from a greater centralization of operations to a reassessment of the role of members and the relationship of the centre to the periphery (e.g. constituencies, local campaigns). In probably all cases, more care has been taken to deal with communication and to reflect and alter the processes and content of communication to meet the challenges that have arisen from the changing nature of media, changing nature of government and the changing nature of the parties themselves.

The decline of the political party's traditional position of pre-eminence within the political process (and in the media) leads to a greater questioning of how they must operate in competitive elections, in the present but also in the future. By and large, in a situation where citizens have become less supportive of political parties, less trusting of the political system and more likely to abstain, there is likely to be a greater incentive to employ those skilled in the arts of communication and marketing – the professional consultants, communicators and organizers – to help the political parties position themselves in the minds of the citizen/voter.

At an organizational-operational level of political parties, there have been large changes as well. Some, such as the view that organizations should operate with a single vision and should communicate that throughout, have infected political parties and the ways in which they interact with their members, the media and others; others, such as the need to act in a 'professional' way, have also entered the vocabulary and the practice of organizations, as well as individuals.

> In other words, it is highly likely that those who are internally active in the political parties of European democracies also hold intra-party or elected offices. Or, to overstate this point somewhat, hardly any active grassroots members are left in the parties to provide a linkage between

party elites and mass publics at large. However, the membership organization of political parties is but one organizational linkage that is,
in principle, available to party elites when they wish to connect with
their wider constituency. Historically, the major parties on the Left
and on the Right have relied on alliances with organized religion and
organized labor in order to stabilize their electorates. However, these
linkages have undergone similar processes of erosion.

> (Van Biezen and Poguntke, 2012, p. 209)

Another indication of these changes is the process of centralization, not only
in political parties but also in government, which has created a tight framework for the control and conduct of communication functions. In probably
all cases, more care has been taken to deal with communication and to
reflect and alter the processes and content of communication to meet the
challenges that have arisen from the changing nature of media, changing
nature of government and the changing nature of the parties themselves.

CHANGES IN POLITICAL COMMUNICATION?

So, what sort of links exist now, and what do media and other forms of
communication require to aid the conduct of political life that in Western
democracies is still perceived to work through political parties? Van Biezen
and Poguntke argue:

> Perhaps, in the age of modern democracy we simply no longer need the
> traditional organizational anchorage of party politicians. … Instead,
> we may need to ask: "What kinds of representative democracy are
> thinkable. And what forms of party (…), if any, are appropriate to
> them?" … Increasingly, when citizens wish to make their voices heard,
> they are more likely to turn to interest groups, advocacy coalitions or
> the media than to political parties. In the past, interest groups tended
> to operate more under party aegis, as a complement to the more estab-
> lished partisan channels. In contemporary polities, however, interest
> groups operate quite independently of the parties, and in many ways
> offer an alternative, if not directly challenge, to the process of interest
> intermediation provided by parties. In this sense, parties have become
> more isolated and more removed from societal demands.

> (vanBiezen and Poguntke, 2012, p. 214)

If we follow the argument that Van Biezen and Poguntke offer, we can begin
to see the outlines of the crisis of political communication. It is a crisis that
is born out of the disconnection between the traditional institutions that
sustained the democratic process and its visceral connection to the public;
it no longer exists in the shape or form of old. Yet we remain wedded to the

notion of political parties and to the notion that it is through political parties that politics must be conducted. We remain wedded to the notion that the media should reflect political debate as represented by political parties and give them primacy as the key actors in the political system.

How we continue to keep those increasingly weakening links in the system of political communication from completely breaking off may be the key issue for the current era. As Mancini argues, example of movements across Europe such as Occupy and the Indignados (Indignants Movement) appear to illustrate "the progressive weakening of traditional mass parties but also (...) the increasing fragmentation of the political landscape that now appears to be open to a number of different competitors very frequently without any previous traditional, political experience." (2013, p. 53) Using new and old media, these forces can muster supporters and become powerful centres of political activity.

CONCLUSIONS

To argue, then, that there is a crisis in political communication is to argue that the political world is no longer able to communicate its messages to the public (voters, citizens) or to communicate those messages as it used to. But this is a problem of the political world more than of the media or the communication practices and techniques used by the politicians and the political parties.

Nor can one convincingly argue the media are the main cause of a general 'crisis' in representative democracy per se. In a representative democracy, direct participation is not possible but through established mechanisms everyone can play a part in political life. As it happens, those established mechanisms include political parties. But to what extent are professional parties representative of the public? Do they listen to the public? Have they failed the public? Put differently, the professionalization of politics – professional politicians, professional election machines – has not only enhanced the established features of professionalized political communication but, and in the process, cemented the detachment of the ordinary citizen. In his work on the most recent US Presidential campaigns and their extensive use of new media, Daniel Kreiss has suggested the new methods of campaigning seemingly connect voters and citizens to their leaders. In practice, they do not. He has argued:

> Despite predictions to the contrary, the book shows that the use of new media in campaigning has seemingly not brought about fundamental changes in the levers of accountability, forms of political representation, quality of democratic conversation, or distribution of power in the American polity.
>
> (Kreiss, 2012, p. 26)

We can take two lessons away from this. The first is that, as in the bad (but not crisis-laden) old days, the public is acted upon, not acting. The second, as in the old days, is that those in charge are not really interested in the public/citizen in any way other than as a potential voter/voters. In which case, has political communication in modern representative democracies now become little more than a conversation between those who have political power and those who have media power to the exclusion of the public? Has the public become no more than by-standers in the processes of political communication? And is this different from the era in which political communication was not in an institutional crisis?

The new media (either web applications or social media like Twitter, Facebook and YouTube) complement and supplement the older forms of communication by creating other sources of information. But as Paolo Mancini has argued (2013, p. 50), media and consequently audience fragmentation will probably increase political polarization, not just in countries where involvement in the public good has been traditionally lower, such Mediterranean, Central and Eastern European countries, "where the government is not able to provide the various resources, services, and policies that make citizens feel part of a community that takes care of them, and where essential rights are not universally ensured and the rules of the democratic game are adapted to different circumstances and actors." (Mancini, 2013, p. 50) Additionally, this may have an effect on other countries in Northern Europe or North America. As studies on the use of new media indicate, the public is not being engaged more but is being micro-managed more (Lilleker et al., 2011; Jungherr, 2014).

In one way or another, regardless of the rise of new political formations, political action is still channeled through political parties, political leaders are still chosen from the political parties and politics is mostly organized as it was before. The core features of representative democracy remain in place, not only because they have been so completely normalized in Western capitalist societies but also because those who have invested most in such structures are themselves able to adapt and co-opt forces of change, which is why political parties will make use of the Internet and why they will modernize themselves.

But political action, movements or riots are no longer organized by the political parties. The new digital media can create new networks of communication, of information and of news. In effect, in the age of digital media, political communication needs no longer to derive from government or party to the citizen or voter; it could include elements of feedback, response, discussion and so on.

The central argument of this chapter has been that the nature and content of political communication in Europe has inevitably changed as well as affected politics. But political communication as a way of communicating messages to the citizens is not in crisis, though the political system may be. Although the political system may ultimately affect the media system, media logic is pervasive in most aspects of political communication and to some extent has been associated with media malaise. We believe European societies have entered a new stage, possibly a digital age of political communication. With a highly fragmented media landscape and with the Internet in place, many elements of the relationships between politicians, the media and the public necessarily change. Politicians in Europe still need to reach, persuade and mobilize the public – and do so in increasingly professional ways – but they do so using both the old and the new media. In turn, the old and the new media develop new ways of reaching the audience as public with the added factor that a section of the public ceases to act as an audience and becomes both citizens and communicators.

To return to a point made at the beginning of this chapter, we have yet to work out just how much new media will alter the parameters of political communication. Is it simply because of the new communication developments that politics has shifted from party democracy to audience democracy to the establishment of the permanent campaigning and the dominance of polls? Any crisis of political communication is part of a larger problem of reaching people/citizens/voters in an effective and persuasive way and of engaging them in the process. It is the political system that does not give answers to the problems the citizens are facing. It is the politicians and political parties – who as part of the framework of representative democracy – who need to begin to address the larger problems posed by political and technological change.

REFERENCES

Barnett, S. (2002) Will a crisis in journalism provoke a crisis in democracy? *The Political Quarterly*, 73(4). pp. 400–08.

Brants, K., de Vreese, C., Möller, J. and van Praag, P. (2010) The Real Spiral of Cynicism? Symbiosis and Mistrust between Politicians and Journalists. *The International Journal of Press/Politics*, 15. pp. 25–40.

Blumler, J.G. and Kavanagh, D. (1999) The Third Age of Political Communication: Influences and Features. *Political Communication*, 16. pp. 209–30.

Blumler, J.G. (2001) The third age of political communication. *Journal of Public Affairs*, 1(3). pp. 201–09.

Blumler, J.G. and Gurevitch, M. (2001) 'Americanisation' reconsidered: UK-US campaign communications across time. In: Bennett, L.W. and Entman, R.M. (eds.) *Mediated Politics: Communications in the Future of Democracy*. Cambridge: Cambridge University Press.

Esser, F. (2013) Mediatization as a challenge: media logic versus political logic. In: Kriesi, H., Lavenex, S., Esser, F., Matthes, J., Bühlmann, M. and Bochsler, D. (eds) *Democracy in the age of globalization and mediatization* (pp. 155–76). Basingstoke: Palgrave Macmillan.

EurActiv (2009) *Twittering not: MEPs fail to embrace Internet craze*. Retrieved from: (http://www.euractiv.com/en/eu-elections/twittering-meps-fail-embrace-internet-craze/article-182511).

Eurobarometer (2014) *Public Opinion in the European Union.* Standard Euroba-rometer 80/ Spring 2014 TNS Opinion & Social. Retrieved from: http://ec.europa.eu/public_opinion/index_en.htm.

Eurobarometer (2013) *Media Use in the European Union.* Retrieved from: http://ec.europa.eu.

Fink, K. and Schudson, M. (2013) The rise of contextual journalism, 1950s–2000s. *Journalism* 15(1). pp. 3–20.

Jungherr, A. (2014) The Logic of Political Coverage on Twitter: Temporal Dynamics and Content. *Journal of Communication,* 64(2). pp. 239–59.

Hartleb, F. (2012) *All Tomorrow's Parties: The Changing Face of European Party Politics.* Centre for European Studies. Retrieved from: http://martenscentre.eu/publications/all-tomorrow%E2%80%99s-parties-changing-face-european-party-politics.

Kreiss, D. (2012) *Taking our country back: the crafting of networked politics from Howard Dean to Barack Obama.* New York: Oxford University Press.

Kuhn, R. (2005) Where's the spin? The executive and news management in France. *Modern and Contemporary France,* 13. pp. 307–22.

Lilleker, D. G., Koc-Michalska, K., Schweitzer, E. J., Jacunski, M., Jackson, N. and Vedel, T. (2011) Informing, engaging, mobilizing or interacting: Searching for a European model of web campaigning. *European Journal of Communication,* 26(3). pp. 195–213.

Mair, P. and van Biezen, I. (2001) Party Membership in Twenty European Democracies 1980–2000. *Party Politics,* 7(1). pp. 5–21.

Mancini, P. (2013) Media Fragmentation, Party System, and Democracy. *The International Journal of Press/Politics,* 18(1). pp. 43–60.

Mancini, P. and Swanson, D.L. (1996) Politics, media and modern democracy: intro-duction. In: Swanson, D.L. and Mancini, P. (eds.) *Politics, Media and Modern Democracy: An International Study of Innovations in Electoral Campaigns and their Consequences* (pp. 1–26). New York: Praeger.

Manin, B. (1997) *The Principles of Representative Democracies.* Cambridge: Cambridge University Press.

Mazzoleni, G. (1987) Media Logic and Party Logic in Campaign Coverage: The Italian General Election in 1983. *European Journal of Communication,* 2(1). pp. 55–80.

Mazzoleni, G. and Schulz, W. (1999) Mediatization of Politics: A Challenge for Democracy? *Political Communication,* 16(3). pp. 247–62.

Mayhew, L. (1997) *The New Public.* Cambridge: Cambridge University Press.

McQuail, D. (1994) *Mass Communication Theory: An Introduction.* London: Sage.

McNair, B. (2006) *Cultural Chaos: Journalism, News and Power in a Globalised World.* London: Routledge.

Meyer, T. (2000) *Media Democracy: How the media colonize politics.* Cambridge: Polity.

Negrine, R.M. (2005) Professionalism and the Milbank Tendency: A Response to Webb and Fisher. *Politics,* 25. pp. 107–15.

Negrine, R.M., Mancini, P., Holtz-Bacha, C. and Papathanassopoulos, S. (eds.) (2007) *The Professionalisation of Political Communication.* Bristol: Intellect.

Negrine, R. (2008) *The Transformation of Political Communication: continuities and changes in media politics.* Basingstoke: Palgrave.

Negrine, R. and Papathanassopoulos, S. (1996) The 'Americanization' of Political Communication: A Critique. *Press/Politics,* 1(2). pp. 45–62.

Nord, L. (2007) The Swedish Model Becomes Less Swedish. In: Negrine, R. M., Mancini, P., Holtz-Bacha, C. and Papathanassopoulos, S. (eds.) *The Professionalisation of Political Communication*. Bristol, Intellect.

Plasser, F. and Plasser, G. (2002) *Global Political Campaigning. A Worldwide Analysis of Campaign Professionals and their Practices*. London: Praeger.

Papathanassopoulos, S., Negrine, R., Mancini, P. and Holtz-Bacha, C. (2007) Political Communication in the Era of Professionalization. In: Negrine, R.M., Mancini, P., Holtz-Bacha, C. and Papathanassopoulos, S. (eds.) *The Professionalisation of Political Communication* (pp. 9–27). Bristol: Intellect.

Papathanassopoulos, S., Coen, S., Curran, J., Aalberg, T., Jones, P., Rojas, H. and Tiffen, R. (2013) Online Threat, But Television Is Still Dominant: A comparative study of 11 nations' news consumption. *Journalism Practice*, 7(6). pp. 690–704.

Reuters Institute (2013) *Digital News Report 2013: Tracking the Future of News*. Newman, N. and Levy, D. A. L. (eds.) Oxford: University of Oxford Press.

Sartori, G. (1976) *Parties and Party Systems*.Cambridge: Cambridge University Press.

Seymour-Ure, C. (1996) *The British Press and Broadcasting Since 1945*. Oxford: Blackwell Publishing.

vanBiezen I., Mair, P. and Poguntke, T. (2012) Going, going … gone? The decline of party membership in contemporary Europe. *European Journal of Political Research*, 51(1). pp. 24–56.

vanBiezen I. and Poguntke, T. (2012) The decline of membership-based politics. *Party Politics*, 20(2). pp. 205–16.

Part IV

Looking to the Future

Policy Perspectives

10 Challenges and Confusion in Media Regulation

A Four-Country Comparison

Hannu Nieminen, Alessandro D'Arma,
Claudia Padovani and Helena Sousa

INTRODUCTION

In this chapter we discuss recent developments and challenges in European media and communication policy, focusing on the period following the 2008 global financial crisis. We are especially interested in the implications of the financial crisis and its political repercussions nationally (austerity measures and cuts to public services, growing anti-politics sentiments and widespread dissatisfaction with free-market capitalism and representative democracy) for media and communication policy, understood here in a broad sense, so as to include all electronic communications, such as the Internet, mobile communications, social media etc. Our overarching concern is with the implications of developments in media and communication policy for the democratic functions of the media in Europe.

We ask whether there is any evidence for the notion that the macro-economic and political conditions of recent years have contributed to a reorientation of prevalent approaches to media and communications policy in Europe. There are three aspects to this. Our main question considers whether there has been a shift away from the neoliberal values that influenced European media policy for much of the past three decades. We are also interested in determining whether the crisis has led the EU to use the opportunity to increase its powers and control within media and communications policy over the sovereignty of its member states. Finally, we ask if there are any signs of the 2008 crisis directly influencing different media and communications policy areas. In our analysis we concentrate specifically on three issues drawn from different policy areas: public subsidies (or state aid) to media content providers; protection of minors in the new technological environment; and national broadband policies.

Has there been a move away from neoliberal values emphasising free markets over state intervention and freedom of expression over regulation to protect social values and vulnerable groups? This could be said to be underway if we were to establish that public subsidies to media content-providers have at least been maintained at previous levels in spite of the financial crisis constraining state budgets; policy-makers have taken concrete actions involving new regulations to address growing societal concerns for the safety of our children in the online environment; substantial public money has been allocated in deploying the national broadband infrastructure, with a view to achieving the goal of universal service.

In the same manner, an increase in EU control of media and communications policy over national sovereignty can be established if the EU Member States now have less sovereignty to decide on public subsidies to media and communications-providers than they had before the crisis; there are increasingly pan-European legal standards for the protection of minors in the digital media environment; there is a unified European broadband policy, decreed and implemented by the EU with the assistance of its member states. Accordingly, we will search for signs of the direct influence of the 2008 crisis in the three policy areas.

We will attempt to find indications as to whether the abovementioned conditions exist by placing our empirical focus primarily (though not exclusively) on four western European countries with different media policy traditions (Hallin and Mancini, 2004): two small countries (Finland and Portugal) and two large ones (Italy and the United Kingdom), the size of a country being in turn a relevant variable in media policy (cf. Just and Puppis, 2012). In addition, and arguably more importantly for our purposes, there are differences in the degree to which these four countries have felt the impact of the global financial crisis on their national economies, the two southern European countries having being engulfed in a deeper economic recession and more political turmoil than either Finland or the UK.

In what follows, we will explore in more detail the three areas of media policy and assess their development in Finland, Portugal, Italy and the UK.

PUBLIC FUNDING AND STATE AID TO MEDIA

Public financing has been a fundamental means of supporting the media in post-war Europe, especially during the first three post-war decades characterized almost everywhere by licence-fee-funded public-service broadcasting monopolies (cf. Humphreys, 1996).[1] Even after the introduction of commercial television in the 1980s and 1990s throughout much of Europe, public financing continued to play an important, and in some cases a predominant, role within national media environments. Here we will focus on public funding to support news media organizations, namely broadcasters and newspaper publishers. They have been the primary destination of the public money channelled into the media, largely due to the major contribution they are expected to make to the democratic process as the main source of political information and commentary on issues of public relevance in contemporary societies. But it should be noted that other media producers (e.g. film companies, animation studios, documentary-makers and video-game developers) often benefit from substantial amounts of public money obtained through various mechanisms (cf. Grant and Wood, 2004; Gibbons and Humphreys, 2011), not least through public-service broadcasting itself, whose remit, of course, includes not only news and current affairs provision but also provision in popular entertainment genres and support for domestic film and audiovisual industries.

Unlike licence-fee-funded broadcasting in post-war Europe, newspapers, while recognized as serving the public interest, were initially not state-subsidized, as this was interpreted as a potentially distortive influence on press freedom. However, in the 1960s and 1970s, when the newspaper sector showed its first signs of decline, several countries adopted public policies to support the press with the stated aim of promoting a diversity of titles and viewpoints (Murschetz, 1998; Humphreys, 2006). Different forms of press subsidies were introduced and have operated within Europe ever since, including both untied and earmarked subsidies (e.g. for delivery); targeted subsidies for special purposes (e.g. to support party newspapers); tax reductions and VAT exemptions; and reduced postal tariffs. There have been considerable national variations within Europe in the modalities and extent of press subsidies, reflecting, as put by Peter Humphreys (2006, p. 39), "national political, economic and cultural characteristics." While providing indirect subsidies to the whole sector (e.g. preferential rates of VAT) has been commonplace throughout the EU, direct selective subsidies have tended to be adopted only in countries characterized by either strong welfare and social democratic traditions (such as the Nordic countries) or strong state-interventionist traditions (southern Europe), while more liberal-oriented countries, like the UK, have eschewed them.

These various forms of subsidy schemes in favour of the press have always sat rather uneasily with the EU's single market policy. According to EU treaties, state aid is not permissible when it distorts competition.[2] On this basis, there has been growing pressure on EU member states to suspend their various subsidy schemes (e.g. CEC, 2009; generally on EU press policy see Lichtenberg, 2008; Hutchinson, 2007). The case of public-service broadcasting, however, is different. While funding public-service broadcasting also qualifies as state aid from the EU's perspective, the Protocol on Public Broadcasting to the EU Amsterdam Treaty of 1997 recognized that public-service broadcasting is "directly related to the democratic, social and cultural needs of each society,"[3] and accorded member states the freedom to fund public-service broadcasting providing the compensation is proportionate to their public service remit.

Notwithstanding this authoritative source of legitimation, life has been far from assured for public-service broadcasters (PSBs) around Europe during the past twenty years. For instance, the European Commission's 2009 Communication on State Aid to Public Service Broadcasters was characterized by what has been described as a more restrictive approach to PSBs' online expansion than was previously the case (Brevini, 2013; see also Donders and Moe, 2012). Overall, however, it is fair to say the institution of public-service broadcasting has shown remarkable resilience in Europe, especially considering the set of challenges it has faced over a long period.

Prior to the global financial crisis of 2008, the challenge to the PSBs was primarily an ideological one, based on a technologically driven argument forcefully put forward by rival commercial interests and their political backers. Simply put, the argument has been that technological advances, most notably new delivery technologies such as digital broadcasting and the Internet, by eroding barriers to entry also remove the main market failures associated with television and thus undermine the rationale for significant public intervention in the form of large stand-alone publicly funded organizations. Even more vociferously, commercial rivals have accused PSBs of crowding out private provision by entering new media sectors where there are no apparent market failures justifying their presence. In many parts of Europe, notably southern and eastern European countries (though by no means only there), PSBs continue to be widely perceived as overly politicized, biased and wasteful organizations, failing in important respects to fulfil their public service remit.

Since the 2008 global economic crisis, the argument against public-service broadcasting has been presented, especially in those parts of Europe worst affected by the crisis, in more pragmatic, almost fatalistic, terms. Indeed, it is argued that European societies facing a prolonged economic downturncan can simply no longer afford the luxury of funding PSBs, and the political pressure for smaller, scaled-down PSBs is mounting (cf. Lowe and Berg, 2013; Snoddy, 2013). The second half of 2013 saw the unprecedented closure of two southern European public broadcasters, the Greek ERT (replaced by a new, scaled-back organization) and RàdioTelevisió Valenciana (RTVV), one of Spain's regional public broadcasters. Several other PSBs, including those in continental and northern Europe, have had severe funding cuts inflicted, which has led to drastic downsizing.

This also applies to the BBC in the UK – in comparative terms, a PSB traditionally enjoying a strong level of political support. However, the corporation has been under increasing political pressure in recent times after a series of managerial blunders. The BBC Charter is due for renewal in 2017, and it is widely expected the government will use this opportunity to narrow the BBC's public service remit and to continue the financial freeze announced in 2010 that amounts to a sixteen per cent real-terms cut in BBC funds by 2017. The financial squeeze has already forced the BBC to reduce investment levels and the range of services it provides.

In Italy, in recent years RAI's licence fee has been allowed to increase in line with inflation. However, it remains low by comparative standards and is widely evaded (over one in four Italians do not pay it). During the same period, RAI's advertising revenues have been in free fall, in the context of the country's economic recession. Thus RAI is facing severe financial pressures, given its historic dependence on commercial revenue, with the situation worsened by the decision to freeze RAI's licence fee for 2014. As in Italy, in Portugal the PSB RTP has historically been underfinanced and has experienced difficult times recently, amid talk of privatisation (eventually rejected) and a new funding deal announced in late 2013 that further reduces its already meagre budget.

There are exceptions to this rather bleak scenario for public-service broadcasting in Europe. One is Finland, which was one of the first European countries to move from a licence-based financing system to a (generous) wholly tax-based system in 2013. To prevent the government from intervening in the use of this income, the tax is collected in a separate fund used exclusively to finance public broadcaster Yle.[4] The new financing model has arguably strengthened the overall position of Yle, not only financially but also in terms of public trust.

In the case of press subsidies, there has been a clear trend towards the gradual reduction, or even the complete abandonment, of subsidy schemes in Europe (Murschetz and Trappel, 2014). The reduction in press subsidies, however, predates the financial crisis of 2008–2009. Finland, historically one of the European countries with the most extensive system of press subsidies, slashed almost all direct state aid to newspapers in 2007; the only significant remaining form of subsidy is a reduced VAT rate for print newspapers (cf. Lehtisaari, et al., 2012). Therefore, Finland's approach to press subsidies now appears more restrained than even the UK's, where the only form of state aid to the press is the VAT exemption.

Like Finland, Italy and Portugal have a long tradition of subsidizing the press, but in recent years they have reduced levels of support. In Italy, relatively substantial press subsidies have remained in place, although the system was simplified and the level of support decreased in 2012.[5] The conclusions of a recent comparative study on public support for news media, which included the UK, Finland and Italy, was that direct subsidies to the press were becoming less common, and that in any case, they are less significant than indirect forms of support (i.e. VAT exemptions or reductions). The latter are "a much more significant form of public support for the media than is commonly realized, worth hundreds of millions of euros per year." (Nielsen, 2011, p. 4) Another significant finding related to the lack of innovation in public-funding policies, and the author remarked on the lack of public-sector support for online-only media organizations.

Since the adoption of the European State Aid legislation in the late 1960s (cf. Thomas, 2000) there has been pressure for a unitary application of this policy in the area of media and communication. Although the EU State Aid policy is officially based on an economic argument – that public subsidies interfere with the free market principle – there is obviously a strong ideological influence of neoliberalism, which aims to deny the public-service principle and approaches media content merely as a commodity.

From the viewpoint of the EU versus nation states, it seems that, based on the Lisbon Treaty (2007) and the Treaty on the Functioning of the European Union (2010), the EU can use its powers to overcome the sovereignty of the nation states in relation to the positive content regulation, at least in the form of public subsidies. However, the member states still have some means to defend their traditional state aid policies, if they choose to use them.

PROTECTION OF MINORS

Public debates on the need to tackle the dangers children face when using audiovisual media started in the UK and Finland as early as the 1960s. Initially focused on film and television, concerns are now widespread and linked to the digitalization of the media, especially the Internet, social-media platforms and game cultures. Inviting regulatory responses nowadays are issues such as grooming and paedophilia, pornography, excessive violence, advertisements aimed at minors, cyber-bullying, the presentation of children in the media and game dependency.

At the EU level, the protection of minors is addressed in the Audiovisual Media Services Directive (2007, Articles 27 and 12)[6] and E-commerce Directive (2000). The European Commission does not monitor programmes on an individual basis but rather indicates a minimum set of common rules covering aspects such as advertising and protection of minors in the 'single European TV market' (Directive 2010/13/EU[7]), while monitoring the performance of member states in general. At the same time, the EU has formulated strategies to deal with the particular needs and vulnerabilities of minors using the Internet, with the aim of making the Internet a place of opportunities where children can access knowledge, communicate and develop their skills. One such initiative, part of the EU Digital Agenda, is the Strategy for a Better Internet for Children (COM/2012/0196 final),[8] which proposes a series of actions to be undertaken by the Commission, member states and the whole industry. Also relevant are initiatives like the Safer Internet Forum,[9] an annual EU-supported international conference where different actors come together to discuss the latest trends, risks and solutions related to children's online safety, and projects such as EU Kids Online,[10] a multinational thematic network that aims to stimulate and co-ordinate the many nation-based investigations into children's online uses, activities, risks and safety.

A strong emphasis on industry self-regulation arguably characterizes the EU approach to minors' protection,[11] while the implementation clearly remains the responsibility of the individual member states, where such responsibilities are shared, to differing degrees, by public authorities, audiovisual industries, Internet service-providers, education professionals and parents. At the national level, we can draw a distinction between 'hard instruments' (legislation and technical tools) and 'soft means' (information and education, support for parental guidance) in the protection of minors. In the four countries observed in this study, it appears there are significant differences in arranging the protection of minors, both in regulatory terms and in relation to the crucial role of parents in supporting/accompanying children.

According to a recent EU Kids Online[12] study on children's online risks and parenting practices across Europe, Finland, together with other Nordic countries, belongs to a group of countries where minors can be defined as 'supported risky explorers.' The underlying assumption is that minors cannot be effectively protected from exposure to unwanted content, hence a major role is envisioned for educators and parents, since instead of adopting restrictions to content, the focus is on strengthening trust relationships between minors and educators. Consistently, in Finland the emphasis is on 'soft means' such as information campaigns and media education.

Regarding the anticipated harm resulting from exposure to unwanted content, Finnish statistics show there is no evidence that bullying in general, and online bullying specifically, has increased among adolescents in the past ten years. A long-term trend of about five per cent of children having experienced bullying, either through social media or by other means, has remained stable over time (cf. Jokiranta, 2008; Luopa, Pietikäinen and Jokela, 2008). In contrast to the Finnish approach, according to the same EU Kids Online study, the other three countries – the UK, Portugal and Italy – belong to a group where minors are 'protected by restrictions.' In these cases, Internet use is limited, and largely restricted to practical activities. Such restrictive mediation may prevent risks, but it may also lead to children missing out on online opportunities.

In Italy, we find a mix of measures, with an emphasis on legally enforced co-regulation. The Code of Auto-Regulation of Media and Minors,[13] concerned with both minors' representation and exposure to content, was adopted in 2002, signed by all public and private television companies, and became a law (112/2004) to which all audiovisual content-providers are subject.

Since 2006 (law 38/2006), all Italian Internet service-providers are required to indicate unlawful activities and obliged to institute filtering mechanisms to prevent access to sites and materials containing child pornography. Implementing the law is the responsibility of the National Centre to Counter Paedopornography (Postal Police)[14] and the Observatory to Counter Paedophilia and Pornography of Minors (Department of Equal Opportunities of the Presidency of Ministers)[15]. Growing concern in the country also relates to bullying on social networking sites, especially due to tragic events involving teenagers committing suicide that have attracted public and media attention since the end of 2013.

Such an issue is also of great public concern in the UK. Followings several cases of teenagers committing suicide after being subjected to online bullying, there have been calls to introduce legislation to criminalize cyber-bullying. Under current UK legislation there is no specific law that makes cyber-bullying illegal but, according to experts, it can be considered a criminal offence under legislation such as the Protection from Harassment Act and the Criminal Justice and Public Order Act.[16]

The Conservative British Prime Minister recently announced a "war" against online pornography, describing it a corrosive influence on childhood.[17] British plans to fight child pornography include requiring Internet service-providers to introduce family-friendly filters as default options on domestic Internet connections (the so-called opt-in policy, to be implemented by the end of 2014), and criminalizing the possession of extreme pornography, which includes scenes of simulated rape. The plans have been heavily criticized both on practical grounds (for being technically impossible to implement) and on substantive grounds (by libertarians).

In Portugal, considerable attention has been paid to the representation of minors in the media. The state media regulatory body, the ERC, created in 2005, systematically monitors television content that represents minors. According to Article 34, Number 1, of the Television Act, all TV broadcasters must comply with "the observance of broadcasting ethics that ensures respect for human dignity, for fundamental rights and other constitutional values, especially the development of children and adolescents' personality." In a recent report, the ERC found that in 2009–2010, approximately sixty per cent of the items monitored on television did not use any concealment technique to protect the identity of the children or young people shown (ERC, 2011, p. 46).

To protect children, in 2006 television broadcasters adopted a self-regulatory agreement regarding the classification of programmes,[18] with the main goal of providing consumers with a guide to television programming appropriate for children's ages and of providing educators with guidelines on programme viewing. Episodic initiatives are also taken by the regulatory body in different domains, such as hate speech or exposure to extreme violence, based on individual complaints. Nevertheless, mechanisms of restraint created by the operators for the prevention of specific situations seem inadequate and ineffective. 'Soft' measures are also adopted, as demonstrated by a resolution of the Assembly of the Republic of Portugal in 2008, which recommended the promotion of a national campaign to encourage awareness and prevent the risks children face when using the Internet.[19]

The protection of minors is high on the public agenda in all four countries. The rapid diffusion of media technologies and the liberalization of online commercial activities are challenging traditional media regulation, and there is a significant difference in the approaches adopted by public authorities. In Finland, 'soft' measures such as education, providing information and self- and co-regulation are preferred; in the other three countries, it appears the emphasis is on restrictive policies and statutory regulation. Here, different national and cultural traditions clearly narrow the EU's influence and restrict its influence in monitoring and informational activities. It seems obvious that more and in-depth research is needed to increase our understanding of the real challenges and opportunities minors are confronted with in the digital environment, to inform governing arrangements and to determine an adequate balance between 'soft' and 'restrictive' measures.

BROADBAND ROLL-OUT

The promotion of a high-speed broadband network is one of the EU's main targets as part of its Digital Agenda 2020. The main motivation is that, according to the EU, "it is estimated that a 10% increase in broadband penetration brings up the GDP by 1–1.5%." [20] The targets for full European coverage were set by the EU in 2010 as follows:

- "Basic broadband for all citizens by 2013 (target met – satellite broadband is available to raise the coverage to 100 per cent in every Member State);
- Coverage: Next Generation Networks (NGN) (30 Mbps or more) for all by 2020;
- Uptake: 50 per cent of households having 100 Mbps subscriptions or higher." [21]

The EU strategy is largely based on the expectation that the goals will be met by commercial operators, who will, by 2020, offer almost universal high-speed connectivity in Europe, both to companies and households. Only where there is a clearly defined market failure (i.e. high-speed connections are not commercially viable) will public subsidies be deployed. [22] Even then, state aid can be applied only if approved beforehand by the EU. [23]

The EU is constantly monitoring the implementation of the European high-speed broadband policy, [24] and provides recommendations on its execution to the member states. [25] However, despite the EU's attempts to co-ordinate the rollout, there are major differences, both between the countries and within the countries. For example, while connectivity is almost univer-sal in some of the EU's northern member states (the Netherlands, Denmark), it remains much less advanced in many southern members (Romania, Greece). Meanwhile, in many urban centres the availability of connections of 100 Mbps or more is abundant, while rural areas often still lack even basic connections. [26] Additionally, the EU member states differ widely in their geographies and levels of urbanization, with the effect that the costs of constructing networks differ hugely. The more sparsely populated the areas and the more demanding the geographical conditions, the less commercially viable the construction of the network. [27]

In Finland, although the promotion of high-speed broadband is a govern-mental priority, there has been very little public effort deployed to promote its implementation effectively. In 2008, the government adopted a two-stage broadband strategy, according to which by summer 2010, a connection of 1Mbps became a universal service obligation, binding all network operators to offering an affordable Internet connection to all potential customers in their market area. By 2015, a 100 Mbps connection was to be made avail-able to every household. [28] The strategy was proclaimed as market-led, as only the connection of five per cent of the most remote households and companies was to be supported by public subsidies (requiring a total of €66-million).

The implementation was left therefore to commercial operators, except for the five per cent in which regional and local authorities were engaged.

There was very little further national guidance available, and no central co-ordination. The state aid was granted only retrospectively, which forced the local and regional actors (municipalities, small companies, co-operatives) to engage in complicated negotiations on bank loans to finance the network construction (cf. Nieminen, 2013). By autumn 2013, two interim assessments had allowed stakeholders to voice their concerns.[29] As part of this process, the Regional Mayor of the Regional Council of Southwest Finland (the country's second largest council), Juho Savo, stated the strategy had failed totally and the responsibility lay with the Ministry of Transport and Communications and its reliance on the market. The problem is that the network operators are only interested in building 4G networks in the densely populated areas that promise quick profits, rather than investing in the fibre-optic broadband that will take several years to produce a profit.[30]

In Italy, the National Plan for the Development of Broadband[31] was adopted in 2010, based on previous laws in 2009 and 2010 stipulating the administrative and financial provisions.[32] The goal was to eliminate the digital divide by 2013 – which in 2008 still involved more than eight million Italians – mainly through the development of infrastructures (with ADSL connections and, in the most remote areas, also through satellite technologies), and to bring broadband to the whole population with a connection speed of between 2 and 20 Mbps. The plan was amended in July 2013 when Telecom, the Italian incumbent operator, received an authorization from the national regulatory authority (AGCOM) to offer fibre-optic 30 Mbps connections nationally.

Despite the activity of public authorities, the rollout of high-speed broadband has been less successful than hoped. The Italian country evaluation in the EU Digital Scoreboard 2013 reveals a generally problematic situation. "Italy has a relatively low take-up of fixed broadband and a low availability of Next Generation Access. The share of high-speed connections (at least 30 Mbps) is significantly lower than average. Nevertheless, in mobile broadband, take-up on large screens remains above average. Italy should foster further the investment in infrastructure in order to increase the availability of high-speed broadband."[33]

The national broadband policy in Portugal has changed quite considerably since 2011 under the direction of the neoliberal post-troika coalition led by Pedro Passos Coelho. The previous socialist governments of 2005–2011 developed an ambitious technological plan,[34] but this was suspended in 2011. In line with the Lisbon Agenda, the socialists aimed at developing a knowledge-based economy, with the promotion of high-speed broadband as an important dimension. There was a belief in business innovation and on overcoming scientific and technological backwardness. Several programmes were actually implemented, such as Ligar Portugal/Connecting Portugal,[35] with the aim of promoting Portugal to the top five countries in terms of the technological modernization of schools through the expansion of Internet use for students and teachers. Despite the political disputes caused by some initiatives (the one-laptop-per-child Magalhães programme was probably the most controversial), the socialists' technological plan democratized the Internet in an unprecedented way for the middle classes.

However, the Lisbon Agenda demanded resources and a political will that were simply impossible to achieve after the troika intervention in Portugal. Since then, the promotion of a high-speed broadband network has been left to market operators. The EU Digital Scoreboard 2013 states that Portugal "has a relatively low take-up of fixed broadband, but does considerably better than average regarding the availability of Next Generation Access. In mobile broadband, take-up is lower than average but LTE[36] availability is relatively high."[37]

In the UK, the coalition government that took office in 2010 set the objective of having the best superfast broadband network in Europe by the end of the parliamentary term (by spring 2015 at the latest). The rollout of broadband and superfast broadband networks (at least 30Mbps) has been mostly market-led[38] and driven by private investment. In the words of the government minister Jeremy Hunt during the summer of 2010: "(…) When it comes to superfast broadband, there is no question that the market must lead the way. …"[39] Additional public funding has been made available by both the government and local authorities to ensure superfast broadband reaches some of the most rural and hard-to-cover areas (the 'final third of the country').

Thus far, the government is committed to investing £1.6-billion of public funds to extend superfast broadband to ninety-five per cent of premises by 2017.[40] With regard to mobile networks, licensing and regulatory obligations representing a policy tool used to achieve public interest goals (i.e. the universality of service). The national regulator Ofcom has included coverage obligations in one of the 4G spectrum licences for mobile networks in an effort to ensure near universal availability of broadband. This will provide indoor coverage to ninety-eight per cent of consumers at speeds of 2Mbps by 2017, with at least ninety-five per cent coverage being provided in each of the UK home nations.

The UK national target for fixed broadband networks is for superfast broadband coverage of at least ninety per cent by 2016 and ninety-five per cent by 2017. Currently, the government is exploring options with industry as to how to extend coverage to ninety-nine per cent. However, there is increasing public criticism of the implementation of the government's broadband policy, especially in rural areas. The claim is that when promoting a practical monopoly of only one incumbent company, British Telecom (BT), the government has neglected supervision of the execution. According to the critics, BT has not provided the connections and services promised.[41]

According to the evaluation of the EU Digital Scoreboard 2013, "The United Kingdom has a relatively high take-up of fixed broadband and does considerably better than average regarding the availability of Next Generation Access. In mobile broadband, the take-up is one of the highest in the EU."[42]

The rapid expansion of the high-speed broadband network in Europe involves one of the EU's major industrial and technological initiatives, its

Digital Agenda for Europe 2020. The main expected benefits are industrial and commercial, while it is anticipated it will bring about significant savings in the public service areas of health care, education, social services, etc. From this perspective, the use of the broadband network for information and media services is auxiliary, and this use is only promoted providing it advances the broadband network's rapid deployment.

The problem is that although the Digital Agenda for Europe covers all member countries, its success depends on national resources. Here, the neoliberal ideology and the EU State Aid policy create a hindrance. As the evidence from our four countries clearly indicates, and contrary to the expectations of EU policy, the high-speed network cannot be created on a purely commercial basis. The commercial network operators are not willing to invest in the networks unless they view them as profitable, and this restricts their interest to densely populated regions, cities and suburban areas.

From the viewpoint of the relationship between the EU and its member states, the situation appears to have reached a stalemate. The nation states cannot use their own resources, even if they had them, because of the EU's State Aid policy, while the EU does not have power over national markets.

CONCLUSIONS

The four country cases do not provide a basis for firm conclusions. However, we will offer here some thoughts and suggestions for further policy research.

On the Europeanisation of Media and Communication Policy

Our examples seem to confirm there is no unitary European policy in the areas of media and communication; instead, there are different policies in different policy areas. First, in the case of the protection of minors, the competence of the EU is based on two directives, the Audiovisual Media Services Directive and the E-commerce Directive. Issues other than those covered by these directives belong to the national sovereignty of EU member states.

With regard to public information about the protection of minors and media education, the role of the EU is that of a co-ordinator of national policies and promoter of good practices, while responsibility for the practical implementation lies with national authorities. Furthermore, there is a major cultural divide in Europe concerning the understanding of how best to protect minors from unwanted media content. In northern Europe, the emphasis is on information and education, while countries in central and southern Europe stress control and restrictions.

Secondly, concerning state aid to media, the EU applies a strict market-based policy, according to which public subsidies are permitted only in the case of significant market failure. On the level of EU member states, we can identify a clear push towards a unified European policy in relation to the media. In the case of newspapers, although a number of EU member states practise a policy of VAT exemption for the press, there appears to be increasing pressure to streamline state aid policy along the EU official line and to stop all direct and indirect forms of subsidies. In contrast, in the case of public-service broadcasting, the EU has guaranteed national sovereignty to its member states in how the fundingis arranged, provided it fulfils the general conditions stipulated originally in the Amsterdam protocol of 1997. As a result, there is traditionally a large variety of funding arrangements, ranging from tax-based (Finland) to a combination of licence fees and advertising (Italy).

Thirdly, the roll-out of high-speed broadband is part of the EU's flagship Digital Agenda 2020 programme, which set numerical targets for 2020 that member states are expected to fulfil. The execution of these targets is left to the member states. There are, however, wide differences between the member states' financial and technological competences. Additionally, there is a lack of effective European-level co-ordination of the implementation. As the target was originally to be achieved by market operators – private telecommunications companies – state aid was to be used only to cover the construction of the network in commercially non-viable areas. However, it has been clear during the process of implementation that this market-driven policy will not be sufficient to reach the EU's 2020 target.

On the Effects of the 2008 Crisis on Media Policy and Regulation

It is difficult to offer general conclusions based on the evidence presented in this chapter. However, in relation to the issue of the protection of minors, it may be possible to state that the financial crisis and increasing competition has led the content and service industries to lower their ethical standards. Additionally, the enhanced possibilities offered by Web2.0 and different social media applications have arguably led content-providers to supersede national and European regulatory mechanisms, and as a result expose children to uncontrolled and unmonitored content.

In relation to state aid for the media, it may be possible to claim that as a product of the crisis, there seems to be political ambivalence between the ideological imperatives of neoliberal policies and the dire reality of the media industries. According to neoliberalist policy doctrines, public subsidies to the media should be rejected, but both European creative industries and the European socio-political stability apparently continue to require public subsidies if they are to survive.

The same is true of high-speed broadband policy. From the viewpoint of the future of European industry and trade, Europe needs an effective high-speed broadband network as soon as possible. The problem is that, contrary to the ideological policy doctrine, the markets have not been able to provide it as expected, and in this regard the application of more public subsidies starts to become a necessary alternative.

On the Necessity of a New Balance between Commercial and Democratic Needs

Based on our comparison, it appears there is an increased need to find a new balance in media and communication policy between economic interests and democratic, social and cultural needs. There is currently much confusion as to how to (re)construct this balance in the new converging environment, and the long-lasting effects of the crisis that began in 2008 do not make this task any easier. One way of interpreting the situation is that we should not expect the EU to solve the problems on the level of a common European communication policy. Instead, what looks like confusion can be seen as a variety of different contexts and problem-solving-oriented approaches, leaving room for the EU members to implement national resolutions. However, one clear conclusion seems to arise from our analysis: the recognition that the state still matters. Our examples indicate that at least in the areas we discussed, the EU has not been able or willing to form a pan-European regulatory framework for all media and communications.

This may be because the European financial crisis has led to a deepening social and political polarization, the results of which will only become apparent later. However, this perspective appears set to complicate all European policy issues well into the future.

NOTES

1. The UK and Finland were two exceptions to this predominant historic pattern. The UK was the first European country to launch commercial television financed by advertising, ITV (Independent Television), in 1954; Finland was the first Nordic country to allow commercial television in 1957.
2. Retrieved from http://eur-lex.europa.eu/en/treaties/new-2-47.htm.
3. Retrieved from http://eur-lex.europa.eu/LexUriServ/LexUriServ.do?uri=CELEX: 11997D/pro/09:en.html.
4. Retrieved from http://www.lvm.fi/web/en/pressreleases/-/view/1280864?cssType= normal.
5. Law 103 in 2012; see also Presidency of the Council of Ministers, Department for News and Publishing, Contributions to Publishing Initiatives 2011. Retrieved from http://www.governo.it/DIE/dossier/contributi_editoria_2011/index2011. html.
6. Retrieved from http://ec.europa.eu/avpolicy/reg/tvwf/protection/index_en.htm#27. These rules are supplemented by previous Recommendations on the Protection of Minors and Human Dignity (98/560/EC and 2006/952/EC). An Implementation Report on the Protection of Minors and Human Dignity Recommendations was published in 2011 (http://eur-lex.europa.eu/LexUriServ/LexUriServ.do?uri= CELEX:52011DC0556:EN:NOT).

7. Retrieved from http://eur-lex.europa.eu/LexUriServ/LexUriServ.do?uri=OJ:L:20 10:095:0001:0024:EN:PDF.

8. Retrieved from http://eurlex.europa.eu/Notice.do?checktexts=checkbox&val= 677844%3Acs&pos=1&page=1&lang=en&pgs=10&nbl=1&list=677844% 3Acs%2C&hwords=&action=GO&visu=%23texte.

9. Retrieved from http://www.cvent.com/events/better-internet-with-you-th-/event-summary-e6c8907d87cf4e719aceb823e13c3463.aspx.

10. Retrieved from http://www.lse.ac.uk/media@lse/research/EUKidsOnline/Home. aspx. Relevant is the database of European research on children and young people's online activities, accessible at http://www.lse.ac.uk/media@lse/research/ EUKidsOnline/DB/home.aspx?query=.

11. Retrieved from http://ec.europa.eu/digital-agenda/en/self-regulation-better-internet-kids.

12. Retrieved from http://www.lse.ac.uk/media@lse/research/EUKidsOnline/EU% 20Kids%20III/Classification/Home.aspx.

13. Retrieved from http://www.agcom.it/default.aspx?message=visualizzadocument &DocID=3100.

14. Retrieved from http://www.poliziadistato.it/articolo/455Centro_nazionale_per_ il_contrasto_alla_pedo_pornografia_su_internet/.

15. Retrieved from http://www.pariopportunita.gov.it/index.php/organismi-colle-giali/osservatorio-per-il-contrasto-della-pedofila-e-della-pornografia-minorile.

16. See the Public and Commercial Services Union (PCS). Retrieved April 14, 2014, from http://www.pcs.org.uk/en/resources/health_and_safety/hazardsatoz/bullying-guidanceformembers.cfm.

17. Retrieved from http://www.telegraph.co.uk/technology/internet/10194073/Online-porn-David-Cameron-declares-war.html.

18. Retrieved from www.gmcs.pt/ficheiros/pt/acordo-de-auto-regulacao-sobre-a-classificacao-de-programas-de-televisao-13-09-2006.pdf.

19. Retrieved from http://www.gmcs.pt/pt/resolucao-da-assembleia-da-republica-n-382008-proteccao-das-criancas-na-internet?crian%C3%A7as.

20. Retrieved from http://ec.europa.eu/digital-agenda/en/high-speed-broadband.

21. Retrieved from http://ec.europa.eu/digital-agenda/en/broadband-strategy-policy.

22. Retrieved from http://eur-lex.europa.eu/LexUriServ/LexUriServ.do?uri=OJ:C:2 013:025:0001:0026:EN:PD.F

23. Retrieved from http://ec.europa.eu/competition/sectors/telecommunications/ broadband_decisions.pdf.

24. Retrieved from http://ec.europa.eu/digital-agenda/en/digital-agenda-europe; http://ec.europa.eu/digital-agenda/en/scoreboard.

25. Retrieved from http://ec.europa.eu/information_society/newsroom/cf/itemdetail. cfm?item_id=7948.

26. See Commission Staff Working Document: Digital Agenda for Europe - AGood Start and Stakeholder Feedback. Retrieved from http://ec.europa.eu/digital-agenda/en/news/digital-do-list-new-digital-priorities-2013-2014; https://ec.europa. eu/digital-agenda/sites/digital-agenda/files/DAE%20SCOREBOARD%20 2013%20-%202-BROADBAND%20MARKETS%20.pdf.

27. For example, because of different qualities of the ground within Finland, the costs of laying fibre-optic cable vary from 1 euro/metre to more than 20 euro/ metre.

28. Retrieved from http://www.lvm.fi/en/broadband.

29. See a 2011 report, retrieved from https://ec.europa.eu/digital-agenda/en/blog/getting-the-finnish-broadband-strategy-up-to-date.
30. Retrieved from http://www.aamuset.fi/naista-puhutaan/uutiset/maakuntajohtaja-savo-laajakaista-kaikille-2015-hanke-totaalinen-floppi.
31. National Broadband Plan/Piano nazionale Banda Larga. Retrieved from http://www.sviluppoeconomico.gov.it/images/stories/documenti/adi/TESTO-INTEGRALE-PIANO-NAZIONALE-BANDA-LARGA.pdf.
32. Laws and normative framework for the implementation of broadband in Italy. Retrieved from http://www.mise.gov.it/index.php?option=com_content&view=article&idarea1=1699&idarea2=0&idarea3=0&idarea4=0&andor=AND&sectionid=0&andorcat=AND&partebassaType=0&idareaCalendario1=0&MvediT=1&showMenu=1&showCat=1&showArchiveNewsBotton=0&idmenu=3049&directionidUser=0&viewType=2&cattitle=Leggi.
33. Retrieved from https://ec.europa.eu/digital-agenda/sites/digital-agenda/files/IT%20%20-%20Broadband%20markets.pdf.
34. In the government programme of the XVII Constitutional Government, 2005–2009. Retrieved from http://www.portugal.gov.pt/media/464060/GC17.pdf.
35. Retrieved from http://www.ligarportugal.pt/.
36. LTE = Long Term Evolution; refers to next-generation technology.
37. Retrieved from https://ec.europa.eu/digital-agenda/sites/digital-agendafiles/PT%20%20-%20Broadband%20markets.pdf.
38. Retrieved from http://www.beyondbroadband.coop/kb/government-policy-next-generation-broadband.
39. Jeremy Hunt, Secretary of State for Culture, Media and Sport, July 15, 2010. Retrieved from http://webarchive.nationalarchives.gov.uk/20110709203937/http://discuss.bis.gov.uk/bduk/about/.
40. DCMS 2013, p. 7.
41. Retrieved from http://www.theguardian.com/technology/2013/sep/26/digital-britain-government-accused-rural-broadband.
42. Retrieved from https://ec.europa.eu/digital-agenda/sites/digital-agenda/files/UK%20%20-%20Broadband%20markets_0.pdf.

REFERENCES

Ariño, M. and Llorens, C. (2008) Back to the future: New media, same principles? Convergence regulation re-visited. In: Ward, D. (ed.) *The European Union and the culture industries* (pp. 125–44). London: Ashgate.

Black, J. (2002) Critical reflections on regulation. *Australian Journal of Legal Philosophy*, 1(27). pp. 1–35.

Brevini, B. (2012) European Commission media policy and its pro-market inclination: The revised 2009 Communication on State Aid to PSBs and its restraining effect on PSB online. *European Journal of Communication*, 28(2). pp. 183–97.

CEC (Commission of the European Communities) (2009) *State aid: Commission proposes appropriate measures to bring Swedish press aid into line with single market.* IP/09/940. Retrieved from: http://europa.eu/rapid/press-release_IP-09-940_en.htm.

Christensen, J. G. (2010) *Public interest regulation reconsidered: From capture to credible commitment.* Paper presented at Regulation at the Age of Crisis, ECPR Regulatory Governance Standing Group, 3rd Biennial Conference, University College, Dublin. June 17–19.

Donders, K. (2012) *Public service media and policy in Europe*. Basingstoke: Palgrave Macmillan.

Donders, K. and Moe, H. (eds.) (2012) *Exporting the public value test: The regulation of public broadcasters' new media services across Europe*. Gothenburg: Nordicom.

Freedman, D. (2008) *The politics of media policy*. Cambridge: Polity.

Gibbons, T. and Humphreys, P. (2011) *Audiovisual regulation under pressure: Comparative cases from North America and Europe*. London and New York: Routledge.

Grant, P. and Wood, C. (2004) *Blockbusters and trade wars: Popular culture in a globalised world*. Vancouver: Douglas and McIntyre.

Hallin, D. and Mancini, P. (2004) *Comparing media systems: Three models of media and politics*. Cambridge: Cambridge University Press.

Harcourt, A. (2006) *European Union institutions and the regulation of media markets*. Manchester: Manchester University Press.

Harcourt, A. (2008) Institutionalizing soft governance in the European information society. In: Ward, D. (ed.) *The European Union and the culture industries* (pp. 7–31). London: Ashgate.

Harold, A. (2008) European film policies and competition law: Hostility or symbiosis? In: Ward, D. (ed.) *The European Union and the culture industries* (pp. 33–57). London: Ashgate.

Humphreys, P. (1996) *Mass media and media policy in Western Europe*. Manchester: Manchester University Press.

Humphreys, P. (2006) Press subsidies in the context of the information society: Historical perspective, modalities, concept and justification. In: Fernández Alonso, I., de Moragas, M., Blasco Gil, J. and Almirón, N. (eds.) *Press subsidies in Europe* (pp. 38–54). Barcelona: Generalitat de Catalunya.

Hutchison, D. (2007) The EU and the press: Policy or non-policy? In: Sarikakis, K. (ed.) *Media and cultural policy in the European Union* (pp. 183–202). Amsterdam, New York: Rodopi.

Ilmonen K., Lyytinen, E., Salokangas, R. and Vihavainen, T. (1996) *Yleisradion historia 1926–1996*, 3 kirjaa [*The History of the YLE;* three volumes]. Helsinki: Yleisradio.

INDIREG (2011) Indicators for independence and efficient functioning of audiovisual media services regulatory bodies for the purpose of enforcing the rules in the AVMS Directive (SMART 2009/0001). Final report by Hans Bredow Institute for Media Research (lead partner); Interdisciplinary Centre for Law & ICT (ICRI), Katholieke Universiteit Leuven; Centre for Media and Communication Studies (CMCS), Central European University; Cullen International Perspective Associates (sub-contractor). Retrieved from: http://ec.europa.eu/avpolicy/docs/library/studies/regulators/final_report.pdf.

Jokiranta, E. (2008) *"VÄLILLÄ VAKAVAA, VÄLILLÄ EI"*. *Nettikiusaaminen nuorten keskuudessa* [*"SOMETIMES HEAVY, SOMETIMES EASY": Cyber bullying among young people*]. Bachelor's thesis. Jyväskylän ammattikorkeakoulu [Jyväskylä University of Applied Sciences]. Retrieved from: http://www.mediakasvatus.fi/files/u4/Opinn__ytety___-_Elias_Jokiranta.pdf.

Jääsaari, J. (2007) *Consistency and change in Finnish broadcasting policy: The implementation of digital television and lessons from the Canadian experience*. Åbo: Åbo Akademi Förlag. Retrieved from: https://www.doria.fi/bitstream/handle/10024/5995/JaasaariJohanna.pdf?sequence=3.

Klimkiewicz, B. (2008) Media pluralism and enlargement: The limits and potential for media policy change. In: Ward, D. (ed.) *The European Union and the culture industries* (pp. 81–104). London: Ashgate.

Körber, T. and Kamecke, U. (2008) Technological neutrality in the EC Regulatory Framework for Electronic Communications: A good principle widely misunderstood. *European Competition Law Review*, 29(5). pp. 330–37.

Lehtisaari, K., Karppinen, K., Harjuniemi, T., Grönlund, M., Lindén, C.G., Nieminen, H. and Viljakainen, A. (2012) *Media convergence and business models: Responses of Finnish daily newspapers*. Communication Research Centre (CRC), Department of Social Research, University of Helsinki. Retrieved from: http://www.samk.fi/download/26895_Media_Convergence.pdf.

Levi-Faur, D. (2011) Regulation and regulatory governance. In: Levi-Faur, D. (ed.) *Handbook on the politics of regulation* (pp. 2–13). London: Edward Elgar.

Levy, D. (1999) *Europe's digital revolution: Broadcasting regulation, the EU and the nation state*. London: Routledge.

Lichtenberg, L. (2008) Press concentration, convergence and innovation: Europe in search of a new communications policy. *Central European Journal of Communication*, 2 (1). pp. 49–61.

Lowe, G. F. and Berg, C. E. (2013) The funding of public service media: A matter of value and values. *International Journal on Media Management*, 15(2). pp. 77–97.

Lunt, P. and Livingstone, S. (2012) *Media regulation: Governance and the interests of citizens and consumers*. London: Sage.

Luopa, P., Pietikäinen, M. and Jokela, J. (2008) *Koulukiusaaminen peruskoulun yläluokilla 2000–2007* [*School bullying in secondary school 2000—2007*]. Opetusministeriön julkaisuja 2008:7 [Ministry of Education 2008:7]. Helsinki: Ministry of Education.

Michalis, M. (2007) *Governing European communications: From unification to coordination*. Plymouth, US: Lexington Books.

Murschetz, P. (2006) State support for the daily press in Europe: A critical appraisal – Austria, France, Norway and Sweden compared. *European Journal of Communication*, 13(3). pp. 291–313.

Murschetz, P. and Trappel, J. (2014) State aid for newspapers: A summary assessment. In: Murschetz, P. (ed.) *State aid for newspapers: Theories, cases, action* (pp. 375–91). Heidelberg, New York, Dordrecht, London: Springer.

Nielsen, R. K. (2012) *Ten years that shook the media world: Big questions and big trends in international media developments*. Reuters Institute for the Study of Journalism. Retrieved from: https://reutersinstitute.politics.ox.ac.uk/fileadmin/documents/Publications/Working_Papers/Nielsen_-_Ten_Years_that_Shook_the_Media.pdf.

Nielsen, R. K. and Linnebank, G. (2011) *Public support for the media: A six-country overview of direct and indirect subsidies*. Reuters Institute for the Study of Journalism. Retrieved from: https://reutersinstitute.politics.ox.ac.uk/fileadmin/documents/Publications/Working_Papers/Public_support_for_Media.pdf.

Nieminen, H. (2013) *Sadan megan maakunta: loppuarvio* [*One hundred megabit region: A final assessment*]. Communication Research Centre (CRC). Helsinki: University of Helsinki.

Prosser, T. (2010) *The regulatory enterprise: Government, regulation and legitimacy*. Oxford: Oxford University Press.

Psychogiopoulou, E. (ed.) (2012) *Understanding media policies: A European perspective*. Basingstoke: Palgrave Macmillan.

Rajab, A. (2009) Technological neutrality. *Lex Electronica*, 14(2) (Automne/Fall 2009). Retrieved from: http://www.lex-electronica.org/docs/articles_236.pdf.

Schejter, A. and Han, S. (2011) Regulating the media: Four perspectives. In: Levi-Faur, D. (ed.) *Handbook on the politics of regulation* (pp. 243–53). London: Edward Elgar.

Simpson, S. (2008) The changing totems of European telecommunications governance: Liberalization, market forces and the importance of the EU regulatory package. In: Ward, D. (ed.) *The European Union and the culture industries* (pp. 105–24). London: Ashgate.

Snoddy, R. (2013, December 11) The future of public service broadcasting. *Mediatel Newsline*. Retrieved from: http://mediatel.co.uk/newsline/2013/12/11/the-future-of-public-service-broadcasting/.

Sousa, H., Trützschler, W., Fidalgo, J. and Lameiras, M. (2013) *Media regulators in Europe: A cross-country comparative analysis.* CECS – Communication and Society Research Centre. Braga, Portugal: University of Minho. Retrieved from: http://www.lasics.uminho.pt/ojs/index.php/cecs_ebooks/article/view/1533/1436.

Statistics Finland (2012) *Turnover of electronic media doubled since 2001.* Retrieved from: http://tilastokeskus.fi/til/jvie/2011/01/jvie_2011_01_2012-12-12_tie_001_en.html.

Storsul, T. and Syvertsen, T. (2007) The impact of convergence on European television policy. Pressure for change – Forces of stability. *Convergence.The International Journal of Research into New Media Technologies 2007*, 13(3). pp. 275–91. Retrieved from: https://www.duo.uio.no/bitstream/handle/10852/27244/88331_storsul.pdf?sequence=3.

Thomas, K. P. (2000) *Competing for capital: Europe and North America in a global era.* Washington: Georgetown University Press.

Trappel, J. and Nieminen, H. (2011) Media serving democracy. In: Trappel, J., Meier, W. A., d'Haenens, L., Steemers, J. and Thomass, B. (eds.) *Media in Europe today* (pp. 135–51). The Euromedia Research Group. Bristol, Chicago: Intellect.

11 Renewing the Public Service Media Remit

Barbara Thomass, Hallvard Moe and Leen d'Haenens

Public Service Broadcasting (PSB) and Public Service Media (PSM) in Europe are more than ever changing rapidly. Digitization, convergence, internationalization and globalization are the key words for the shifting mediascape. Nevertheless, the situation across European countries is very diverse, not the least as a result of the economic crisis and the ways in which it has been affecting public broadcasters. The convergence between media, telecommunications and computing necessitates new strategies that keep the balance between policies for mass audiences and fragmented audiences at the same time. As any service in the multiplatform communication system, PSM have to encompass the characteristics of mobility, time-shifting, on-demand personalization and social sharing. Beyond that, PSB, which is by tradition and definition a national undertaking, have to answer to diversity requirements in migrating societies and respond to the Europeanization of public spheres.

This chapter discusses these changes and challenges, analyzing the policies concerning Europeanization strategies and integration of staff with a migrant background. Furthermore, it looks at the digitization strategies of PSM and gives options for what the renewal of the PSM remit could look like. In this chapter, we refer to the notion of public service media as the public service broadcasters, which expand their services to the various platforms of digital and mobile communication. The underlying hypothesis is that public service broadcasting and its new media are running the risk of becoming less relevant if they do not relate to changing social environments. Nevertheless, PSM, which are strong and well connected to civil society, may be able to mitigate the effects of the crises, which could otherwise result in a further disintegration of society.

MAIN CHALLENGES FOR PSM

In a 1992 article titled "Which Public, Whose Service," cultural studies pioneer Stuart Hall criticized the BBC and argued the united national public had always been a construct and public service could only survive if it adapted by "pluralizing and diversifying its own interior worlds." (1992, p. 34) Broadcasting, Hall continued, needed to be turned into "the open space, the 'theatre' in which this cultural diversity is produced, displayed and represented." (Hall, 1992, p. 36) At that point in time, broadcasting was analogue and the first web browser, Mosaic, was yet to be launched. Hall's critique reminds us that the challenge of serving a public is immanent for public service broadcasting, and it takes different forms related to different technological, political and social contexts.

Twenty years on, the challenge can be related to the convergence between media, telecommunications and computing, which necessitates new strategies to keep the balance between policies for mass audiences and fragmenting audiences at the same time. In a media landscape where new and established actors alike scramble to utilize the plethora of available services to reach and connect with an audience, public service broadcasters have to encompass the characteristics of mobility, time-shifting, on-demand personalization and social sharing (e.g. Lowe and Steemers, 2012). But the institutions have to do so without throwing their core remit away. Public service broadcasters have to reach the public at large while also incorporating tools that allow for more specialized communicative modes.

The dilemma infiltrates a range of activities relevant to European public service broadcasters. Take social network sites such as Facebook, which have become staples in everyday life across the continent, offering a perfectly individualized communication environment for each and every one of us. For media organizations in general, social network sites offer opportunities on different levels. For one thing, journalistic work can be done more efficiently and potentially better by involving users in different ways.

Secondly, and on a more prosaic level, the services are thoroughly integrated in the journalistic output on most mainstream news websites, urging readers to spread the word via their own networks. In addition, media organizations have ventured into such services with their own content with the aim of reaching new users. Such is also the case for public service broadcasters, many of which employ social networking sites in their provision (e.g. Moe, 2013). For these organizations, an additional challenge has to do with commercial aspects. These public service broadcasters can be seen as national non-commercial entities that enter the domain of global commercial enterprises. But how can public service broadcasters' use of social network sites contribute towards striking the balance between serving a general public and catering to the fragmented users? Such is the dilemma at the forefront of public service broadcasting today.

In addition, the necessary aspiration to relate more closely to audiences requires that PSB as an institution gets away from the scrutiny and the grip of politicians who try to maintain their view of how politics have to be presented to the audience. A strong political influence – as it is still the case in many PSBs – cannot be reconciled with serving civil society. The recent decision of the German constitutional court on the constitution of the ZDF's broadcasting and administrative council, which includes an excessively large number of state representatives, is a clear sign of the necessity to find new forms of involving civil society in PSB governance.

In what follows, we address these dilemmas on four levels. First, laying the basis for any discussion of renewal, we look at how European public service broadcasting institutions have fared when facing the recent economic downturn. Secondly, we focus on the challenge of migrating societies – that is, how public service broadcasters can find an answer to changing diversity requirements. Thirdly, the issue of a European level is discussed in terms of how public service broadcasters relate to the Europeanization of the public sphere. Fourthly, we show their main digitization strategies and possible alternatives.

Before looking at possible responses and strategies by public service media organizations to on-going fundamental changes, this chapter will look at the striking variety of public broadcasters in terms of sources of income across large and small European countries from 2008 to 2011.

PSM IN EUROPE: A STRIKING VARIETY AS TO FUNDING, CONTENT PROVISION AND MARKET PROMINENCE

Given its public mission and the notions of independence attached to it, one could expect public funding to be the major source of income for public broadcasters. However, the share of public funding is very different from country to country. In general, the clearest financial fracture can be identified in public-broadcasting systems such as France, Germany and Sweden, with a still steady public-income ratio between eighty and ninety-five per cent. In France, the financing issue was hotly debated in recent years, as less advertising income had to be compensated for by taxes levied on private broadcasters, mobile telephone operators and Internet service-providers.

Countries, small and large ones alike, such as Belgium, Italy, the UK, Switzerland and Slovenia, tend to rely on public funding for two-thirds of their total budget. Evidently a country's market size matters a great deal (e.g., Lowe and Nissen, 2011). Hence large discrepancies remain in terms of total income. Whereas in large countries such as the UK and Germany the income fluctuates between seven and a half to almost nine billion Euro, their smaller Belgian, Slovenian, Baltic and Scandinavian counterparts have to make do with a budget ranging from between 18.9 million (Lithuania) and 828 million Euro (Denmark) (European Audiovisual Observatory, 2012).

The demand to renew the PSB mission statement first became acute subsequent to the Amsterdam Protocol (1997) and the Communication on State Aid (2001). The main contextual drivers stimulating PSB to become PSM are digitization, globalization, convergence, fragmentation, individualization and a paramount market logic (see also Bardoel and d'Haenens, 2008). In its Communication on the application of state-aid rules to public service broadcasting (2009), the European Commission stipulates that the definition of the public service mandate should be:

as precise as possible. It should leave no doubt as to whether a certain activity performed by the entrusted operator is intended by the Member State to be included in the public service remit or not. (…) Without a clear and precise definition of the obligations imposed on the public service broadcaster, the Commission would not be able to carry out its tasks.

From this it is clear that on the basis of 'subsidiarity,' the European Commission leaves it to the member states to formulate the task – broad if necessary – of public service broadcasting, while at the same time making it quite clear that as far as the Commission is concerned, this task cannot be concrete enough.

Obviously a central component of the mission is the programme assignment of public broadcasting. The current debate on this issue can be summarized by the catchwords 'comprehensive or complementary.' In practice, most of the broadcasters have chosen, principally or pragmatically, the middle way of compensation. The discussion about the future of PSB revolves around two competing visions: that of the pure "monastery model" on the one hand and the "full portfolio model" on the other (Jakubowicz, 2003). The former vision is shared by critics of the commercialization of PSB and the latter is likely to be adopted by most of the public service broadcasters and policy-makers who hold PSB dear.

Among them are the Digital Strategy Group members of the EBU, unmistakably stating in their Media with a Purpose (2002) that the public service broadcasters should meet the diverse needs of all audience members and therefore remain a 'full portfolio' content-provider – a position that is renewed and developed within the "Vision 2020" project.[1] Although there is much debate in most countries on the mission of public service broadcasting, no country has made the choice to really restrict the task and focus. In response to this critical debate, most public service broadcasters look for arguments in favour of the full-scale model and want to stress their distinctiveness more than ever before.

Market failure has become the main rationale for public service media. The market failure argument goes as follows. As commercial broadcasters are mainly supplying popular programmes, an undersupply of information, education and cultural programmes may be a consequence should public service media not exist. Therefore the latter have the mission to correct market failure and to guarantee content as a merit good. In light of the current state of media markets in many EU competitive markets, one may wonder whether market failure will indeed continue to be a valid policy argument to be supported as an institutional public arrangement.

Europe's fragmentation as regards languages and cultures may be considered an asset, but it does have adverse consequences for the marketing potential of European audiovisual products. The smaller linguistic and cultural communities in particular find it difficult to generate enough home-made production, let alone show it outside their own borders. Berg has shown a positive correlation on the relative influences of size with regard to small and large populations and economy in relation to TV market volume and domestic TV content (Berg, 2012, p. 228). The Italian (TSI 1) and French-language (TSR 1) channels in Switzerland, for example, broadcast respectively 33.1 and 44.8 per cent European-originated fiction, including TV films, series and soaps, TV animation, feature films and short films, of which only 4.8 and 3.2 per cent are national (European Audiovisual Observatory, 2012).

The imposition of a quota system is not always appreciated and it is, at any rate, no solution to the financial problems. European countries differ with respect to the broadcasting of foreign television fiction production originating in Europe and outside Europe. Commercial channels tend to broadcast more non-European productions than public service channels do, the differences being highest in Germany, France, The Netherlands and Sweden.

An explanation often voiced by private channels broadcasting more foreign (often US) productions is that the latter are considerably less expensive than producing programmes themselves and therefore more cost-effective (Steemers, 2004). The UK shows a somewhat different picture. With an average of sixty-three per cent for ITV 1 and 2 against sixty-eight per cent for BBC 1 and 2, the commercial broadcaster follows the BBC closely in broadcasting European fiction (including national). Despite this peculiar situation, the BBC maintains its strong position in transmitting national fiction in Europe (a total of 80.75 per cent on BBC 1 and 2 in 2011). The German PSB follows with an average 68 per cent national fiction.

These findings tend to underline the public service broadcaster's distinctiveness when it comes to its central carrier's role of home-grown and European fiction production. In general, European fiction outnumbers non-European output. On commercial channels, the opposite is true. Here fiction mainly originates from outside Europe, with a clear preference for US productions.

A sound relationship with the public and civil society has become of vital importance, since a relation with politics has proven to have its drawbacks. Popular support can also compensate for an all too close relationship with, or dependence on, politics – a problem that is most prevalent in many Eastern European countries where the grip of politicians on PSB institutions is strong and civil society is not robust enough to combat this influence. A key problem is the gradually diminishing reach of public service broadcasters among 'problematic groups' such as younger generations, migrants and the less educated. Collins et al. (2001, p. 8) introduce the term "audience universality," which is achieved "by serving all, the poor as well as the rich, with a range of programs, including those which may be unprofitable."

The position of public service broadcasters on the viewer market also differs among countries. In the large countries (except for France), the public service broadcasters still stand their ground against commercial competitors. The same situation holds for small countries such as Switzerland, the Benelux (except for the French Community of Belgium) and the Scandinavian countries. Public service broadcasters in these countries continue to be major players on the broadcasting market, with shares ranging from thirty up to forty-five per cent. However, the sister institutions from the Mediterranean basin and the Baltic States have to leave the biggest chunk of the market to their private counterparts, ending up with a mere ten to twenty per cent (European Audiovisual Observatory, 2012).

PUBLIC SERVICE BROADCASTERS VIS-À-VIS THE ECONOMIC CRISIS

In order to assess how the recent economic crisis has impacted on public service broadcasters and to discuss what the consequences might be, we cannot emphasize enough that public service broadcasting arrangements come in different forms in different countries. One possible way to classify them is by separating systems with broad regulatory interventions and strong public service broadcasters; systems with some public service intervention, usually in order to stimulate domestic programming, and a lower level of public funds available; and systems with minimalist intervention, a low level of public funding and marginal public service broadcasters (Moe and Syvertsen, 2009; see also e.g. Berg and Lund, 2012).

The latter category would include Southern European countries such as Greece, Italy, Portugal and Spain, as well as New Zealand and the United States and some Eastern European countries. The middle category would fit, for example, France, Australia, Canada and South Africa, while the first – the one with the most wide-ranging policy interventions – historically has had its stronghold in Japan and Northern Europe: the UK, Germany, Belgium, The Netherlands and the Nordic region (see also Mendel, 2000).

Importantly, this is not a static categorization. Countries move between categories along with shifting policies and economic contexts. New Zealand, for instance, saw a rapid change to its media policy, public service broadcasting included, following radical deregulation from the late 1980s (e.g. Comrie and Fountaine, 2005). More recently, in Europe, a country such as Spain could be said to have moved from the second category to the third partly as a result of the recent economic crisis.

Such a separation, then, seems to make sense considering recent developments as well. In fact, one might argue the economic downturn could have strengthened the differences between public service broadcasting in different countries. The most obvious example is the unprecedented closing of the Greek public service broadcaster ERT. Seventy-five years after its establishment, the partly publicly funded institution was closed down overnight in June 2013 to wide public protests. The months that followed brought further controversies, as the government sought to launch a replacement broadcaster while the ERT crew managed to continue producing and distributing content, partly via satellite and partly via web TV. At the time of writing, the situation remains unclear. What is clear, however, is the status of public service broadcasting in Greece is alarming. It is also quite clear the developments follow from a situation in which the institution has been marginalized and also in the transformation from catering to a broadcast audience to communicating with multiplatform users.

Looking at the situation in media systems with broad regulatory interventions and historically strong public service broadcasters, we see quite different effects of the crisis. The revision of the funding schemes is one very concrete case in point. The licence fee on radio and television sets – the original way of funding public service broadcasters – has been abolished in country after country. Yet the systems that have replaced the licence fee are telling for the political and public support of the institutions, as well as for their economic well-being.

Germany opted for a household fee, specifically set aside for funding the country's public service institutions. A similar set up was introduced in Finland in 2013, when the licence fee was replaced by a so-called YLE tax, named after the country's public service broadcaster. The tax, which applies to individuals, includes a grading system to account for persons with low income such as retirees (cf. Ala-Fossi, 2012). These solutions seem, at least at the outset, to be constructed with an attention to the need for retaining an arm's-length distance between political powers and the media institutions.

A different revision has been introduced in another of the countries with historically strong public service broadcasters: Denmark. There, the licence fee was kept but extended to include not only traditional television sets but also PCs and handheld devices capable of receiving audiovisual media content. Such attempts at future-proofing the funding schemes for public service broadcaster stand in stark contrast to the situation in other parts of Europe and serve to illustrate the ways in which history and political context fundamentally matter (e.g. Micova, 2012, for discussion of recently established institutions in South East Europe; Brevini, 2010, for a Southern European perspective).

PSM AND DIVERSE SOCIETIES

Referring to Hall's suggestion that PSB should pluralize and diversify "its own interior worlds" (1992, p. 34), the following section looks at PSB having been by tradition and by definition a national undertaking. Language and remit are the areas in which the national scope of PSM is still very persistent. In the spheres of law and culture, we can observe strong tendencies of transgressing borders taking place – within law, the role of the EU regulation leading the way creates more and more transnational conditions for PSM.

Culturally speaking, PSM has started to open to the world, although the cultural understandings and the laws for broadcasting are still very much framed by the nation state. This entails a contradiction, which creates crisis symptoms for PSM institutions.

This national understanding and range of public service media are still true when it comes to their actual performance and programming. But because of far-reaching developments within processes of transnationalization, internationalization and globalization, this needs to be questioned with a view to the future. Two border-transgressing phenomena are discussed further. One is the demographic reality of all European societies that have a relevant part of population with migration histories. PSM in Europe and its performance for diaspora, ethnic minorities and immigrants is discussed in this paragraph. The other phenomenon refers to the process of European integration, which – notwithstanding the present financial crises – requires an equivalent to the national-dimensioned public spheres and will be elaborated upon in the following paragraph.

European societies are in no way nations with a homogenous ethnic population but are ethnically and religiously fragmented in many ways. In addition to long-lasting diversities throughout history, nearly every European state is the address of desire for many migrant people for many different reasons. But the coexistence and living together of the majority in societies with their migrant minorities are not without frictions. Some ideas about identity and otherness are helpful for understanding the challenges. As one of the core remits of PSB in many countries is to further the integration of society, it can and should be expected that it gives answers to these new challenges.

Nations are not natural objects but had been created by ideology, politics and social processes. They build on inclusion and exclusion. They form images of themselves as well as images of the other. Minorities are used to form an image of identity, and often these images are hostile and stereotyped. Integration, inclusion and exclusion are forms by which societies in their majority deal with the otherness of minorities. Media are a factor and forum where these images of otherness are constructed and negotiated.

They do it by different mechanisms that mark the difference of otherness in appearance, behaviour, habits and language, although ideally, these 'minorities' should no longer be regarded as 'other' (Roth and d'Haenens, 2011). In spite of this, otherness is shown in TV or film as a danger and menace for the life of the viewer, as an inferior position that has to adapt to the existing hierarchy, as the traced element that has to be cared for or as a funny or weird appearance (Hickethier, 1995, p. 21).

Research on the representation of migrants in mainstream media has shown many stereotyped, one-sided or distorted images. They include a syndrome of criminality, overrepresentation of allegedly undesired groups in the published opinion, defining foreign people as a problem, syndrome of negativity, syndrome of topicality, dramatization, semantics of danger and right radicalism. Especially audiovisual media tend to concentrate on showing violent occurrences where migrants are involved (Ruhrmann and Demren, 2000, p. 71).

D'Haenens and Mattelart illustrate the mechanism of how mainstream media represent ethnic minorities and come to the result of a "stereotypical image of minorities as relegated to specific secluded spheres of society linked to crime and deviance at the negative end and celebrities at the positive end." (d'Haenens and Mattelart, 2011, p. 240) Thus media can enforce disintegrative tendencies in society (Dorer and Marschik, 2006, p. 24).

Nevertheless, media can also choose to play an important role in reducing prejudices, stereotypes and discrimination, as they are able to replace and enhance individual encounters with migrants to a certain degree by media-based confrontation with issues of migration (Holzer and Münz, 1996, p. 45). Hafez (2005) elaborated the different fields in which media can show effects with respect to integration of migrants: they contribute to civic integration, to social and to cultural integration. Depending on whether and how media pick up and frame issues of minorities, questions of the integration of migrants or reproduce stereotyping or negative representations of the other, they can be helpful or prevent social processes of integration.

Diversity is both a reality and a necessity in European societies. Having said this, and taking into account that integration is one part of the remit of public service media in nearly all European countries, we can argue this remit has to be renewed, interpreted and implemented in an advanced way. This means PSM have to answer to diversity requirements in migrating societies.

The establishment of diversity as normality will only succeed if intercultural information, entertainment and education are imparted that connect the interests of minorities and majorities, and if the potentials embedded within the concept of diversity is recognized, used and promoted. As public service media have by origin and legitimation always been grounded on remits that serve social purposes, the latter have to take into account the social and cultural changes within the societies catered for.

Although public service broadcasters have made efforts to increase the fair and balanced portrayal of ethnic diversity in programming and employment, they are far away from showing diversity as a given normality in society. Pilot studies in different European public service media institutions show how weak the approach to develop diversity still is. In the German-speaking countries, the percentage of citizens with a migrant background is about one-fifth, thus they are a fair distance away from being represented fairly and proportionally in the public-broadcasting institutions.[2]

In Austria, 18.6 per cent of the population has migrant roots. However, the visibility of ethnic minorities in the media in general and within the public broadcaster ORF is marginal. There are no data available on the migrants' representation in ORF and no policies to promote young media professionals within the broadcaster. In Germany, North Rhine-Westphalia is the country state with the highest percentage of people with a migrant background – 23.5 per cent. The regional broadcasting corporation WDR hence is one of the federal broadcasters within the ARD, which has the comparatively most advanced policy in Germany. Here 13.9 per cent of the staff has a migrant background and the corporation has an authorized representative for migrant issues and a developed human-resources approach to the issue. Within the ZDF, the national public broadcaster, a working group on diversity has started an initiative to look into diversity issues on various levels. Data on the representation of migrants within the staff had not been collected until now.

Switzerland has an even higher share of population – 23 per cent – with migrant roots, two-thirds of them stemming from EU/EFTA member states. The multicultural construction of Switzerland is reflected in an obvious sensitivity to the issue within the documents of the public broadcaster SRG. Although there is no representative for migrant issues and no documentation of the number of staff with migrant backgrounds, the communication department of SRG claims employees from forty nations work within the broadcaster and contribute to diversity open-mindedness.

In the Netherlands, a law was in place until 2004 but was abandoned, which forced corporations to promote as well as publish the ethnic diversity of their staff. Since then, public broadcasters tend to pay less attention to diversity mainstreaming (Thomass and Radoslavov, 2014, p. 19). In the United Kingdom, the Diversity Strategy of the BBC includes not only gender, sexual orientation, age and handicapped people but also ethnicity, and obliges the corporation to refine policies to promote and showcase diversity.

In consequence, d'Haenens and Mattelart ask for more intercultural content in mainstream media in order "to provoke a process in which audiences could reach out to others, to reconcile value differences, to work on conflict resolution and generally motivate everyone to go beyond their own interests." (d'Haenens and Mattelart, 2011, p. 247) PSB and PSM could and should be first addressed with this demand. A reinterpretation of their remit – especially with respect to the aim of integration – is therefore needed.

One far-reaching way to live up to these aspirations would be to create intercultural channels such as the Special Broadcasting Services (SBS) in Australia (Thomass, 2013). In Canada, special licences are attributed to so-called multicultural channels, which broadcast sixty per cent multicultural content. Such a channel would create production, employment and audiences as a brand for which multicultural living together is a ground, remit and aim of existence. Although there are arguments against this idea, as it might provoke a push away from intercultural dialogue in niche media, it can be defended as specialized channels with diversity programming and employment. Such a multi-cultural channel could also serve as a centre of competence for the mainstream channels, as is for example the case with Funkhaus Europa, a radio channel produced by the German public service corporation WDR (WestdeutscherRundfunk) (Zambonini in Geißler and Pöttker, 2005, p. 285).

Aside from such a strong commitment, PSM have to develop policies by which the principle of better presentation through representation can be put into practice so PSM contribute to a society that is no longer defined by homogenous ancestry, culture or religions, nor by unchangeable demarcations of inclusion and exclusion, but by the plurality of a vibrant citizenship. This refers to the vision of Stuart Hall about broadcasting cited in the beginning of this chapter, according to which public broadcasting is "the 'theatre' in which this cultural diversity is produced, displayed and represented." (Hall, 1992, p. 36)

PSM AND THE EUROPEAN PUBLIC SPHERES

The second border-transgressing phenomenon that questions the national understanding and range of public service media refers to Europe. Renewing the public service remit has to take into account the European cross-border influences and relations as a significant issue for public service media in the sense there is a need for a response to the Europeanization of public spheres. The performance of PSM with respect to a democratic communication culture must respond to the changing societal environment in order to make it relevant for its users as well as for the future.

Besides the migration topic, another topic is concerned with changes in the communications space that was created by the European integration process. Although the crises of financial markets, of the Euro and in consequence of European politics at large might suggest the euphemistic idea of a Habermas-oriented European public sphere is outdated, the argument that is laid out here postulates that Europe needs more than ever integrated and networked communicated spaces in which European issues can be dealt with beyond national borders.

Discourses on the Euro crisis give the impression that more than before, national perspectives are dominant, distances and differences to other countries in Europe are underpinned and a 'we versus the others' is the prevalent perception of the relations between European countries. This is the ground on which stereotypes such as the lazy Southern European states, the eager tiger state like Eastern Europeans and the dominant Germans, ruling the roost, are a living resurrection (Gottschalck, 2013).

This means more Europe-related content in all media and all genres is necessary in order to surmount purely national perspectives, to address European issues with supranational orientations and to allow for media experiences in the reception of the viewers and users that widen the window to political, economic, social and cultural conditions in other European countries in order to get involved in debates that are relevant in these countries. But even in public service broadcasting, Europe is not a strong issue, which opens the perspectives for audiences on near or far neighbours (Thomass, 2006). The reason for this reluctance to represent more of European issues is manifold and lies mainly in the strong focus of PSB on audience figures. Europe as a topic in the light of the European crises is not an attractive content for programming.

The prerequisite for media presenting European issues is that there is a certain amount of attention paid to Europe. If not, commercial media do not have an incentive to attract audiences with these issues. This market for European topics – either in news or, even more, in entertainment – is even more difficult to develop in small state markets (Lowe and Nissen, 2011). But it is especially this variety of small and big markets, small and big language spaces, that is a given fact for European public sphere.

It is not only the economic ratio that requires European content at large but a political and cultural one, which can be better answered by PSM, as they are linked to a remit with social, political and cultural purposes. Thus PSM can be an instrument for developing and networking European public spheres, if they are connected to this task. The broadcasting laws in Europe do not spell out the need for contributing to European public spheres, but it is evident that there are adequate points of connection between broadcasting laws and the above-described prerequisite. If public service broadcasting is considered in the Amsterdam Protocol as "directly related to the democratic, social and cultural needs of each society" (EC 97 C/340/01), if it has a central role to play in national media systems for reflecting and accompanying social reality in an encompassing way, it must consider fundamental processes, one of which is Europeanization. Having said this, any considerations of PSM in a national frame are too narrow. Of course broadcasting acts are adopted in every state but also by the European Union. On the other hand, national public broadcasters have to take into account the European directives.

For the time being there are many pan-European channels that offer a program of European issues to audiences (Chalaby, 2002). But there are many more activities to be imagined and promoted that will position PSM more consequently as a factor of European public spheres. In this perspective, political procedures in the EU institutions, issues of European politics and supranational, relevant debates in European countries have to be given more time and space in programming.

It is imaginable that communicative spaces in areas with shared languages are constructed in a systematic way by broadcasting across borders. This would be possible if broadcasters agree on taking over the programs of smaller states in their networks, which would give more attention to their concerns and discourses. Co-operation between public broadcasters in border-transgressing regions is another way to enlarge communicative spaces, which could be elaborated all over Europe. The enhancement of the national remit with a European dimension is an indispensable precondition for such a technically and easily built communicative space. This could be further developed in elements of programming. Of course, these perspectives need calibrations among the institutions of PSM, which have with the EBU a body of understanding that should be strengthened.

Diversity with respect to opinions, format and genres etc. is one of the fundamental norms of media politics and program politics as well. The extension and consolidation of this diversity imperative must be interpreted with respect to European realities. Exchange programs could enhance the European perspectives within PSM. Internships of editors and journalists of public broadcasters in different countries within an exchange program would promote mutual understanding and comprehension and – in a practical sense – possibilities of investigation as well. The development and diversification of Europe-related formats and genres may attract audiences to European issues. The existent formats are far away from utilizing the whole spectrum of possibilities. Video bridges, as shown in Arte, or entertainment formats such as the European Song Contest are examples that can be developed further.

All these possibilities need a regulatory framework at the European level. This also implies that some of the legal conditions of PSM would need to be examined. As it is the task of PSM to provide information about all relevant issues in society, and as these issues pertain more and more to the whole European society or European institutions, PSM – if they are to be relevant in future – have to contribute to European public spheres.

ONLINE PRESENCE: PART OF THE REMIT OR NOT?

With the public mission of public broadcasting and the EU Communication on the application of state aid rules to public service broadcasting (2009), the discussion was opened to the question of whether or not online services should be part of the remit of public broadcasters. Most of the arguments brought forward a restrictive interpretation of the mission, leaving online services to the market, starting from a purely competition-oriented argument defending competitors' interests in exploiting new and growing possibilities for content distribution (cf. Coyle and Siciliani, 2013).

These interests are defended more fiercely when more competitors feel their business models are threatened by crisis effects. As many of the EU Member States – as a result of private-competition complaints regarding PSB's funding to the Commission – incorporated the *ex ante* test in their media legislation, public broadcasters had to adapt to the given legislation and to the varying platforms in use (e.g. Donders and Moe, 2011). Hildén concludes that restrictive national legislation seems to limit the online activities of PSBs far more than the pre-evaluation of services within the *ex ante* test (Hildén, 2013). He even considers it possible "that the added bureaucratic burden leads PSBs to refrain from proposing new services." (Hildén, 2013, p. 7) According to his study, PSBs use online options in order to enhance their traditional services. The most important activities are web news and provision of access to programming either via live streaming or as a catch-up service. Most broadcasters provide regional news, while local news – especially in the UK, Germany, Denmark, Austria and Switzerland – is limited by law as a result of claims by newspaper publishers.

Nearly all PSBs offer on-demand services, although the number of programs available differs between ten and ninety per cent of the broadcasts (Hildén, 2013, p. 6). Again, legal limitations prevent the broadcasters from providing more, the most exceptional case being Germany, where the new broadcasting law created a new word, "depublicising," meaning the public broadcasters had to remove from the web material that had been previously published online prior to the implementation of the law (Interstate Broadcasting Treaty, 2013, art. 11d[5]).

Mobile and tablet applications are also common for most PSBs. Sharing content through Twitter or Facebook is regarded as one possibility to access younger audiences. Online archives, due to legal and copyright issues, are only rarely to be found, the Nordic countries being in the fore in this respect. As commercial activities of PSBs often face critique, only few PSBs make commercial use of their content through the possibilities of the web, either by on-demand services for pay or – which is much more common – offering web shops with books and DVDs. More than half of the broadcasters studied had advertising on their websites (ibid., p. 8), although the revenue through online advertising is marginal.

Astonishing as these findings may be, it is surprising that European PSBs do not make use of the possibilities of digitization of content delivery. No multiplatform strategy can be detected, audiovisual content in web news is rarely to be found and the development of new online services is in its infancy. Copyright issues are one reason for this, which should and could be solved at an EU regulatory level.

These findings are in sharp contrast to the scenario the EBU project Vision 2020 presented (Bierman et al., 2013). The 'anything, anytime, anywhere' paradigm of a multiplatform environment (Suaréz Candel, 2012), makes a case for a new role of PSM as a "curator, connector, enabler, filter, trainer, educator, archivist" (Bierman et al., 2013, p. 18) with a comprehensive offer and an integrated strategy with linear and on-demand services for a general audience and for communities and personalized offers, for more interactive and dialogue-orientated services and with a focus on prioritized content genres.

CONCLUSIONS

In conclusion, PSM are in crisis and under pressure for two reasons. On the one hand, media convergence in digitized mediascapes has changed the competitive environment to a degree that their services are questioned and harder to locate in an abundance of media offers. On the other hand, they are in danger of losing their legitimacy and support in the public sphere and the political domain if they cannot show they are indispensable due to their very distinctive programs and services. The institutions of PSM have for too long ignored how desperately dependent they are on a society that accepts their privileged position through public funding.

As societies in Europe are moving away from being national containers, wherein PSB once served a rather homogenous audience, public service media of the future have to give answers to fundamental changes. Europeanization and diversity have been spelled out in this chapter as two main challenges within these ongoing changes, which have hitherto not been discussed very prominently. As was said in the introduction, public service broadcasting and its new media are running the risk of becoming less relevant if they do not relate to changing social environments. To make PSM stronger and well connected to civil society requires answers to changes in the mediascapes as well as to social changes. While effects of the crises may result in a further disintegration of society, a new interpretation of the remit with respect to the value of integration could be able to mitigate these effects of the crises. The suggestion we present here is that PSM, in order to overcome their crisis, create a new legitimation and attract new audiences, have to broaden their remit. Europe as a larger space and cultural diversity as the content of this space are important points of reference of this renewed remit.

NOTES

1. See http://www3.ebu.ch/cms/en/knowledge/vision2020.
2. These and the following findings result from a study of a master class at Ruhr-University of Bochum, in press. (see Thomass, 2015)

REFERENCES

Ala-Fossi, M. (2012) Social obsolescence of the TV fee and the financial crisis of Finnish public service media, *Journal of Media Business Studies*, 9(1). pp. 33–54.

Bardoel, J. and d'Haenens, L. (2008) Public service broadcasting in converging media modalities: Practices and reflections from the Netherlands. *Convergence: The International Journal of Research into New Media Technologies*, 14(3). pp. 351–360.

Beck-Gernsheim, E. (2004) *Wir und die anderen. Vom Blick der Deutschen auf Migranten und Minderheiten*. Frankfurt/Main: Suhrkamp.

Berg, C.E. and Lund, A.B. (2012) Financing Public Service Broadcasting: A Comparative Perspective. *Journal of Media Business Studies*, 9(1). pp. 7–23.

Berg, C. E. (2012) *As a Matter of Size: The Importance of Critical Mass and the consequences of Scarcity for Television Markets*. Copenhagen: Copenhagen Business School.

Bierman, R, Leurdijk, A. and Suárez-Candel, R. (2013) *Vision2020: Future Strategies for PSM: An EBU Project* (presented at IAMCR 2013).

Brevini, B. (2010) Towards PSB 2.0? Applying the PSB ethos to online media in Europe: A comparative study of PSB's internet policies in Spain, Italy and Britain. *European Journal of Communication*, 25(4). pp. 348–365.

Chalaby, J. K. (2002) Transnational Television in Europe: The Role of Pan-European Channels. *European Journal of Communication*, 17. pp. 183–203.

CEC (Commission of the European Communities) (1997, October 2) *Protocol on the System of Public Broadcasting in the Member States Attached to the Treaty of Amsterdam*. Brussels: C 340/109.

CEC (Commission of the European Communities) (2001) *Application of State Aid Rules to Public Service Broadcasting*. Brussels: C 320/04.

Collins, R., Finn, A., McFadyen, S. and Hoskins, C. (2001) Public service broadcasting beyond 2000: Is there a future for public service broadcasting? *Canadian Journal of Communication*, 26. pp. 3–15.

Comrie, M. and Fountaine, S. (2005) Retrieving Public Service Broadcasting: Treading a Fine Line at TVNZ. *Media, Culture & Society*, 27(1). pp. 101–118.

Coyle, D. and Siciliani, P. (2013) The Economics of Public Service Broadcasting – A Research Agenda. In: Picard, R.G. and Siciliani, P. (eds.) *Is There Still a Place for Public Service Television? Effects of the Changing Economics of Broadcasting* (pp. 57–69). Oxford: Reuters Institute for the Study of Journalism.

Donders, K. and Moe, H. (eds.) (2011) *Exporting the Public Value Test: The Regulation of Public Broadcasters' New Media Services Across Europe*. Gothenburg: Nordicom.

European Audiovisual Observatory (2012a) *Yearbook 2012: Television, Cinema, Video and On-Demand Audiovisual Services in 38 European States*. Strasbourg: European Audiovisual Observatory.

European Audiovisual Observatory (2012b) *Yearbook 2012: Television, Cinema, Video and On-Demand Audiovisual Services – the pan-European Picture*. Strasbourg: European Audiovisual Observatory.

EBU Digital Strategy Group (2002) *Media with a Purpose: Public Service Broadcasting in the Digital Age*. Geneva: EBU.

Additional services and information for EEC European Communities (1997): Treaty of Amsterdam amending the Treaty on European Union, the Treaties establishing the European Communities and certain related acts, signed at Amsterdam 2 October 1997 (97 C/340/01).

d'Haenens, L. and Mattelart, T. (2011) Media and Ethnic Minorities. In: Trappel, J. et al. (eds.) *Media in Europe Today* (pp. 235–250). Bristol: Intellect.

Dorer, J. and Marschik, M. (2006) Medien und Migration. Repräsentation und Rezeption des „Fremden" im europäischen Kontext. *medien impulse*, 55 (March 2006). pp. 24–28.

Geißler, R. and Pöttker, H. (2005) (eds.) *Integration durch Massenmedien. Medien und Integration im internationalen Vergleich*. Bielefeld: Transcript.

Gottschalck, N. (2013) Die Eurokrise – eine europäische Krise? Analyse des Diskurses über die Eurokrise in Nachrichtenmagazinen in Deutschland, Frankreich und Großbritannien. In: Bravo, R. F., Henn, P. and Tuppack, D. (eds.) *Medien müssen draußen bleiben! Wo liegen die Grenzen politischer Transparenz?* (pp. 47–66). Berlin: Frank&Timme.

Hafez, K. (2005) Islamismus und Medien – eine unheilvolle Symbiose. In: Klussmann, J. (ed.) *Terrorismus und Medien. Eine komplexe Beziehung* (pp. 55–60). Bonn: Evangelishe Akademie im Rheinland.

Hall, S. (1992) Which Public, Whose Service? In: Stevenson, W. (ed.) *All Our Futures. The Changing Role and Purpose of the BBC* (pp. 23–38). London: British Film Institute.

Hickethier, K. (1995) Zwischen Abwehr und Umarmung. Die Konstruktion des anderen im Film. In: Karpf, E. (ed.) *"Getürkte Bilder". Zur Inszenierung vom Fremden im Film* (pp. 21–40). Marburg: Schüren.

Hildén, J. (2013) *European Public Service Broadcasting Online – Services and Regulation*. University of Helsinki: Communications Research Centre (CRC).

Holzer, W. and Münz, R. (1996) Fremdenfeindlichkeit in Österreich? Einstellungen zu Migration, ausländischer Bevölkerung und staatlicher Ausländerpolitik. In: *Demographische Informationen 1995/1996* (pp. 45–53). Wien: Institut für Demographie.

Jakubowicz, K. (2003) Bringing public service to account. In: Lowe, G.F. and Hujanen, T. (eds.) *Broadcasting & Convergence: New Articulations of the Public Service Remit* (pp. 147–67). Gothenburg: Nordicom.

Lowe, G.F. and Steemers, J. (eds.) (2012) *Regaining the Initiative for Public Service Media. RIPE@2011*. Gothenburg: Nordicom.

Lowe, G.F. and Nissen, C.S. (eds.) (2011) *Small Among Giants: Television Broadcasting in Smaller Countries*. Gothenburg: Nordicom.

Mendel, T. (2000) *Public service broadcasting. A comparative legal survey*. Kuala Lumpur: UNESCO, Asia Pacific Institute for Broadcasting Development. Retrieved from: http://www. unesco.org/webworld/publications/mendel/jaya_index.html.

Micova, S.B. (2012) Born into Crisis: Public Service Broadcasters in South East Europe. In: Lowe, G. F. and Steemers, J. (eds.) *Regaining the Initiative for Public Service Media* (pp. 131–48). Gothenburg: Nordicom.

Moe, H. (2013) Public Service Broadcasting and Social Networking Sites: The Norwegian Broadcasting Corporation on Facebook. *Media International Australia* (146). pp. 114–122.

Moe, H. and Syvertsen, T. (2009) Researching Public Service Broadcasting. In: Wahl-Jörgensen, K. and Hanitzsch, T. (eds.) *Handbook of Journalism Studies* (pp. 398–412). New York, London: Routledge.

Roth, L., d'Haenens, L. and Lebrun, T. (2011) No longer 'the other': A reflection on diversity in Canadian fiction television. *The International Communication Gazette*, 73(5). pp. 380–399.

Ruhrmann, G. and Demren, S. (2000) Wie Medien über Migranten berichten. In: Schatz, H. and Holtz-Bacha, C. (eds.) *Migranten und Medien. Neue Herausforderungen an die Integrationsfunktion von Presse und Rundfunk* (pp. 69–81). Wiesbaden: Westdeutscher Verlag.

Scannell, P. (1995) Britain: Public Service Broadcasting: From National Culture to Multiculturalism. In: Raboy, M. (ed.) *Public Broadcasting for the 21st century* (pp. 23–41). Academia Monograph University of Luton Press: John Libbey Media.

Schönhagen, P. (2000) Evaluation des Integrationspotentials von Massenmedien – theoretische und methodische Überlegungen. *Medien- und Kommunikationswissenschaft*, (4). pp. 554–570.

Steemers, J. (2004) *Selling Television: British television in the global marketplace*. London: British Film Institute

Suaréz Candel, R. (2012) *Adapting Public Service to the Multiplatform Scenario: Challenges, Opportunities and Risks*. Working papers of the Hans Bredow Institute, No. 25.

Thomass, B. and Radoslavov, S. (2014) *Discovering, Narrating and Representing Diversity in European Public Service Broadcasting. Paper for RIPE@2014.* Retrieved from: http://ripeat.org/wp-content/uploads/tdomf/3622/Thomass%20_%20Radoslavov%20RIPE%20paper%202014.pdf .

Thomass, B. (2015) (ed.) Migration und Vielfalt im öffentlichen Rundfunk. Bochum: Westdeutscher Universitätsverlag (forthcoming)

Thomass, B. (2013) Diversity als Programm – Vielfalt als Auftrag des öffentlich-rechtlichen Rundfunks. *epd medien* (9). pp. 6–8.

Thomass, B. (2006) Public Service Broadcasting als Voraussetzung europäischer Öffentlichkeit – Leistungen und Desiderate. In: Langenbucher, W.R. and Latzer, M. (eds.) *Europäische Öffentlichkeit und medialer Wandel* (pp. 318–328). Wiesbaden: VS Verlag für Sozialwissenschaften.

Thompson, M. (2005) Foreword. In: Helm, D., Green, D., Oliver, M., Terrington, S., Graham, A., Robinson, B., Davies, G., Mayhew, J. and Bradley-Jones, L. (eds.) *Can the Market Deliver? Funding public service television in the digital age* (pp. vii–x). Eastleigh UK: John Libbey Publishing.

12 Can Civil Society Mitigate Consequences of Crises?

Anker Brink Lund

This chapter discusses how different civil society norms have developed over time in the United Kingdom, Denmark, Italy and the Czech Republic. The aim is to understand if and how these rather different normative traditions may (or may not) motivate civic engagement in times of media crisis. The claim is that if a sustainable balance between market competition, government regulation and public participation cannot be struck, business turmoil and political tumult may develop into crisis of legitimacy affecting the very existence of a civilized public sphere for exchange of news and views. On the other hand, civil society norms may also motivate active citizenship and non-profit philanthropy in times of crisis.

'Civil society' is a flexible and contested concept, containing conflicting norms related to active citizenship beyond the spheres of family, market and state. Jeffrey C. Alexander (1998, p. 7) defines it as a sphere that "is exhibited by 'public opinion', possesses its own cultural codes and narratives in a democratic idiom, is patterned by a set of peculiar institutions, most notably legal and journalistic ones, and is visible in historically distinctive sets of interactional practices like civility, equality, criticism, and respect." What Alexander calls "journalistic institutions" legitimate their role in society as servants of informed citizenship within the public sphere, at arms length from advertiser as well as government control. In so doing, a never-ending, often crisis-ridden quest for independence is taking place within historically informed civil society. Jürgen Habermas (1999, p. 388) puts it thus: "[T]he basic condition is that autonomous public spheres must be anchored in a free civil society and be embedded in liberal patterns of political culture and socialization."

In line with the normative value approach (presented in detail in Chapter 1), this chapter asks if consequences of crisis can be mitigated by applying civil society norms to crisis management, facilitating virtuous circles of reciprocity, deliberation and philanthropy. Our claim is that voluntary associations, non-profit foundations, co-operatives and employee-owned enterprises in the so-called third sector may motivate change and initiate self-governed media activities (Dahlgren, 2000). On the other hand, we should not automatically expect civic engagement to bloom in times of crisis (Kosselleck and Richter, 2006). The aim is to understand if and how different normative traditions may (or may not) motivate civic engagement in times of crisis.

From research in community media development (Jiménez and Scifo, 2010) we know that governments – in line with the recommendations from the Council of Europe – have been supporting experiments of local radio and television since the media crises of the 1970s. Civility of this kind may be short-lived and vulnerable, but have nonetheless, in most European countries, matured into independent non-market and non-state institutions in their own right, challenging not only private media business but also mouthpieces of special interests. Evaluations of self-organized initiatives at the grass-root level, however, document that civic voice is only one possible response to crisis. In Eastern Europe, community media never really succeeded (Dolivwa and Rankovic, 2014), and exit from civic engagement in general and media activism in particular are just as likely to be triggered by crisis than advocacy and non-commercial co-production (Scholte, 2013).

Inspired by Habermas (1975 and 1999) we discuss these public sphere responses within a framework of civil society valuation, claiming that financial trouble may develop into fundamental crises of legitimacy and crisis of motivation beyond simple market and government failures. Crises of legitimacy emerge when market and government failure spill over into the political system, threatening civic confidence and general loyalty towards social institutions of state and market. In this process, financial steering problems can impact fundamental values of business and politics, provoking civil disobedience and critical voices demanding social change. Crises of motivation relate to situations in which loss of legitimacy becomes so massive that apathy rather than political voice is the dominant impact on the general public. In crises of the latter kind, a decisive number of citizens react by cynicism and exit – not by demanding social change and actively engaging in self-organized alternatives. Within this crisis context, non-government and non-market media alternatives cannot be studied merely as community radio and television (Council of Europe, 2009). We must dig deeper into the inherent civil society norms framing media activism and other forms of self-organized civic engagement – or lack of same.

In the next section, a normative framework for valuation analyses (Lund and Langer, 2000) is presented in order to address the fundamental research questions of the chapter: Can civil society mitigate legitimacy and motivational consequences of contemporary crises? And what strands of civil society norms, developed over time in different national contexts, may be more or less instrumental and consequential in crisis management of this kind?

VARIETIES OF EUROPEAN CIVIL SOCIETY

In order to offer tentative answers to the research questions stated above, self-organized media initiatives beyond family, state and market have been surveyed and contextualized within a civil society framework, containing historically distinct but partly overlapping traditions. Inspiration has primarily been found in political theory (Cohen and Areto, 1992; Kaviraj and Khilnani, 2001), supplemented with input from comparative media-systems analysis (Blumler and Gurevitch, 1995; Hallin and Mancini, 2004).

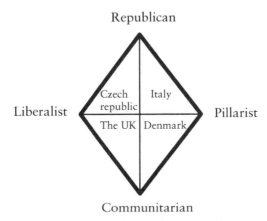

Figure 12.1 A Normative Framework for Civil Society Valuation.

Republican civil society norms, e.g. active citizenship valued as a civic duty to take part in community checks and balances of public affairs (*res publica*). Have been propagated by classical scholars such as Aristotle, Cicero and Machiavelli (Skinner, 1998) and labelled 'critical republicanism' or 'civic humanism.' The contemporary vitality of this tradition has been challenged, especially because active citizenship faces what Jeffrey C. Alexander (1998, p. 3) has termed "dilemmas of institutionalization." Most grass-root initiatives fall short of their republican and humanitarian aims, and if activism succeeds by becoming mainstream, that may *per se* be regarded as a sell-out from the activists' point of view, because original ideals have been compromised in the process of political influence (Dahrendorf, 1999). Historically, the printing press became instrumental in active citizenship of the republican kind, but also in propaganda by the authorities. More recently, self-organized media initiatives have been booming on the Internet, but most social media initiatives either tend to become commercialized or marginalized.

Liberalist civil society norms, e.g. individual rights related to speech and assembly under rule of law, have influenced European media systems all over the world. Liberal protagonists of third-sector values invest hope in contract-based solutions to state/market/individual relationships (Keane, 1988). Historically, the rise of the modern, market-based newspaper press can be seen as a paradigmatic answer to the legitimacy crisis of an authoritarian system of censorship. More recently, neoliberalist norms have been instrumental in commercial businesses, challenging the legitimacy of government regulation of media markets. From the beginning of the 1980s, state monopolies in telecommunications were privatized and public broadcasters were forced to contract out services. Critical scholars warned against the negative side effects of this deregulation, suggesting these liberal norms produce market failure rather than pluralism of voice (Couldry, 2010), especially damaging in small media markets with an immature public-service tradition (Splichal, 2001).

Pillarist civil society norms, e.g. organization of self-interest associations to maximize membership benefits by collective bargaining, has also been labelled 'segmented pluralism,' 'associational democracy' and 'corporatism' (Katzenstein, 1985). Regarded from a civil society valuation point of view, the main feature of this tradition is the institutionalization of conflicting interests by means of state co-ordination (Leiphard, 1968). Pillarism has been particularly strong in social settings where political and religious interest groups have been recognized as co-producers of social order by official authorities, including media management. Pillarist media may mitigate republican as well as liberalist market failures by offering membership-based, non-government and non-market alternatives to commercial and licensed media. Especially in times of crisis, voluntary associations can compensate for-profit media failings by strengthening self-organized communication channels, hiring partisan journalists and initiating public campaigns on a non-profit basis. The potential down side of pillarist media systems consists of tendencies towards clientelism and political parallelism (Hallin and Mancini, 2004). In short, this civil society tradition of this strand struggles to maintain a balance between membership media delivered with political strings attached versus open interaction with public sphere communication writ large.

Communitarian civil society norms, e.g. reciprocity related to civic engagement within a shared habitat, can be regarded as consensus-seeking in order to reduce free riding behaviour in an increasingly fragmented world of libertarian individuals, pillarist rent-seekers and republican activists (Etzioni, 1995). The core civil society value in the communitarian tradition is local patriotism across religious, class and other conflicting interests, sometimes labelled 'responsive mutualism' or 'romantic communalism,' particularly salient within so-called "small platoons" (Cohen and Areto, 1992). Social clubs and voluntary associations embedded in local precincts and neighbourhoods may develop into larger, imagined communities, supported by regional or national media. Public-service broadcasting of the BBC type has been instrumental in building national bridges across polarized communities (Berg, Lowe and Lund, 2014). Furthermore, community radio and other non-profit media have supported responsive mutualism by diffusing close to home news and views (Browne, 2012). This, in turn, may also mediate chauvinist patriotism at the potential expense of excluding outsiders from the public sphere (Vandevelde, 1997).

Our claims are that all four civil society traditions have different upsides and downsides, regarded from a normative public sphere valuation point of view, and varieties of them are at play in European media systems of the twenty-first century. Based on former research (European Journalism Centre, 2011; Kelly, Mazzoleni and McQuail, 2004), four cases have been selected for tentative study, controlling for varieties of media market size and public-service media (PSM) maturity: the United Kingdom (large market with long PSM tradition), Denmark (small market with long PSM tradition), Italy (large market with relatively short PSM tradition) and the Czech Republic (small market with a very short PSM tradition).

The case approach at hand is not to be regarded as an in-depth study of single units but rather comparative illustrations of a theory-driven framework "to elucidate features of a larger class of similar phenomena." (Gerring, 2004, p, 341) In other words, the four cases represent extremes within the normative civil society framework (see Figure 12.1). We take our point of departure from the British case because paradigmatic scholarship (Couldry, 2010; Hallin and Mancini, 2004; Marcinkowski, Meier and Trappel, 2006) regards liberalist norms, originating from the UK, as the current motor of media system convergence. Against this backdrop, the country cases are discussed in terms of media development in order to historically frame the impact of the 2008 financial crisis, especially with regard to legitimacy, motivational voice and exit related to activist, non-profit, special-interest and community journalism (Meyer and Lund, 2008).

LIBERALIST COMMUNITARIAN NORMS

The United Kingdom has a large commercial media market catering to a population of sixty million in twenty-five million households and an even larger audience outside the UK. Eight separate companies distribute national newspapers, and one of these – News Corps. – is also a major player in the television market, in competition with the ITV channels and the BBC, also doing radio, supplemented with 250 local commercial and over 200 non-profit community radio station.

In the late nineteenth century, British liberalism paved the way for private, profit-driven newspapers performing civil society functions at arm's length from government. Compared to other European countries, party subsidies to the press have been limited. This relative independence was made possible by handsome advertising revenues and mass circulation. The liberalist norms, however, never stood unchallenged. The militant labour movement promoted its own values, and succeeded in establishing its own media, accommodating the rank and file on a non-profit basis. In the longer run, however, these pillarist channels of union-oriented communication were not able to maintain sufficient membership, loyalty and non-market reciprocity to offer the commercial tabloids effective competition (Curran and Seaton, 2010).

A more pervasive challenge to market-driven mass communication is the BBC, organized as a public-service institution in the communitarian tradition, with a consensus-seeking, non-partisan and non-commercial remit. John Reith, the first Director-General of the BBC (quoted from Marris and Thornham, 1999, p. 123), wanted the 'the wireless' to avoid controversy and social conflicts, "making the nation as one man." The means by which this was accomplished were the provision of a variety of high-quality content framed within the brute force of monopoly. In so doing, the public-service model represented a non-market and non-government alternative to the liberalist tradition of advertising-based newspapers. Furthermore, the communitarian norms of the BBC were instrumental in mitigating pillarist class conflict by offering a patriotic and paternalistic diet.

Within the carefully balanced BBC remit, the monopoly of radio broadcasting was amended with television from 1936 but modified with the creation of ITV in 1955, creating a duopolistic system with consensual public-service norms. The communitarian norms did not become seriously challenged until the 1980s during the Thatcher administration when neoliberal values of deregulation prevailed. This challenged the pillarist norms of civil society in general and labour union organizations in particular. Subsequently it also created a period of concurrent crises at the BBC, weakening the communitarian solidarity behind public-service broadcasting. This, in turn, assisted multinational entrepreneurs headed by Rupert Murdock in building an influential media conglomerate including newspapers such as *The Times*, *The Sun* and the *News of The World*, incorporated with satellite-based Sky Television. In 1986, the Thatcher-Murdock alliance delivered a final blow to previously powerful labour unions by moving the print business to a high-tech plant in Wapping (Melvern, 1986).

Since the financial crisis of 2008, London has been mediated as the European epicentre for irresponsible banking and shortcomings of anti-statist deregulation in tandem with Wall Street in New York. Bankers and brokers of the City were accredited the lion's share of blame for the building and bursting of the housing bubble and its negative consequences for the Western world writ large. The UK, however, neither experienced massive collective action of the occupy-movements type nor large crowds of protesters taking to the streets (Fuchs, 2014). Consequently, it could be argued that the contemporary legitimacy crisis has turned into a motivational one, not primarily prompting critical voice but rather exit and apathy (Scholte, 2013).

More specifically, the UK media crisis has been diagnosed as a series of neoliberal market failures, creating legitimacy and motivational problems for commercial as well as public-service media. Spectacular scandals have motivated criticism of commercial as well as public-service journalism, including the Hacked Off Campaign, triggered by the *News of the World* scandal. This civil society-based campaign has been funded by Res Publica, Media Standards Trust and other NGOs, monitoring the Leveson Inquiry on media ethics and pressing for substantial reform of press regulation. But the UK currently occupies merely the twenty-ninth place on the Press Freedom Index (Reporters without Frontiers, 2013), and few sustainable, self-organized media initiatives have emerged after 2008.

In order to mitigate the effects of the current crises, official spokespersons for the government as well as the Labour opposition have appealed to civil society actors more in in line with communitarian rather than liberalist and pillarist ones. All leading parties increasingly argue that voluntarism, non-profit philanthropy and small platoons must be mobilized in order to supplement business and tax-based services. The Conservative/Social Liberal coalition has synthesized these policies under the heading Big Society (in contrast to big business and big government). A skeptical Labour opposition rejected most of the specifics, but agreed in principle that a more self-organized public service is necessary. In terms of self-organized media initiatives, however, little action has originated from the communitarian appeals (Edwards, 2012).

COMMUNITARIAN PILLARIST NORMS

Denmark contains a relatively small and homogeneous media market containing five million inhabitants constituting two million households. Historically, newspaper coverage has been high with eight national titles and twenty-two local ones in 2014. The two public service-providers, DR and TV2, hold a sixty-eight per cent share in television and a seventy-six per cent in radio.

In 2005, the Mohammed Cartoon Crisis, which originated at the regional newspaper *Jyllands-Posten*, demonstrated how the ambiguities of the free-speech norm can be interpreted very differently in civil societies around the world. In Danish journalism, the global events were regarded as a moral panic, initiated by publishers preoccupied with costly cut-throat competition on a mature and demanding market. This, in turn, deflected innovative resources from the adjustment of print to web media. Consequently, the 2008 financial crisis actually came as a relief. The foreign investors were hit much harder than their Danish competitors, leaving room for mainstream media consolidation.

To some extent this development can be attributed to a pillarist tradition of non-profit media management, originating in the party press – the so-called four-paper-system. Not until the 1970s did Danish newspaper publishers break off parallelism with political parties. Today, the majority of media companies have transformed themselves to self-governed foundation ownership by acquiring their own stocks (Lund, 2007). Outside Denmark, this type of non-profit, co-op media ownership is rarely found. In the UK, for instance, among major media players only *The Guardian* has a similar organization with the explicit aim to safeguard journalistic freedom.

Foundation ownership allows private media to employ civil society norms on non-commercial terms, e.g. publishers organized in this fashion need not make quarterly profits for external shareholders as long as staff and subscribers are satisfied. Management, so to speak, can afford to make public service for private money in close co-operation with the well-organized Danish union of journalists, which, in turn, has been able to avoid massive redundancies in the aftermath of the 2008 financial crisis. In this fashion a party-pillarist tradition is countered by communitarian public-service values, dating back to the 1920s when the Danish government imitated the BBC model. At first, the party press lobbied for full newspaper control of the air waves. But the limited number of frequencies for broadcasting made this solution technically unfeasible. Instead, the press association was granted monopoly of radio news reporting, and DR was excluded from editorializing and from advertising revenues in order to reserve these vital streams of income for print publishers.

The DR broadcasting monopoly was strengthened further by the introduction of television in the 1950s, not modified until the late 1980s when commercial players were allowed access to radio and television. Until then, the majority of political parties and most civil society actors argued that only communitarian planning, guided by pillarist representative politics, would provide the full range of quality content, construed as merited goods available for the general public. Digitalization as such has had limited impact on this well-funded public-service regime, motivating a multitude of niche channels directed at a fragmented mass audience. DR amended its dominance from radio and flow television into comprehensive production and distribution of online services.

This, with new emphasis after the financial turmoil post-2008, has made private players challenge the legitimacy of licence-fee operations online. Basically the argument has been one of enforcement and failure of government regulation. In times of digitalization, the technical argument of scarcity is no longer regarded as legitimate to mandate the communitarian governance of broadcasting. Warning side effects on market incentives and structural solutions are called for in order to limit the remit of DR and reduce its current presence in new media platforms. Compared to the heated debate in the UK, however, the public-service situation in Denmark can hardly be characterized as a motivational crisis. Ninety-two per cent of Danish households pay their voluntary licence fee with little protest.

In sum, Danish journalism has shown few serious crisis symptoms after 2008 in spite of the turmoil of the global economy and dot-com media market failures. On the print platform, financial problems have resulted in some redundancies, a couple of newspapers have merged, a couple of free sheets have folded, some lifestyle magazines were closed because of failing advertising revenue and privately financed web media ventures went belly up. The Danish Union of Journalist has been quite successful in mitigating layoffs, and serious publishers have been compensated for losses by way of public subsidies. Foundation ownership and handsome licence fees have also been instrumental in maintaining media pluralism measured in terms of content diversity, securing Denmark an impressive sixth place on the Press Freedom Index (Reporters without Frontiers, 2013). The downside to this robust combination of communitarian and pillarist initiatives has been high barriers of entry for non-subsidized media upstarts.

PILLARIST REPUBLICAN NORMS

Italy is a relatively large media market (sixty million residing in twenty-three million households) but contains few widespread newspapers with national coverage. The media market is regionalized and subsidized by special-interest corporations, e.g. industrial groups and affluent individuals with political ambitions. Cross ownership is not uncommon, with the Berlusconi-owned Finn Invest as the dominant private player not only on print but also in television, second in audience share only to the public-service provider RAI, also active in radio, supplemented by numerous local stations.

The Italian press was never a liberal institution in the British civil society tradition, and when the newspaper *L'Indipendente* recently attempted market-based experiments on objectivist and non-aligned journalism, the attempt did not succeed in a civil society dominated by republican and pillarist norms. Originating in the late nineteenth century in tandem with the uneasy national unification, most Italian newspapers were born with strong party or church affiliations but limited readership. Furthermore, this freedom of expression in newspaper as well as radio was suspended during the fascist period from 1922 until the passing of the republican constitution of 1947–48.

Civil society norms stressing the value of arm's length from government and political parties have never been rooted in Italy. The politicizing biases of most Italian newspaper journalism may indeed be regarded as very civilized within pillarist and republican civil society traditions (Putnam, 1993). From a liberal communitarian point of view this is regarded as a weakness, because it motivates opinionated and confrontational rather than middle of the road media content. In spite of these non-liberal standards, the Italian public is offered a wide variety of competing voices, not only within the regionalized press but also in special-interest magazines and local radio.

In spite of liberal reform, Italian public-service media also contain remnants of the so-called principles of *lottizzazione* – pillarist power-sharing between dominant political parties (Hanretty, 2010). But when the established party system experienced a perpetual crisis in the 1970s, little regulation of broadcasting was implemented. At first the vacuum was filled by activists. Challenging the RAI-monopoly, more than a thousand local radio- and television-stations went on air, initiating a republican 'wild west' of community radio on the FM band. This phase of radical republicanism was brief, however. Commercial players established private broadcasting networks across Italy, and in 1992, when Italian politics experienced a serious legitimacy crisis, most of the local and regional initiatives had been boiled down to two conglomerates (Viroli, 2011). One of the winners was instrumental in assisting its owner, Silvio Berlusconi, to became prime minister 1994–95, 2001–6 and 2008–11.

The international financial crisis hit Italy very hard, with gross domestic product falling and unemployment rising, which subtracted 6.5 percentage points from economic activity over the period 2008–2010. Italy is one of the most indebted countries in the Euro zone. Massive cuts in advertising budgets legitimized massive layoffs in the media business. This trend seem to have continued, and FNSI, the Italian union of journalists, estimates major newspapers and RAI together have and will cut at least six hundred jobs in the period 2013–15. In the republican civil society tradition, however, the current crisis has also regarded as an '*occasione*,' a moment of disorder that offers opportunities for new beginnings. A large number of civic action groups has been organized around innovative Internet journalism. Opinionated critics of the political system, e.g. *Il Blog di Beppe Grillo* (Beppe Grillo's Blog), run by a TV entertainer, generated a massive following in cyberspace and paved the way to parliamentary politics for a considerable number of his followers in the 2013 election.

In spite of the financial crisis, new online activities have motivated plurality of content as well as redundancies in mainstream media. It has been estimated that the percentage of Italians depending on television as their sole news source decreased from 46,6 in 2006 to 26,4 in 2009 (Mazzoleni, Vigevani and Splendore, 2011, p. 4). Another notable initiative is *Ammazzatecitutti.org* ("Kill us all"), an anti-mafia movement organizing a variety of non-commercial and non-government media (Cayli, 2013). The Facebook-based Move On Italia campaign has demanded more direct citizen participation in Italian politics, and self-organized social media also played important parts in 2010 when bloggers across Italy united in formulating a joint declaration mobilizing public support against the so-called gagging law aimed at shutting up government critics. The campaign motivated modifications in the legislation passed in the Italian parliament, and inspired a reform for RAI, demanding larger degrees of market and government independence for public-service media.

In sum, one may characterize the Italian situation as a crisis of legitimacy, both in terms of media and politics, originating at least back to the mid-1970s and reinforced once again by the 2008 financial turmoil. This has reduced public confidence in mainstream journalism, market-based as well as government controlled, and influenced voluntary participation of the pillarist kind. In contrast to other parts of Southern Europe, however, the contemporary crisis has hardly fuelled a full-blown motivational crisis. On the contrary, few countries have more pluralist and non-conformist voices on popular community and online media. Voter turnout is still quite high, as is membership of cultural and political associations. During the current crisis Italy actually advanced to forty-ninth place on the Press Freedom Index, receiving this consolation: "The only positive evolution in the south is to be found in Italy, which has finally emerged from a negative spiral and is preparing an encouraging law that would decriminalize defamation via the media." (Reporters Without Frontiers, 2013)

REPUBLICAN LIBERALIST NORMS

The Czech Republic was formed in 1993, when Czechoslovakia split into two independent countries. In the same year, a national radio (CR) and a state-owned television company (CT) were deregulated on a neoliberal public-service remit. The 4.3 million households containing 10.5 million residents make the Czech Republic a small media market with a relatively short public-service tradition. Currently the Czech-speaking population is served by nine national and eighty regional newspapers, four major national TV channels and eighty-two radio stations, primarily locally run and commercially financed.

Intellectuals warned against pillarist as well as neoliberal haste in the top-down development of post-communism, pledging bottom-up community-building based on republican norms (Dahrendorf, 1999). Historically, republicanism of this kind can be dated back to opposition against the Catholic Church and the Habsburg monarchy. More recently, these civil society values were included as motivators for the 1968 Movement by reform socialism, and were activated again during the so-called Velvet Revolution of 1988–89 (Havel, 1992).

Charta 77, Civic Forum and other system-critical groups applied republican norms as vehicles of system criticism, producing mimeographed pamphlets and cassette tapes distributed hand to hand. After the fall of the Wall, however, few of these civic and associational voices succeeded in the transformation to mainstream journalism on market and statist terms. After a brief period of republican euphoria, the political culture turned predominantly neoliberal. Václav Havel, the first democratically elected president, propagated republican ideals of "non-political politics." But practical governance has stressed market economics rather than civic engagement as the prime mover of progress. After a brief interlude of co-operative and employer-based ownership, the national for-profit TV licences and most of the print publishers were bought by foreign capital. Labour unions and other pillarist associations never succeeded in creating sustainable media of their own (Ekiert and Ziblatt, 2013).

In the radical transformation from regulated communism to neoliberal market economy, it has been no easy task to establish a public sphere on a non-market and non-governmental basis. The public-service-providers, CR and CT, have decreased their audience share and reach. In the wake of the 2008 financial crisis, advertising revenues dried up all over Europe and in the Czech media market, the downturn triggered limitations on commercials sold by CT. This political decision privileged two commercial players, Nova and Prima, with a mutual sixty per cent share against CT's thirty per cent of the TV audience. Consequently, CT in particular has experienced failure by triggering a crisis of legitimacy, including political demands for more government-enforced control. In 2011, a proposal to abolish the licence fee and replace it with direct funding from the state budgets (with accompanying strings attached) was defeated by a single vote in the Czech senate. According to a survey of licence-payers, forty per cent of them indicated they would vote for the abolishment of the licence fee all together, and in order to collect the current fees, public-service-providers have considered to make a joint venture with electric power companies because of increasing non-compliance (Rabková and Riháčková, 2013, p. 29).

Notwithstanding, the Czechs were hit less severely by the global financial crisis than comparative economies. Financially this was mainly due to a relatively slow development of the domestic mortgage market and the fact that Czech banks are not fully integrated into the global banking system that has been the motor of the current crisis. National and private debt are generally low and no dramatic decrease in employment has been taking place. This is partly due to harsh lessons learned from the financial strain in the early 1990s, prompting cutbacks in civil services and deregulation of the business world with profitable banking laws (Riishøj, 2007).

This, in turn, has motivated some self-organized non-market and non-government initiatives (Loeser, 2013). An important driver in supporting this kind of open access to civil society-oriented debate has been the Open Society Foundation, funding volunteer socio-political activities, especially critical websites such as NásStát.cz, which challenge government decisions (Browne, 2010, p. 899). On a smaller scale, foundations like the German Friedrich-Ebert-Stiftung attempt to balance commercial dominance and market failures of structure and existence by promoting the idea of community radio in the Czech Republic. Foundation-based programmes also include media research, journalism education and lobbying for social, legal and economic reform (Dobek-Ostrowaska and Glowacki, 2011, p. 125–131). A dozen online news rooms have emerged in the wake of the 2008 global crisis, supplementing one-person blogs and social-media forums for special-interest debate. Some of them have become self-reliant based on voluntary donations and membership fees, fuelling debates on free speech, political pluralism and critical journalims (Rabková and Riháčková, 2013, p. 35).

In sum, the republican civil society heritage revitalized by the underground media of the 1980s has gradually turned into neoliberal and market-driven journalism, marked by crises of legitimacy and motivation – especially in relation to the rather young PSM operation in a relatively small media market. Nonetheless, the Czech Republic holds sixteenth position on the Press Freedom Index (Reporters without Frontiers, 2013), outranking not only neighbouring countries but also Italy and the UK. General trust scores are also relatively high compared to other Eastern European countries (Vajdová, 2005), and the Czech-language Internet portal seznam.cz has been able to compete successfully with Google to a much larger extent than is the case with national language search engines in the other three countries studied here.

CONCLUSIONS

The data generated by the case studies have documented a variety of non-market and non-government journalism across Europe, not only in the form of community media but also as pillarist membership communication, republican web activism and liberal free speech advocacy. Data confirm that media systems are path-dependant structures with taken for granted institutions, positioned within their specific historical context including voices of more or less critical citizenship, grass-roots advocacy and self-organized production of media content.

Active citizenship and non-profit journalism, however, are not one-way streets. Civil society values may mitigate the consequences of market and regulation failures, but in times of crisis these influences also work the other way around, i.e. market and government regulation may influence civil society in different ways. Civic engagement, blogging and community media can be found in all four countries under study, but they neither advocate uniform messages nor act under identical civil society norms. We have found signs of communicative crisis of legitimacy related to all civil society traditions under study, but only in the UK and the Czech Republic have we found marked tendencies towards crisis of motivation. One common denominator is a heavy leaning towards neoliberal norms, challenging public-service media and heralding commercial players as solutions to rather than causes of the current crisis. In Denmark and Italy, on the contrary, alleged market failure has inviting new rounds of government intervention. In the aftermath of the 2008 crisis, the legitimacy and efficiency of neoliberal civil society values have been questioned. Cut-throat competition and pressure on public-service media are increasingly regarded as contributors to market failure in the form of ownership concentration, reducing plurality of public-sphere voices and critical journalism.

Civil society values, of course, can hardly be championed as the sole reasons for varieties of media crisis management in these cases. Nonetheless they appear to have an impact on how consequences of crisis may be mitigated. In this respect, third-sector, non-commercial and non-government media cannot be reduced to self-seeking websites and community radio but must be regarded as a multitude of mediated organizational forms with fluid boundaries, most importantly supported by voluntary associations and philanthropic foundations. Active citizenship plays a particularly important guardian role, attempting (with more or less success) to keep market-driven and voter-dependant journalism in line – offline as well as online. This may be done not only by offering opportunities for voluntary participation online but also by threatening exit and civil disobedience offline.

The roughly sketched case studies highlight shifting impacts on the media systems under study. Amateur attempts to provide a sustainable mix of independent, self-organized, non-subsidized and non-profit journalism tend to disappoint. A few non-commercial and non-subsidized media initiatives succeed in their own right. Some develop into special-interest platforms of the pillarist kind, but most of them become marginalized at the fringes of the liberal public sphere. In the wake of the 2008 financial crisis, some novel and experimental initiatives have emerged, inviting civil society actors to co-create and innovate communicative practices in a non-commercial and non-licenced fashion, but surprisingly few have succeeded in becoming popular platforms for news and views (Scholte, 2013). In the same vein, civic willingness to pay for public-service broadcasting is under pressure, risking stronger state and/or commercial influence on programming. Structurally, the net result is a taken for granted mix of commercial publishers and public-service suppliers, supplemented by rather marginal grass-roots initiatives and foundation-subsidized media at arm's length from both advertisers and governments. All in all, serious journalism offering civic participation and critical debate has been suffering losses, not only financially but also measured in terms of audience share, political legitimacy and civil motivation.

A proactive lesson to be learned from the work at hand is that co-created and user-generated content frequently fails to make a social impact unless some permanent means of financial support is offered. All four case studies demonstrate that media initiatives based on civil society norms cannot stand completely alone of their own accord. Self-satisfied journalists can of course operate in splendid isolation, but civic initiatives with mass communication ambitions cannot. In order to become sustainable content-providers in an over-communicated society, subsidies are required either from state, market or self-reliant institutions of civil society. Most scholarship has been directed towards government sources. But civil society contains understudied types of monies with stamina and arm's length principles, i.e. membership fees, crowd-sourcing and grants from philanthropic foundations (Westphal, 2009).

The majority of post-2008 non-profit and non-government media in Europe are actually run by membership organizations and/or subsidized by philanthropic foundations. The first is inherently special-interest-driven, making use of social media in order to supplement input by way of market-based and government-controlled communication. The latter, on the other hand, may offer means for more independent plurality in content. The Danish newspaper business, for instance, has developed foundation ownership, offering what may be labelled 'public service for private money.' Important parts of Italian community journalism find support in regional savings-bank foundations with philanthropic remits. In the Czech Republic, foreign foundations have been instrumental in balancing commercial players and government intervention, and in the UK, the Res Publica Trust was a driving force behind the so-called Hacked Off Campaign. Media subsidies provided by charitable trusts and other wealthy foundations are no magic bullet, of course. As is the case in market-driven and state-subsidized journalism, strings may very well be attached in civil society transactions. Furthermore, private donors of the foundation type lack the legitimacy of the ballot box. Money speaks, and in spite of noble intentions, foundations "remain ultimately elitist and technocratic institutions." (Arnove and Pinede, 2007, p. 422)

Consequently, serious doubts have been voiced by critical journalism in relation to trust- and charity-funded journalism and public debate. Among the frequently cited criticisms are private donors serving hidden agendas and special interests, encouraging journalists to anticipate and promote ideological and idiosyncratic "whims of funders." (Browne, 2010, p. 891) On the other hand, without subsidies from charitable foundations and other benevolent philanthropists, civil society initiatives tend to fall prone to market and state subordination. Government and mainstream media funding of community content and other types of grass-roots experiments have not exactly mushroomed in the aftermath of the 2008 events on the financial markets. Neither have activist crowd-funding and other types of collective fundraising.

All in all, the short answer to the research question raised in this chapter is that financial turmoil and political tumult do tend to trigger crises of legitimacy, but do not automatically translate into crisis of motivation. Applying a non-market and non-state perspective, the core claim is that such differences may be related to historically informed and taken for granted civil society norms. More empirical research is needed, however, in order to determine how different forms of engaged citizenship more specifically mitigate the adverse consequences of media crisis.

ACKNOWLEDGEMENTS

The author would like to thank members of the EuroMedia Research Group, particularly Aukse Balčytienė, Claudia Padovani and Jeanette Steemers and Václav Štětka, for critical and constructive comments.

REFERENCES

Alexander, J.C. (ed.) (1998) *Real Civil Societies: Dilemmas of Institutionalization*. London: Sage.
Anheier, H.K. (2013) *Nonprofit Organizations*. London: Routledge.
Arnove, R. and Pinede, N. (2007) Revisiting the "Big Three" Foundations. *Critical Sociology*, 33. pp. 389–425.

Berg, C.E., Lowe, G.F. and Lund, A.B. (2014) A Market Failure Perspective on Value Creation in PSM. In: Lowe, G.F. and Martin, F. (eds.) *The Value of Public Service Media* (pp. 105–26). Gothenburg: Nordicom.

Blumler, J.G. and Gurevitch, M. (eds.) (1995) *The Crisis of Public Communication.* London: Routledge.

Browne, D. (2012) What is 'community' in community radio? A consideration of the meaning, nature and importance of a concept. In: Gordon, J. (ed.) *Community radio in the twenty-first century.* Oxford: Peter Lang Publications.

Browne, H. (2010) Foundation-Funded Journalism: Reasons to be Wary of Charitable Support. *Journalism Studies*, 11. pp. 889–903.

Cayli, B. (2013) Italian Civil Society against the Mafia: From Perceptions to Expectations. *International Journal of Law, Crime and Justice*, 41(1). pp. 81–99.

Cohen J.L. and Areto, A. (1992) *Civil Society and Political Theory.* Cambridge, MA: The MIT Press.

Council of Europe (2009) *Declaration of the Committee of Ministers on the Role of Community Media in Promoting Social Cohesion and Intercultural Dialogue.* Council of Europe.

Couldry, N. (2010) *Why Voice Matters: Culture and Politics after Neo-Liberalism.* London: Sage.

Curran, J. and Seaton, J. (2010) *Power without Responsibility: Press, Broadcasting and the Internet in Britain.* London: Routledge.

Dahlgren, P. (2000) *Television and the Public Sphere - Citizenship, Democracy and the Media.* London: Sage.

Dahrendorf, R. (1990/1999) *Reflections on the Revolution in Europe.* London: Translation Publishers.

Dobek-Ostrowska, B. and Glowacki, M. (eds.) (2011) *Making Democracy in 20 Years: Media and Politics in Central and Eastern Europe.* Wroclav: Wydawnic-two Uniwersytetu Wroclawskiego.

Doliwa, U. and Rankovic, L. (2014) Time for Community Media in Central and Eastern Europe. *Central European Journal of Communication*, 7. pp. 18–33.

Edwards, J. (ed.) (2012) *Retrieving the Big Society.* London: Wiley-Blackwell.

Eikiert, G. and Ziblatt, D. (2013) Democracy in Central and Eastern Europe One Hundred Years on. *East European Politics and Societies*, 27. pp. 90–117.

Etzioni, A. (1995) *New Communitarian Thinking.* Charlottesville, VA: University of Virginia Press.

Fuchs, C. (2014) *OccupyMedia! The Occupy Movement and Social Media in Crisis Capitalism.* Winchester: Zero Books.

Gerring, J. (2004) What Is a Case Study and What Is it Good for? *American Political Science Review*, 98. pp. 341–54.

Hallin, D.C. and Mancini, P. (2004) *Comparing Media Systems: Three Models of Media and Politics.* Cambridge: Cambridge University Press.

Habermas, J. (1975) *Legitimation Crisis.* Boston: Beacon Press.

Habermas, J. (1999) *Between Facts and Norms: Contributions to a Discourse Theory of Law and Democracy.* Cambridge, US: MIT Press.

Hanretty, C. (2010) *Public Broadcasting and Political Interference.* London: Taylor & Francis.

Havel, V. (1992) *Summer Meditations.* London: Faber.

European Journalism Centre (2011) *Media Landscapes.* Retrieved from: http://www.ejc.net/media_landscapes.

Jiménez, N.R. and Scifo, S. (2010) Community Media in the Context of European Media Policies. *Telematics and Informatics*, 27. pp. 131–40.

Katzenstein, P.J. (1985) *Small States in World Markets: Industrial Policy in Europe.* Ithaca: Cornell University Press.

Kaviraj, S. and Khilnani, S. (eds.) (2001) *Civil Society: History and Possibilities.* Cambridge: Cambridge University Press.

Keane, J (1988) *Civil Society and the State: New European Perspectives.* London: Verso.

Kelly, M., Mazzoleni, G. and McQuail, D. (eds.) (2004) *The Media in Europe. The Euromedia Handbook.* London: Sage.

Koselleck, R. and Richter, M.W. (2006) *Crisis: Journal of the History of Ideas*, 87. pp. 357–400.

Leiphart, A. (1968) *The Politics of Accommodation.* Berkeley: University of California Press.

Loeser, H.G. (2013) Community Radio for the Czech Republic – Who Cares? In: Hand, R.J. et al. (eds.) *Radio in Small Nations* (pp. 126–39). Chicago: University of Wales Press.

Lund, A.B. (2007) Media Markets in Scandinavia: Political Economy Aspects of Convergence and Divergence. *Nordicom Review*, 28. pp. 121–34.

Lund, A.B. and Langer, R. (2000) Öffentliches Krisenmanagement und kollektive Meinungsbildung. *Publizistik*, 45. pp. 163–79.

Marcinkowski, F., Meier, W.A. and Trappel, J. (eds.) (2006) *Media and Democracy. Experiences from Europe.* Bern: Haupt Verlag.

Marris, P. and Thornham, S. (eds.) (1996) *Media Studies Reader.* Edinburgh: Edinburgh University Press.

Mazzoleni, G., Vigevani, G. and Splendore, S. (2011) *Mapping Digital Media: Italy.* Open University Foundation.

Melvern, L. (1986) The End of the Street. London: Methuen

Meyer, G. and Lund, A. B. (2008) The Multiple Translations of a Profession: Varieties of Journalism. *Javnost – The Public*, 15 (4). pp. 73–86.

Putnam, R.D. (1993) *Making Democracy Work: Civic Traditions in Modern Italy.* Princeton: Princeton University Press.

Rabková, E. and Riháčková, V. (2013) *Mapping Digital Media: Czech Republic.* Prague: Open Society Foundation.

Reporters Without Frontiers (2013). *Press Freedom Index.* Retrieved from: http://www.en.rsf.org/press-freedom-index.

Riishøj, S. (2007) The Czech Experience – Liberalism with a "Czech Face". *Arbejderhistorie*, 2. pp. 24–36.

Scholte, J.A. (2013) Civil Society and Financial Markets: What is Not Happening and Why. *Journal of Civil Society* 9. pp. 129–47.

Skinner, Q. (1998) *Liberty before Liberalism.* Cambridge: Cambridge University Press.

Splichal, S. (2001) Imitative Revolutions: Changes in the Media and Journalism in East-Central Europe. *Javnost – The Public*, 8. pp. 31–58.

Vajdová, T. (2005) *An Assessment of Czech Civil Society after Fifteen Years of Development.* Prague: Civicus.

Vandevelde, T. (1997) Communitarianism and Patriotism. *Ethical Perspectives*, 4. pp. 180–90.

Viroli, M. (2011) The Liberty of Servants: Berlusconi's Italy. Princeton: Princeton University Press.

Westphal, D. (2009) *Philanthropic Foundations: Growing Funders of the News.* Los Angeles: University of Southern California.

Conclusions

13 Grappling with Post-Democracy
Media Policy Options

Werner A. Meier and Josef Trappel

Throughout this book, media transformations and media crises have been observed and described in different European countries. Common crisis indicators are the slump in advertising revenues, falling turnover and profits in publishing, lower audience reach for core media companies, lower numbers of fully employed professional journalists, precarious labour conditions for many other journalists, and increasing consumer time and attention for social media and online content at the expense of legacy media.

These structural changes have not only led to a fundamental crisis of the European media business but they have the potential to lead to serious problems for policy and democracy. In his Foreword to this volume Denis McQuail calls for media policy that accommodates structural media changes that sustain democratic norms and values. In this concluding chapter we return to this proposition and analyse media policy actions and reactions to these structural changes and crises. First, we apply the debate on post-democracy (Colin Crouch) and post-journalism to media policy. Second, we describe and analyse contemporary media policy from a political economy perspective. Third, we present findings from a recent comparative study on media policy and apply our findings to the highly controversial debate about the legitimacy of press subsidies in democratic political systems. We end by suggesting new directions for media policy in uncertain times.

MEDIA PERFORMANCE UNDER POST-DEMOCRATIC RULES

In his best-seller on post-democracy, the sociologist and political scientist Colin Crouch rhetorically asks: "Are we moving away from societies that are truly democratic, towards something that could more accurately be called 'post-democracy?'" By post-democracy Crouch refers to a situation "when political elites have learned to manage and manipulate popular demands" (2004, p. 19); democratic institutions, like elections, function as before, but results do not matter much. Power has disappeared into the more or less closed circles of political and economic elites (Crouch, 2013, p. 443).

According to Crouch, today large corporations operate across a wide range of countries and some of them have even ceased to have a particular sense of national belonging. They employ workers across large parts of the world, and they market their products globally (ibid., p. 449). While governments remain firmly national, global corporations play governments off against each other, claiming they will concentrate their investments in those countries where they are treated most favourably in terms of taxation, labour laws or planning requirements (ibid.).

When large global corporations develop privileged relations with the political world in this way, Crouch spots signs of post-democracy (ibid., p. 452). To underline this he refers to the financial market crisis as the best example so far of a movement towards post-democracy (ibid., p. 453). If markets become the only source of political action, additional problems occur. What happens to democracy and politics, he asks, when corporations develop from powerful pressure groups into major insider participants in the political process? (2011: ix). What means do people have for raising political concern about diversity if the media are controlled by a small number of large corporations that provide only limited choices? (2011, p. 26). Crouch observes decreasing democratic alternatives delivered by corporate media and a decline of communication on political issues in general. Because of their constant search for commercially successful services, the (mass) media increasingly disregard their public and democratic mission. Fierce competition for the attention of viewers, listeners, readers and users promotes over-simplification and sensationalism to the detriment of political debate. In other words, legacy media no longer provide solutions to the problem of post-democracy but are part of the problem.

Crouch's analysis of post-democratic media might be oversimplistic, but the findings on media crisis in this book confirm his general claim. Indeed, working conditions for journalists have deteriorated (see Chapter 6), commercial media tend to disregard democratic values (Chapter 5) and alternative voices are scarce and often depend on philanthropic organizations to get media access (Chapter 12). The post-democracy era in this situation clearly requires governance rules for public communication.

POLICY ACTIVITIES IN NEOLIBERAL POLITICAL AND ECONOMIC STRUCTURES

Contentious media and democracy crises can be understood as a gradual process of transformation whereby institutional pillars erode or become marginalized. Performance with regard to public responsibilities deteriorates, together with the will, intention and ultimately the ability of these actors to deliver their contribution to the democratic process of public deliberation. Such gradual transformation calls for policy reactions. Observations from the perspective of the political economy of communication largely comply with the case Crouch makes. Des Freedman's account of neoliberal media policy (2008) on the one hand and Jonathan Hardy's view on media convergence and communications regulation (2014) on the other refer to similar developments.

For Hardy, neoliberalism has been the dominant ideological force in media policy and its dominant tool has been marketization, a term used to describe a shift in governing values that privileges and promotes freedom of action for private business and market mechanisms over state regulation and public provision (Hardy, 2014, p. 178f). For Freedman, deregulation, liberalization, privatization and marketization have driven neoliberal media policy since the early 1980s (Freedman, 2008, p. 47). Freedman claims neoliberalism's discursive attachment to free markets, individual rights, personal choice, small government and limited regulation is now a firmly established part of contemporary life (ibid., p. 36). In this way, neoliberalist policy approaches actively promote the interests of commercial media corporations. Media policy formation, Freedman claims, is a highly ideological process that privileges the frameworks and priorities of the powerful and marginalizes those who challenge these priorities (ibid., p. 29). In short, media policy-making is "exclusive, unequal, distorted and fundamentally undemocratic." (Freedman, 2008, p. 29)

Against this background the following working hypotheses on the contemporary status of media policy at times of crisis can be deducted:

- If neoliberal paradigms such as the free market, free trade, individual rights, the primacy of market regulation and market competition are the dominant ideology, media policy is likely to be low key and corporation-friendly.
- If post-democratic paradigms such as the primacy of national and international corporate expansion prevail, no government policy initiative can be expected to run counter to these interests.
- If media policy decisions are taken by governments in consultation with post-democratic lobby groups and economic elites, the application of a variety of media governance instruments can be expected, such as public-private-partnerships.
- As long as governmental regulation is discredited as inefficient, counterproductive and bureaucratic, no political action can be expected unless dominant media industry actors take the initiative and request governments to act.
- As long as the mass media are not considered system-relevant (in analogy to some banks), no government media policy action is to be expected.
- As long as the market and competition are broadly and principally accepted as exclusive economic co-ordination mechanisms, no government media policy action is to be expected.

What we usually expect from neoliberal-minded governments in the frame of media governance is the firm belief that markets will work their magic, customers will assert their preferences and particular media structures, plat-forms and practices will follow as a result. For Freedman, "(…) many governments claim to be firmly adhering to a policy agenda that emphasizes the efficacy of markets to promote innovation, competition and consumer sovereignty, the need for government and the state to remain 'small', and for media policies to act, above all, as a 'support mechanism' for private economic activity in the communications field." (Freedman, 2014, p. 62)

In the most radical interpretation of the free press theory (cf. McQuail, 2013, p. 34–37), the state not only has to be defensive in its role but also has to be regarded as a potential threat to media freedom. The state is conceptualized "as the main danger and state power viewed as potentially the main barrier to the unrestricted circulation of ideas." (Freedman, 2014, p. 62f) Commercial media companies have to be "free *from* state interference and control as well as the capacity to be free *to* challenge arguments proposed by representatives of the states and to monitor their activities." (ibid., p. 63; emphasis in original)

However, what sounds clear in theory does not always apply in practical terms. Even under the neoliberal paradigm, several different types of state intervention can be observed. In times of crises, the following policy options are principally available:

a   No government action, retreat into symbolic media policy (state as observer);
b   Government undertakes some positive action and monitors its measures (state as moderator);
c   Government actively interferes (state as crisis manager of the crisis).

State as observer (option a): As a matter of principle the government (the state) refuses to take any policy action. The government (the state) denies any responsibility and avoids being associated with the crisis. This passive attitude is justified by not placing any unnecessary regulatory burden on the shoulders of media companies in times of crisis. In such times, additional rules and regulations are inappropriate, especially if they concern issues such as media pluralism, ownership concentration or other rules on competition. Avoiding such regulation is tantamount to indirect support for crisis-affected media companies. In return, politicians can expect a lower level of policy critique within the media and, in general, a less adversarial attitude by journalists, not the least because of crisis-induced limitations on resources allocated by the media to investigative reporting. There is then a fair chance that the government (the state) is strengthened by the crisis, having successfully avoided being trapped by unpopular and contested media policy decisions. Non-intervention is the safe option for the state.

State as moderator (option b): The more that unambiguously powerful corporate stakeholders call for active government policy intervention, the more governments and administrations can be expected to intervene during times of crisis. In a first step, parliamentary commissions or administrative task forces are requested to monitor and inquire what problems are most urgent. The UK communications regulator Ofcom has carried out over 800 consultations since its inception in 2003. For Freedman, this qualifies as "hyper-activism that seems to be at odds with both the caricature of the media policy environment as lax and reactive and the view that the market, if left alone, will deliver the networks and service that are necessary for life in a digital age." (2014, p. 64) Again, non-intervention by monitoring and moderating is a safe policy option for the state.

State as manager of the crisis (option c): Active media policy at times of crisis is risky and politically dangerous. The media remain an essential resource for political success even if they are weakened by the crisis. Therefore, governments apply extra care when attempting to manage the crisis. Communication infrastructures as well as public-service media are politically easier to handle as their respective constitution is based on positive legislation (contrary to the press). "Traditionally, press policy has taken the form of having no policy, and the functioning of newspapers has been left largely to market forces." (Curran and Seaton, 2009, p. 357) Consequently, state intervention to actively manage the media crisis can only be expected in rare and exceptional cases. However, inequalities created by the Internet both as a critical infrastructure and platform for editorial content as well as quintessential cause of the crisis of incumbent media might require active policy management.

MEDIA POLICY PERFORMANCE: TWO CASES

In this section, we will first present findings from a comparative research project on media policy in times of crisis and, second, discuss in more detail the media policy case of press subsidies.

The point of departure for the Swiss Science Foundation-financed research project[1] was the assumption that media policy would be responsive to critical changes and transformation in the media industry. The core research question asked what the role of media policy was in times of crises, its performance and its actions, as well as its capability to cope with crises and transformation. It was assumed media policy would adequately respond to crises that challenged the democratic functions of the media.

Media policy is understood as a process involving private (companies, associations) and civil society stakeholders as well as the state (government). According to Freedman, media policy actors continuously fight for their interests. "Every step of the way is marked by fierce competition for, or deployment of, resources, influence and power." (2008, p. 3) Media policy research is required to identify inequalities and imbalanced power relations, including the analysis of success and failure of political and economic elites. At times of crisis, it can be expected that the neoliberal policy order would privilege the vested interests of private commercial media companies against those of civil society stakeholders. Thus changes of this order are unlikely during times of crisis, as neoliberal values do not favour political interventions.

To answer the research question, media policies were analysed in seven countries (Austria, Canada, Germany, the Netherlands, Sweden, Switzerland and the United Kingdom). Based on desk research as well as expert interviews, media policy decisions were collected and analysed for each country from 1999 (before the so called dot-com crisis) to 2012 (after the financial market crisis).

Each media policy decision was allocated to one or more core policy values, such as quality, competition, diversity, accountability, access, etc. Furthermore, each policy decision was evaluated with regard to policy content (e.g. financial rules, media concentration regulation, content regulation, rules for journalistic labour) and potential beneficiaries (private-commercial media companies, public-service operators, non-commercial service-providers). Semi-structured face-to-face interviews were conducted with representatives of these different beneficiaries, as well as representatives of regulatory authorities and politicians in all seven countries. These were the core findings:

Representatives from governments and regulatory authorities, along with press publishers, tend to ignore or even deny any media crisis. Some accept secluded symptoms of crises, but these are not considered important enough to justify any particular or targeted policy action. Within their discourse, media policy and media crises were incidents isolated from one another. Unless the media crises reach thresholds that threaten, for example, the existence of the market leading media companies, no specific media policy action would be justified in their view.

In the field of media policy, government and state actors tend to work reactively, not proactively, irrespective of the actual state of the media crisis. In most cases, the state acts as both observer and moderator, rather than as the manager of the crises. At best, existing rules are either relaxed or applied with less rigour. Self-regulation gains in relative importance over co-regulation and statutory (state) regulation. Media freedom for media companies enjoys increased importance compared to the individual freedoms of citizens. Despite the crises, statutory media policy emphasizes the primacy of competition rules, thereby supporting private media companies and further restricting public-service operators.

During times of crises, private commercial media companies enjoy privileged access to statutory media policy actors and manage to intensify their lobbying activities. Within national boundaries, they lobby for self-regulation at the expense of state regulation; at the international level they ask for protection against global players such as copyright protection related to Google. Crises seem to facilitate mutual exchanges between private commercial media and the state (government). One result is relaxed rules for television advertising for commercial operators (e.g. endorsement of split-screen and virtual advertising), together with additional restrictions for their public-service competitors (notably in Austria, Germany, the Netherlands and Sweden).

Public-service media, in contrast, did not profit from the media crises. Their budgets were cut in parallel to the market crises. Before the dot-com crisis in 2000/2001, several public-service media were empowered to increase their licence fee-based revenues (Sweden, Switzerland). During and after that crisis, as well as during the financial market crisis, licence fee revenues decreased and their operations were substantially restricted. For example, German and Austrian public-service broadcasters are obliged to remove digital copies of their broadcasts from their public archives no later than seven days after first transmission. Additional restrictions followed from public value tests, which were decreed by the European Commission. All new digital services of public-service media have to pass an *ex-ante* test for their potential to distort markets – and for their capacity to respond to democratic, social and cultural needs – before they are allowed to start (for more details see Donders and Moe, 2014; Donders and Pauwels, 2010). At times of rapid change, this requirement constitutes a substantial burden for the development of public-service operators.

Media crises facilitate changes in market power calibration. Throughout all seven countries under scrutiny, small third-sector community media failed to improve their legal and market status, and some were confronted with substantial budget cuts. Statutory media policy set different priorities. Larger media companies were literally encouraged to expand market control. Licensing policy in Canada, for example, contributed in 2010 to the increase of market power of leading media companies. In Germany, media policy was concerned to strengthen national media companies against their global competitors such as News Corporation, Google and Yahoo.

Media policy representatives as well as representatives from the media business confirmed the assumption that during times of crises, self-regulation is the preferred mode for media policy. They argue this preference allows for making the best use of knowledge accumulated within media companies, which corresponds favourably with the increasing complexity of the issues at stake (traditional issues such as quality, content variety and ownership concentration, but also contemporary issues such as open access and net neutrality). In this way statutory media policy avoids conflicts, which is a welcome side effect.

Finally, values and norms of media policy tend to change during times of crises. While media policy can generally be understood as a delicate calibration of economic and cultural-democratic values, media policy activities at times of crises privilege the former against the latter. Constitutional rights to freedom of opinion are used as arguments to abstain from media policy interventions. In particular, claims for regulation in favour of content diversity and against ownership concentration are rejected in times of crises. Cultural and democratic values are obviously considered less important than economic values.

In conclusion, media policy in times of crises does not follow any strategic concept. It is best described as reactive, not proactive, and it declines – to the extent possible – any responsibility for the crisis. Rather, statutory media policy invites media business actors to take the lead by suggesting self-regulation, normally leading to further deregulation. It should be noted, however, that the study does not propose any direct cause-effect relation between the crises and media policy action. As a rule, media policy does not act immediately to respond to changes in media markets, and media policy regulation takes years from its initiation to enter into force (in particular at the level of the European Union). Nonetheless, this research shows that times of crises provide political advantages to neoliberal concerns and values.

The second case concerns the contested concept of direct press subsidies for media companies. Although subsidies in general contradict neoliberal economic values, the obvious beneficiaries of press subsidy schemes are private commercial publishers who take advantage of lower tax burdens (in this case, value added tax – VAT) or even direct payment by the state (in the case of selective aid).

Despite the fact that EU legislation on state aid rules out any form of state subsidies, more than two-thirds of all countries in Europe support their press with direct selective production aid, and almost all of them provide indirect aid, mostly in the form of reduced value-added taxes (Puppis et al., 2014). In Belgium, Denmark, Norway and the United Kingdom, press sales are entirely exempt from VAT. Remarkably, this main form of state support has remained largely unchanged over decades, despite rapid changes in the media landscape and despite more rigid controls by the European Commission (Nielsen, 2011). There is only one exception to this rule: Finland abolished its scheme for direct selective press subsidies (Nieminen et al., 2014, p. 180). Apparently, press policy remains the domain of nation states with no indication of attempts at transnational regulation.

At the national level, results from press subsidies, as reflected in the literature, are not convincing. Nonetheless, the status quo is not likely to change any time soon, in particular if the media crisis persists (Picone and Pauwels, 2014, p. 151). What has gained momentum, however, is the call for and the debate about the efficacy of innovation support for the press, as it is confronted with fundamental structural change (ibid.). Dal Zotto and van Kranenburg observed that "media firms are less responsive to innovation and change compared to other firms. There is in the industry an increasing appearance of innovation fatigue, that is, a weariness and desire to stop innovation, caused by the speed of continuous innovation." (2008: xvii)

Following the claim of Meikle and Young (2012, p. 183) that government funding of innovation would ensure the development of new media technologies and forms retains a public good dimension, Picone and Pauwels (2014) distinguish three forms of newspaper innovation support: innovation for marketplace competition, innovation to facilitate the journalistic process and innovation of journalistic output. What sounds convincing in theory shows flaws in practise. The emphasis on technology, product and business innovation might, according to Picone and Pauwels, go at the expense of content quality (2014, p. 158f). Instead of concentrating on the democratic tasks of newspapers, "the 'app' becomes more important than the content." (ibid., p. 159) Despite such flaws, the authors recommend developing an innovation policy that might allow "available resources to be invested in the otherwise too expensive practices of in-depth journalism." (ibid., p. 160)

One example of active innovation support is the Netherlands. In September 2009, the Minister of Education, Culture and Science decided to allocate eight million Euro to the Press Fund, earmarked for press innovation. Funds can be used for research and the development of models to better exploit and distribute news and Dutch journalism, or for renewing and strengthening the links between journalism and society. The Press Fund provides up to fifty per cent of the project's cost (Lichtenberg and d'Haenens, 2014, p. 282f). The authors believe "that such supportive policy is of great help especially when cutbacks in future media policy expenditures are inevitable in times of general economic and financial crisis." (ibid., p. 287)

The media industries in other countries are much more sceptical about press subsidies. In Germany and the UK, for example, any selective support is rejected. In Switzerland, the Federal Media Commission suggested in 2014 supporting media innovation projects. Despite obvious symptoms of the crisis, press publishers indignantly rejected this attempt.

Both cases (comparative media policy study and press subsidies) indicate the dominance of neoliberal media policy paradigms during times of crises. Divergent or alternative policy concepts focusing on quality, diversity or content in general have not been developed in any of the countries, and even positive media policy propositions such as support for innovation are much more the exception than the rule.

OLD AND NEW CHALLENGES OF MEDIA CONVERGENCE AND MEDIA GOVERNANCE

Post-democracy, post-journalism and neoliberal paradigms seem not only to survive the media crises but also to prevail as the dominant ideological foundation of policy. Denis McQuail reminds us in his Foreword to this volume of the enormous valorization of the Internet world, new forms of monopoly control by major media owners and service-providers, as well as the massive surveillance of society. Media and communication policy is thus confronted with old (marketization, concentration) and new challenges (surveillance, corporate globalization). New global actors not only enhance competition at the national level, they also question the fundamentals of media policy, which still is primarily nation-based, marginally European and not at all global – contrary to the communication business.

Scientific reflection on media and communication policy should not restrict itself to the critique of traditional policy concepts. Rather, old and new media need to be conceptualized within a wider framework, including concepts such as 'creative commons' and 'net neutrality.' The media crises might serve as a valid starting point for the analysis of alternative forms of financing journalism and content, as well as for the elaboration of new forms of institutionalizing media and communication that serve democratic norms and values.

Civil society perspectives need to be integrated more centrally in the media policy debate, as well as the large variety of different forms of public voice. It is time to develop media and communication policy models based on principles of democracy, participation and accountability to civil society, as an alternative to the neoliberal paradigm that has, after all, contributed to the structural media crises.

NOTE

1. "Medien- und Kommunikationspolitik in der Krise. Neue Spielräume, neue Handlungszwänge?" Subproject 7 within the Sinergia framework "Krise und Wandel der Medien in der Schweiz. University of Zurich, 2014.

REFERENCES

Crouch, C. (2004) *Post-Democracy.* Cambridge, UK, Malden, US: Polity Press.
Crouch, C. (2011) *The Strange Non-Death of Neoliberalism.* Cambridge: Polity Press.
Crouch, C. (2013) Democracy's Fatigue: Are we moving toward Post-Democracy? In: H. Kriesi and Müller, L. (eds.) *Democracy: An Ongoing Challenge* (pp. 439–59). Zürich: Lars Müller Publishers.
Curran, J. and Seaton, J. (2009) *Power without Responsibility*, 7th edition. London: Routledge.
Dal Zotto, C. and van Kranenburg, H. (2008) Introduction. In: Dal Zotto, C.and van Kranenburg, H. (eds.) *Management and Innovation in the Media Industry* (pp. ix–xxiv). Cheltenham, UK: Edward Elgar.
Donders, K. and Pauwels, C. (2010) The introduction of an ex ante evaluation for new media services: Is 'Europe' asking for it, or does public service broadcasting need it? *International Journal of Media and Cultural Politics*, 6(2). pp. 133–148.
Donders, K. and Moe, H. (2014) European State-Aid Control and PSB: Competition Policy Clashing or Matching with Public Interest Objectives? In: Donders, K., Pauwels, C. and Loisen, J. (eds.) *The Palgrave Handbook of European Media Policy* (pp. 426–41). Basingstoke, UK: Palgrave Macmillan.

EMEK (2014) *Medienförderung: Standortbestimmung und Empfehlungen für die Zukunft*. Schweizerische Eidgenossenschaft, Biel.

Freedman, D. (2008) *The Politics of Media Policy*. Cambridge: Polity Press.

Freedman, D. (2014) *The Contradictions of Media Power*. London, Delhi, New York, Sydney: Bloomsbury.

Hardy, Jonathan (2014) *Critical Political Economy of the Media: An Introduction*. London: Routledge.

Lichtenberg, L. and d'Haenens, L. (2014) The Netherlands: Initiatives to Subsidise Press Innvovation. In: Murschetz, P. (ed.) *State Aid for Newspapers, Media Business and Innovation* (pp. 271–89). Heidelberg, Berlin: Springer Verlag.

McQuail, D. (2013) *Journalism and Society*. London, Thousand Oaks, CA, New Delhi, Singapore: Sage.

Meikle, G. and Young, S. (2012) *Media Convergence: Networked Digital Media in Everyday Life*. Hampshire, New York: Palgrave Macmillan.

Murschetz, P. and Trappel, J. (2014) State Aid for Newspapers: A Summary Assesment. In: Murschetz, P. (ed.) *State Aid for Newspapers, Media Business and Innovation* (pp. 375–91). Heidelberg, Berlin: Springer Verlag.

Nielsen, R.K. and Linnebank, G. (2011) *Public Support for the Media: A Six-Country Overview of Direct and Indirect Subsidies*. Report. University of Oxford: Reuters Institute for the Study of Journalism.

Nieminen, H., Nordenstreng, K. and Harjuniemi, T. (2014) Finland: The Rise and Fall of a Democratic Subsidy Scheme. In: Murschetz, P. (ed.) *State Aid for Newspapers, Media Business and Innovation* (pp. 179–94). Heidelberg, Berlin: Springer Verlag.

Picone, I. and Pauwels, C. (2014) Belgium: Big Changes in a Small News Economy. In: Murschetz, P. (ed.) *State Aid for Newspapers, Media Business and Innovation* (pp. 149–61). Heidelberg, Berlin: Springer Verlag.

Puppis, M., Schweizer, C., Künzler, M. and Studer, S. (2014) *Public Financial Support for News Organizations in the Digital Era: A Comparative Analysis of Media Subsidies and Public Service Media Funding in 18 Countries*. Paper presented at ICA in Seattle.

Contributors

Auksė Balčytienė, Department of Public Communications, Vytautas Magnus University, Kaunas, Lithuania.

Laura Bergés Saura, Department of Catalan Studies and Communication, University of Lleida, Spain.

Alessandro D'Arma, Communication and Media Research Institute, University of Westminster, London, United Kingdom.

Leen d'Haenens, Institute for Media Studies, University of Leuven, Belgium.

Willem Joris, Institute for Media Studies, University of Leuven, Belgium.

Kristina Juraitė, Department of Public Communications, Vytautas Magnus University, Kaunas, Lithuania.

Anker Brink Lund, CBS Center for Civil Society Studies, Copenhagen Business School, Denmark.

Denis McQuail, School of Communication Research (ASCOR), Amsterdam University, Netherlands.

Werner A. Meier, SwissGIS – Swiss Centre for Studies on the Global Information Society, University of Zürich, Switzerland.

Hallvard Moe, Department of Information Science and Media Studies, University of Bergen, Norway.

Ralph Negrine, Department of Journalism Studies, University of Sheffield, United Kingdom.

Hannu Nieminen, Department of Social Research, Media and Communication Studies, University of Helsinki, Finland.

Claudia Padovani, Department of Politics, Law and International Studies, University of Padova, Italy.

Stylianos Papathanassopoulos, Department of Communication and Media Studies, National and Kapodistrian University of Athens, Greece.

Karin Raeymaeckers, Department of Communication Sciences, Ghent University, Belgium.

Karen Ross, Media and Communication Design, Northumbria University, Newcastle, United Kingdom.

Helena Sousa, Communication and Society Research Centre, University of Minho, Portugal.

Jeanette Steemers, School of Media, Arts and Design, University of Westminster, London, United Kingdom.

Barbara Thomass, Institute for Media Studies, Ruhr University Bochum, Germany.

Josef Trappel, Department of Communication Studies, University of Salzburg, Austria.

Elena Vartanova, Faculty of Journalism, Moscow State University.

Index